The Islamic Antichrist Debunked

A Comprehensive Critique

CHRIS WHITE

CWM Publishing
P.O. Box 272
Ducktown TN 37326
chris@chriswhiteministries.com

The Islamic Antichrist Debunked – A Comprehensive Critique / Chris White

ISBN: 978-0-9912329-4-9

Cover image by M. S. Corley - corleyms@yahoo.com

Editing by Rene' Holt

First Edition

Further information available at the author's website:
http://BibleProphecyTalk.com

Dedication

To Connie, my wife and best friend.

CONTENTS

Preface

The theory that the Antichrist will be a Muslim has become increasingly popular in the years following 9/11. The rise of extremist groups like ISIL/ISIS and Al-Qaeda have also contributed to many Christians asking themselves or their pastors if it's possible that the great enemy of last days, the Antichrist, might in fact be a Muslim.

I myself used to hold to the Islamic Antichrist theory, and I, therefore understand and sympathize with many of the arguments that people make for it. However, I have since come to believe that the Islamic Antichrist theory, when examined closely, does not line up with the Bible and that many of the arguments made in its defense can be shown to be false with certainty.

This book is intended to be a comprehensive refutation of all the major arguments that are used to support the Islamic Antichrist theory. Though many great scholars and teachers have written articles against this theory, there has not to date been a resource that attempts to systematically refute all the points that are raised in defense of the view.

Since it is my sincere hope that this book will be useful to as many people as possible, I have tried to keep my own personal views about the origin and nature of the Antichrist to an absolute minimum, choosing instead to argue against the Islamic Antichrist theory without presupposing an alternative origin for the Antichrist. In other words I wrote this book in a way that the reader can agree with, no matter what his views on the Antichrist are.

The first and longest part of this book will describe and refute the primary arguments that Islamic Antichrist proponents make in support of their theory, whether those arguments are from Scripture or are based on circumstantial evidence. Examples of the types of arguments in this section include the Islamic Empire being in view in Daniel 2 and 7, the Assyrian in Isaiah and Micah 5 referring to the Antichrist, and the Mark of the Beast being an Arabic word and not a number, among many others.

The second part of this book will examine the claims of Islamic Antichrist proponents regarding Islamic eschatological figures such as the Mahdi, Isa, and the Dajjal. The Islamic Antichrist theory relies greatly upon comparisons of these figures with Christian counterparts such as The Antichrist, The False Prophet, and Jesus. I will spend quite a lot of time discussing the origin of Islamic eschatology, and then take the claims of Islamic Antichrist theorists about these Islamic eschatological figures one by one in an effort to refute their arguments.

In the third section of this book I will look at some of the logical inconsistencies with the claims of the Islamic Antichrist theorist using the doctrines that what we know to be true about the Antichrist from Scripture.

In the fourth and final section, I will discuss why I believe the Islamic Antichrist theory is not just wrong but extremely dangerous. In this section I will break my self- imposed limitations on discussing my own personal views about the nature and origin of the Antichrist, and though I will not argue for my personal position, I will ask the reader to consider the potentially disastrous results that the Islamic Antichrist theory could cause if my view is correct.

In this book I will be quoting extensively from Joel Richardson, who I believe is the most intelligent and articulate advocate for the Islamic Antichrist theory. I respect Mr. Richardson greatly, both as a fellow brother in Christ and as a researcher. On occasion I will also reference Walid Shoebat's views, particularly on issues that Richardson has not published, like the Mark of the Beast, and Mystery Babylon. These two men are the most responsible for the promotion of the Islamic Antichrist theory, and it is often their work that is referenced when pastors teach this view. Therefore, I have intentionally limited the authors I will be directly referencing to these two men. I want to say at the outset that I appreciate Shoebat and Richardson greatly, especially because through their efforts a large number of Christians are considering end times matters seriously for the first time. Though I may disagree with them on certain issues, as Christians we agree on what matters the most.

Part 1
Examining the Arguments

Chapter 1
Nebuchadnezzar's Dream

The second chapter of the book of Daniel describes Nebuchadnezzar, king of Babylon, having a dream that troubles him greatly. In his dream he saw a statue of a man consisting of four metals, a head of gold, a chest and arms of silver, a belly and thighs of bronze, and legs of iron. The bottom part of this statue's legs was mixed with both iron and clay.

In verse 36 Daniel begins to interpret Nebuchadnezzar's dream. He explains that the different metals in the statue represent different kingdoms that will appear on earth. He explicitly tells us that the head represents Nebuchadnezzar's Babylonian kingdom, and while he doesn't give us the names of the other three kingdoms, they are believed by the vast majority of Christian scholars to be Medo-Persia, Greece, and Rome, in that order.

Islamic Antichrist theorists, such as Joel Richardson, attempt to make a case that the legs of iron, commonly identified as Rome, is actually the Islamic Empire which existed from 632 AD to 1923. Richardson's main argument centers on Daniel 2:40 which seems to suggest that the "legs of iron" kingdom somehow conquers all the other kingdoms that came before it (Babylon, Medo-Persia, and Greece).

> "And the fourth kingdom shall be as strong as iron, inasmuch as iron breaks in pieces and shatters everything; and like iron that crushes, *that kingdom* will break in pieces and **crush all the others.**" (Daniel 2:40)

Richardson believes that "crushing" all the others is a reference to a kingdom being able to claim that it is holding all the land that the previous empires held in history. He makes the case that Rome cannot be the fourth kingdom because even at its largest point, the geographical borders of the Roman Empire didn't encompass all of the territory that other empires on the list held. For example, Babylon and Medo-Persia held some territories which were much further east than Rome ever reached, and therefore Rome cannot be said to have "crushed the others," but that the Islamic Empire which followed the Roman Empire could make that claim.

There are several good theological, historical, and grammatical reasons why the fourth kingdom in Nebuchadnezzar's dream cannot be a reference to the Islamic Empire and must be a reference to Rome. I will begin with a discussion on the grammar of Daniel 2:40 which is so central to the Islamic Antichrist thesis.

It should be noted that not all English Bibles translate this verse the way it is above. In fact, if a translation does include the words "all the others," it often supplies a footnote to let the reader know that the words have been added and are not in the original Hebrew. Some translations like the King James Version translate this passage in a way that suggests the fourth kingdom is not crushing all the other kingdoms but rather, seem to suggest that Daniel is making a point about how iron, which is stronger than gold and silver, is able to destroy all the other metals.

> "And the fourth kingdom shall be strong as iron: forasmuch as iron breaketh in pieces and subdueth all *things*: and as iron that breaketh all these [as in the other metals], shall it break in pieces and bruise." (Daniel 2:40 KJV)

Notice that "all the others" is not added at the end of this verse.

I emailed a Hebrew scholar to ask him why there was a difference in the way certain English Bibles translated this passage. He said the following:

> "Let me place these words in the order in which they occur in the Hebrew:"

> "And as iron which breaks all these it will crush and break."

Since there are no commas in the original text, translators struggle with whether to include "all these" with the preceding clause [as in] "and as iron which breaks in pieces all these, it will crush and break," or whether to put it with the final clause [as in] "and as iron which breaks in pieces, it will crush and break all these."

In other words it's difficult to tell if the "all these" in this verse is talking about the metals, in which case this is simply a way to express the strength of the final kingdom. In this case it would be saying that the fourth kingdom is stronger than the other kingdoms in the same way that the metal this portion of the statue is made of (iron) is stronger than all the other metals in the statue. If this is the case there is no reason to think the fourth kingdom will need to conquer the other empires at all. On the other hand, if the "all these" is to be applied to the final clause, then it would refer to the other nations and not the metals, in which case we would need to discover some way for the fourth empire to "crush" the other empires, despite the other empires having been dead for hundreds of years.

It should be noted that some translations such as the International Standard Version translate the passage in such a way that suggests the fourth empire will crush "everything" and not specifically the other nations in the statue:

> "Then there will be a fourth kingdom, as strong as iron. Just as all things are broken to pieces and shattered by iron, so it will shatter and crush everything." (Daniel 2:40 ISV)

In this case Richardson's point would again be moot since the fourth kingdom's crushing "everything" could be a reference to its general destructive power, as typified by iron but not necessarily a reference to crushing all the historic kingdoms of the earth.

Getting to the bottom of this is further complicated by the fact that the Greek Septuagint and the Latin Vulgate do not contain certain portions of this verse, which makes it difficult to determine from context how to understand the grammar of this verse.

For the sake of argument I will proceed as if the "all these" in this verse is referring to the legs of iron somehow needing to "crush" all the other empires that came before it, since it could very well be the way this verse is intended to be understood. I only mention the grammatical problems in Daniel 2:40 to suggest that since there is a debate among Bible scholars and Bible translators about how to interpret this verse, we should tread lightly when trying to build doctrine on this passage.

Setting aside for the moment the problem of determining how Rome, or any other empire, could be said to have crushed kingdoms that they had no contact with, I want to discuss some of the other problems with viewing the legs of iron as the Islamic Empire as opposed to the Roman Empire.

Why Skip the Romans?

The other three empires that make up the statue in Nebuchadnezzar's dream all have certain things in common with one another. They are all huge empires that controlled much of the known world, including Israel; they all followed in direct succession to one another; and they were all conquered by the empire that is listed after it. For example, Babylon, the head of gold, was conquered by the next empire in the statue, Medo-Persia; and Medo-Persia was conquered by the next empire in the statue, the Grecian Empire. Since the Grecian Empire was directly followed by and conquered by the Roman Empire, and because it too was a vast empire that was the next to control Israel, it would seem to be a natural fit to the pattern established by the first three empires of the statue. If the Islamic Empire was listed after Greece, it would break this pattern significantly since the Islamic Empire didn't arise until much later. It would mean that this prophecy skipped the Roman Empire altogether despite Rome fitting precisely into the pattern set by the previous Empires.

In response to this criticism Joel Richardson, in his book *Mideast Beast,* essentially says it is okay to ignore the chronology and skip over Rome because even if you assumed that the fourth kingdom was Rome, the list of kingdoms in Daniel 2 would still be overlooking other empires such as the Parthian Empire which existed over 100 years before Rome. So in effect he is saying if chronology matters so much, why exclude the Parthian Empire?

There are a few problems with this argument. The first is that the Parthian Empire, which existed between 247 BC and 224 AD, overlapped the tail end of the Greek Empire and the beginning of the Roman Empire, it was an enemy of both the Greeks and Romans, but never could it be said that it was a world empire like the others or that it conquered either Greece or Rome. It should more properly be seen as one of the many smaller kingdoms that served as an on-again-off-again enemy of the vastly bigger and more powerful world empires of Greece and Rome.

The Parthians were a relatively small kingdom compared to the Greek and Roman Empires, occupying the land of ancient Persia, which was primarily in modern-day Iran. More importantly, the Parthian Empire did not control Israel at any point in its existence, which may very well be the most important thing that links all the empires in Daniel 2.

It should also be noted that the Parthians considered themselves to be a continuation of the Medo-Persian Empire which was conquered by the Greeks. Many of their kings even claimed to be direct descendants of Medo-Persian kings, which might even be true, based on the fact that they seem to have the same genetic diseases as the Medo-Persian kings.

The point is that the exclusion of the Parthian Empire in Nebuchadnezzar's dream does not suggest that chronology doesn't matter; it only suggests that the Parthian Empire doesn't qualify to be on such a list.

It is interesting that later in his book *Mideast Beast*, where Richardson is discussing Revelation 17:10, he includes Rome in the proper place in this chronology. I will quote Revelation 17:10 here so you can get the context of his point.

> "They are also seven kings, five of whom have fallen, one is, the other has not yet come, and when he does come he must remain only a little while." (Revelation 17:10)

Here Richardson interprets this as referring to seven successive kingdoms, including Egypt, Assyria, Babylon, Medo-Persia, Greece, and Rome. If you take out the first two (Egypt and Assyria)--since Daniel was writing after Egypt and Assyria had fallen--you have the same list as the traditional view of the four kingdoms of Daniel 2. The reason Richardson must include Rome after Greece in the Revelation 17 list is because John says of the sixth kingdom, "one is," as in the one that existed in John's day, which is unambiguously Rome and, therefore, impossible to interpret as the Islamic Empire. If his interpretation of the list of kingdoms in Revelation 17:10 is correct, it gives credit to the idea that Scripture is intending Rome to be seen as the fourth kingdom of Daniel 2 because in Revelation 17:10, Rome is clearly placed after Greece, not the Islamic Empire. Richardson tries to deal with this seeming contradiction by saying the following:

> "Some will ask why, if the Roman Empire was not included in Daniel 2 or 7, it is included in the list of empires in Revelation 17. The answer is simply because, while Revelation 17 presents us with a comprehensive list, detailing the full pan-biblical view of all of history's satanic, pagan beast empires, Daniel 2 and 7 do not list every one of Satan's empires. Neither chapter includes

the Egyptian, Assyrian, or Roman empires. As we have seen, these passages simply speak of the empires that would rise after Nebuchadnezzar in Babylon, and the Roman Empire was not included among these. It is not until we come to Revelation 12, 13, and 17 that the full, pan-historical list of Satanic empires is given."[1]

He argues here that in Revelation 17 there are more empires listed because it is a more complete list of Satanic kingdoms than is found in Daniel 2, which is why he says it's OK for Rome to be listed after Greece in that case, but not in Daniel 2. It should be obvious, however, that the reason the list in Daniel 2 does not include Egypt and Assyria is because at the time Daniel was writing, those empires had already come and gone. Nebuchadnezzar's dream in Daniel 2 was about the empires that would come after his own, not the ones that had come before; therefore, mentioning Egypt and Assyria in his dream would have been pointless since the vision was about the future, not the past. The problem still exists for Richardson. The Bible seems to give us a way to check our facts here, and it seems to be telling us in Revelation 17:10 that placing Rome after Greece is the correct way to interpret Daniel 2.

To sum up this point, there is, in fact, a chronological pattern with the kingdoms in Daniel 2. Babylon, Medo-Persia, Greece and Rome were all world empires that controlled Israel and that conquered the world empire that came directly before it. Daniel 2 gives us a perfect and unbroken chain of empires that matches up with what we know of in Scripture and in history. To say that it is okay to abandon this chronological and typological pattern because the Parthian Empire existed at the same time as the Greeks and Romans is to give the Parthian Empire much more significance than it deserves. It would be like saying that Daniel 2 should have also included the Carthiginian Empire, which also existed during and fought against the Greek and Roman Empires, despite the fact that it was relatively small, it didn't conquer either the Greeks or Romans, and it didn't control Israel at any time in its existence.

---

[1] Richardson, Joel (2012-06-08). *Mideast Beast: The Scriptural Case for an Islamic Antichrist* (p. 158). Joel Richardson. Kindle Edition.

The Theological Problem

I think that the greatest problem with the idea that the fourth kingdom in Daniel 2 is the Islamic Empire is the theological problem that it creates. This is because Daniel 2 may very well be a prophecy predicting the first coming of the Messiah, in addition to its many other predictions, and this chapter may also be the very reason that messianic expectations were so high in Jesus' day. That is because Daniel 2 was telling people to expect the Messiah in the days of the empire that would follow the Greek Empire, i.e. during the Roman Empire.

I say this because of the rock that strikes the statue and destroys it in Daniel 2:34 and 44-45. We are told explicitly that this rock is a "kingdom," not a king, and more specifically we are told that this rock is a "kingdom set up by God," i.e. the Kingdom of God. Many people take this rock striking the statue as an end-times event. I sympathize with that view because it is true that Jesus' second coming in the last days should be considered an integral part of the establishment of the Kingdom of God. However, as anyone who has done an extensive study on the biblical idea of the "Kingdom of God" will tell you, it is a multifaceted concept, and at least in some sense the Kingdom of God was said to be established during Jesus's first coming during the Roman Empire.

> "But if I cast out demons by the Spirit of God, surely **the kingdom of God has come upon you.**" (Matthew 12:28, emphasis added)

> "Now at one point the Pharisees asked Jesus when the kingdom of God was coming, so he answered, 'The kingdom of God is not coming with signs to be observed, nor will they say, "Look, here it is!" or "There!" **For indeed, the kingdom of God is in your midst.**'" (Luke 17:20–21, emphasis added)

> "And saying, 'The time is fulfilled, and **the kingdom of God is at hand**. Repent, and believe in the gospel.'" (Mark 1:15,

emphasis added)

> "In those days John the Baptist came preaching in the wilderness of Judea, and saying, 'Repent, for **the kingdom of heaven is at hand!**'" (Matthew 3:1-2)

The reason the Kingdom of God can be said to have started during the Roman Empire, yet not be fully realized until the second coming, is explained by a couple of parables given by Jesus on the subject of the Kingdom of God.

> "Another parable He put forth to them, saying: 'The kingdom of heaven is like a mustard seed, which a man took and sowed in his field, which indeed is the least of all the seeds; but when it is grown it is greater than the herbs and becomes a tree, so that the birds of the air come and nest in its branches.' Another parable He spoke to them: 'The kingdom of heaven is like leaven, which a woman took and hid in three measures of meal till it was all leavened.'.(Matthew 13:31–33)

These two parables describe the Kingdom of God as starting small and then growing large over time. This may refer to Christianity which started with only twelve disciples in Jesus' day but will ultimately culminate in in the largest and greatest kingdom that ever existed.

This is interesting because it is exactly the same idea we see described in Daniel 2:35.

> "And the stone that struck the image **became a great mountain and filled the whole earth.**" (Daniel 2:35b)

Here we see that much like the parable about the Kingdom of God concerning the mustard seed, or the leaven, the last empire (Rome) was struck by a small stone (Jesus' establishment of the Kingdom of God during His first coming) that **only later** grew to be a "mountain" and encompass the entire earth.

I will conclude by saying that even if only a portion of this chapter was intended to be a prophecy of the first coming of Jesus, then it would be theologically disastrous to say that that the fourth empire was the Islamic Empire as that would require us to say that Daniel didn't predict the Messiah coming until at least 632AD!

Did Rome Conquer the Other Empires?

As I said before, though I think there are grammatical issues that call into question whether or not Daniel 2:40 is, in fact, telling us that the fourth empire must "crush all the others" that preceded it, I will however assume this is true for the sake of argument and offer some possibilities for understanding this phrase.

The obvious problem is that no matter whether you think the fourth empire is the Roman Empire, the Islamic Empire, or any other empire, there is no way for any more modern empire to conquer an empire that has long ceased to be. For example, neither the Romans nor the Islamic Empire could go back in a time machine and fight Nebuchadnezzar and the Neo-Babylonians, or Cyrus the Great and the Medo-Persians. We must recognize from the outset that we are dealing with something other than a straightforward understanding of how one empire "crushes" another.

As I mentioned, Richardson suggests the way to understand this "crushing all the others" is that the fourth empire must occupy the exact same territory as all the previous empires. While Rome, at one time or another, did occupy most of the areas that the Babylonian Empire held, the Greek and Medo-Persian Empires extended much further east than Rome ever did. Richardson calculates in his book that Rome only held one-fifth of the total area of the Medo-Persian Empire. It should be mentioned that all of the first three empires in the statue placed particular importance in the city of Babylon[2] and Rome did, in fact, conquer Babylon under Trajan. Considering that Babylon was such an important part of this prophecy, this could be significant, though I admit it is only

---

[2] Medo-Persia actually had four capital cities, though Babylon was arguably the most important of these in terms of continual use and symbolic power.

speculation.

Another way to look at this is from an Israel-centric perspective. The only empires that controlled Jerusalem from the time they were carried off to Babylon until the first coming of Christ were Babylon, Medo-Persia, Greece, and Rome, the very nations that are typically identified as the nations in Daniel 2. If you consider the control of Israel as kind of heavyweight championship belt, the prize for defeating the previous champion, it could be argued from this Israel-centric paradigm that Rome was the reigning champion of the other empires. Again I admit this is speculation.

Of the scholars who believe Daniel 2:40 is saying that Rome somehow "crushed" the previous kingdoms, many of them, such as Stephen Miller, believe this is referring to how each of the empires listed in Daniel 2 physically conquered the empire listed before them (Medo-Persia conquered Babylon etc.), meaning that Rome, the last one listed, crushed all the others in that sense. At the same time others make the case that Rome, despite its not covering every bit of the land occupied by Medo-Persia, could be said to have controlled much of the important areas (such as Babylon and Israel). So even if Richardson's understanding of "crushed" is correct, it doesn't mean that Rome would not qualify.

I believe that Richardson has proposed a kind of false dilemma by stating that "crushing all the others" means the fourth kingdom has to hold all the land all the other kingdoms held, even though that nation wouldn't have actually "crushed" the other kingdoms in any real sense. He then proclaims that the only nation that solves his false dilemma is the Islamic Empire, despite all the problems created by forcing the Islamic Empire into this statue imagery. It seems much more likely that either "crushing the others" is referring to the metals and not the nations, as the King James Version has it, or if the crushing is in fact a reference to the fourth kingdom crushing the other kingdoms, then Stephen Miller's view that this refers to each nation having conquered the one that preceded it is correct. In any case I would beg the Islamic Antichrist theorist to recognize that this particular claim relies solely on one phrase in Daniel 2:40 ("all the others"), a phrase that doesn't even appear in the original

Hebrew. The difficulty that translators have with this verse is evident by the many different ways Bible versions translate the passage. It is never wise to build new doctrines on this kind of ground, but it is especially unwise when the new doctrines cause several historical and theological problems to arise as a result.

In this chapter I have listed a few of the problems that come from seeing the fourth empire of Daniel 2 as the Islamic Empire. I have noted the problems with the grammar in the key passage that makes the Islamic Empire view of Daniel 2 even possible. This view also forces us to abandon the pattern set by the first three empires by skipping Rome completely, even though it is clearly included in the later list of kingdoms in Revelation 17:10. It causes theological problems if Daniel 2 is in fact partially a prophecy of the first coming of the Messiah.

Chapter 2
The Four Beasts of Daniel 7

In chapter 7 of the book of Daniel we find another vision that is believed to be a prophecy about future kingdoms. In this case the symbolic picture given is of four beasts instead of a statue with four metals. The four beasts listed in Daniel 7 are a lion, a bear, a leopard, and a very strange beast with 10 horns.

Although there is nothing in the Bible that expressly demands the following interpretation, the four beasts of Daniel 7 have traditionally been equated with the four parts of the statue in Daniel 2. So the head of gold (Babylon) in Daniel 2 would be equivalent with the lion, the silver chest (Medo-Persia) with the bear, the bronze belly and thighs (Greece) with the leopard, and the iron legs (Rome) with the final 10 horned beast.

In his book *Mideast Beast*, Joel Richardson argues that the final beast of Daniel 7 is the Islamic Empire and not Rome. Richardson does not spend too much time trying to prove his belief that the final beast of Daniel 7 is the Islamic Empire, which is probably because he is following the traditional view that equates Daniel 2 directly with Daniel 7. In this view, those who believe they have determined the identity of the legs of iron in Daniel 2 feel at liberty to copy and paste that kingdom into the final beast kingdom of Daniel 7 without much explanation. Since

Richardson, as we saw in the last chapter, has already determined the legs of iron in Daniel 2 to be the Islamic Empire, he also believes that the last beast in Daniel 7 must be the Islamic Empire.

Richardson does offer two arguments for the fourth beast being the Islamic Empire. To interact with those arguments we need to read what is said about this beast in Daniel 7.

> "After this I saw in the night visions, and behold, a fourth beast, dreadful and terrible, exceedingly strong. It had huge iron teeth; it was devouring, breaking in pieces, and trampling the residue with its feet. It was different from all the beasts that were before it, and it had ten horns. I was considering the horns, and there was another horn, a little one, coming up among them, before whom three of the first horns were plucked out by the roots. And there, in this horn, were eyes like the eyes of a man, and a mouth speaking pompous words." (Daniel 7:7-8)

The fourth beast is said to be very destructive—."devouring," "breaking in pieces," and "trampling." Richardson says this is an argument in favor of the fourth beast being the Islamic Empire because the Roman Empire was not very destructive, and the Islamic Empire was.

> "The Roman Empire in many ways was anything but a destructive empire. Instead it was rather constructive, often adding infrastructure, order, and law to the lands it conquered."[3]

While it is true that Rome did build up its empire and attempt to add infrastructure, order, and law to the lands they conquered, the exact same thing could be said of the Islamic Empire. More to the point, the fact that Rome was at times constructive does not negate the fact that they were also very destructive. They fought countless wars, often destroying entire cities. I am reminded of a quote, attributed to Calgacus by the Roman

---

[3] Richardson, Joel (2012-06-08). *Mideast Beast: The Scriptural Case for an Islamic Antichrist* (p. 82). Joel Richardson. Kindle Edition.

historian Tacitus, which says of the Roman Empire: "They plunder, they slaughter, and they steal, this they falsely name Empire, and where they make a wasteland, they call it peace."

Richardson then goes on to suggest that the Islamic Empire was more destructive than the Roman Empire. However, it seems that an evaluation of which of these two empires was more destructive is a very subjective endeavor. They both used their military to conquer new territory, and they both killed countless people on their road to building their empires. At the same time, they both seemed to prefer to use non-violent means to acquire new territory when possible. They both tried, whenever possible, not to destroy major places of worship or cities in their conquests, but rather to convert them to suit their own purposes. Since Richardson's main argument for the fourth beast being the Islamic Empire as opposed to the Roman Empire is that, in his opinion, the Roman Empire was not destructive but the Islamic Empire was, we can dismiss it easily on the grounds that such a distinction between the two empires is by no means clear. Despite Richardson's claim to the contrary, the Roman Empire was most certainly extremely destructive, desolating entire cities when it suited them and killing countless people, including many Jews and Christians.

The only other argument that Richardson makes to explain why the fourth beast of Daniel 7 is the Islamic Empire and not the Roman Empire is regarding the blasphemous words spoken by one of the horns on the head of the fourth beast:

> "As for the ten horns, out of this kingdom ten kings shall arise, and another shall arise after them; he shall be different from the former ones, and shall put down three kings. **He shall speak words against the Most High**, and shall wear out the saints of the Most High, and shall think to change the times and the law; and they shall be given into his hand for a time, times, and half a time. But the court shall sit in judgment, and his dominion shall be taken away, to be consumed and destroyed to the end." (Daniel 7:24–26)

Richardson here makes the case that because one of the horns on the beasts' heads is speaking blasphemies against the most high and killing saints, this should be seen as an Islamic Empire and not the Roman Empire. He says that the Roman Empire was too tolerant for Scripture to describe it in this way.

There are two problems with this argument. The first is most interpreters don't see the actions of the "little horn" in Daniel 7 (the one who speaks blasphemous words) as relating to the ancient Roman Empire in any way. Though they see the fourth beast itself as representative of the ancient version of Rome, or the so-called "revived Roman Empire," they see the actions of the "little horn" on the beast's head as the actions of the Antichrist himself, a man who has yet to come, not a nation. The fact that Daniel 7:25 tells us this horn's actions are primarily limited to three and a half years should be enough to prove that the actions of the little horn of this beast isn't a commentary on the ancient Roman Empire at all since the Roman Empire lasted much longer that three and a half years. In addition, Daniel 7:25 uses the pronoun "him" to describe the horn, suggesting it is a man, not a nation. Richardson's case that the ancient Roman Empire can't be the little horn because Rome was too "tolerant" is totally moot because the part of the beast called the "little horn" is a prophecy about a yet future man, the Antichrist, and is not making a commentary about ancient Rome's tolerance or lack of tolerance in any way.

The second problem with this idea is while the Roman Empire was tolerant of most religions, they were only tolerant if you tolerated their religion as well. This was just fine for most religious people of the day who had no problem with simply adding another god to their lists of gods to honor, but it became a big problem for followers of monotheistic religions like Judaism and Christianity, who would not bow down to gods other than the God of the Bible. Eventually Jewish people and Christians were brutally persecuted and countless numbers of them were killed by the Roman Empire because of this so-called "tolerant" Roman religious system. The Roman emperors were also seen as a part of the Roman pantheon of gods, and people were expected to worship them with a pinch of incense. This would be considered a very blasphemous practice by most standards, and many Christians and Jews were executed because they refused to participate in it. To say the fourth beast cannot refer to Rome because Rome was too tolerant is not a very good argument. If you told the Christians being burned alive, crucified, and fed to lions in the coliseum by the Roman Empire that Rome was tolerant of their religion, I doubt they would have agreed with you.

As I have said before, it is my goal to limit my personal beliefs to a minimum while criticizing the Islamic Antichrist view. However I have included in Appendix 1 a discussion about Daniel 2 and Daniel 7 to explain how I understand these chapters. If I am correct, then Richardson's argument about Daniel 7 is completely irrelevant.

Chapter 3
The People of the Prince to Come

In the ninth chapter of Daniel we find the following phrase:

> "And the people of the prince who is to come shall destroy the city and the sanctuary." (Daniel 9:26)

In context, this verse is a prophecy of the destruction of the city of Jerusalem and the temple. It is almost universally believed to be a prophecy of the destruction of Jerusalem and temple by the Romans in AD 70. The word *prince* in the phrase, "the people of the prince to come," is often taken to be speaking of the Antichrist; in other words, it's saying: "There is a prince to come far in the future (the Antichrist), but he won't be around at the time of the destruction of the temple in 70 AD. Only his people will, and they will destroy the temple." Therefore, this is often taken as a way to determine the nationality of the Antichrist. The idea is that all one has to do is determine the people who destroyed the temple in 70 AD, and that will reveal the people from whom the Antichrist comes.

If we accept this premise, it would seem the most natural method of interpretation would be that the Antichrist would somehow be associated with the Roman Empire since the Roman Empire conquered Jerusalem in

70 AD.

However, Islamic Antichrist proponents have suggested that, because the Romans used legions that were stationed in the east in the war with Jerusalem, a certain percentage of their recruits would have been from the areas in which they were based, i.e. the Middle East. They also point to a reference by Tacitus that the Roman army used some "Arab auxiliaries" in the same war. So the argument goes that since at least some of the Roman soldiers who destroyed the temple were from places like Syria and Turkey, perhaps Scripture is pointing to the ethnicity of the Roman soldiers in the "people of the prince" phrase as opposed to the empire that the soldiers actually fought for, which was Rome.

First let's talk about the Arab auxiliaries that Tacitus mentions. Josephus actually tells us how many of them there were (about 6000); this is compared to the 60,000 men who participated in the war. So at most only 10 percent of the soldiers in 70 AD could have been considered non-Roman. It should be noted here that the reason people joined the auxiliaries was so they could be awarded Roman citizenship at the end of their term of service.

The other 54,000 men were all Roman citizens from the 3rd, 5th, 10th, 12th, 15th, and 18th Legions. Since it was required that a soldier must be a Roman citizen to be in the legionnaires, we can be pretty sure that these 54,000 men were, in fact, Roman citizens.

However, those who hold to the Islamic Antichrist theory claim that, of the 54,000 other troops, at least some of them must have originally been from places like Syria or Egypt because many of the Roman citizens who fought in the Jewish war were stationed in the those areas and there was sure to be a certain amount of recruitment from the Roman citizens within those eastern populations. For example, they will say, "Look at the 10th legion; it was stationed in Syria" (which contained a major military base for Rome in the East). Since this unit was based in Syria, they suggest that most of the legionnaires in the 10th were ethnically Syrian. There are a number of problems with this, but first I should mention that before and after the 10th legion was stationed in Syria, it was stationed in Judea. Using their logic, the 10th legion should have been primarily made up of ethnically Jewish soldiers since it spent a much longer time stationed in Jerusalem that anywhere else.

In truth there is no way for anyone to know exactly how many citizens from the 10th legion, or any other legion, were from the areas where they were stationed. Nobody has that information that I am aware of, but knowing what we do know about the legions, it is very likely that any division in that area at that time was comprised of Roman citizens from all over the Empire. It is true that Roman legions did recruit from the local populations where they were based as long as the recruits were Roman citizens. The citizenship requirement alone restricted local recruits to only the most wealthy or influential families in those regions; and the citizens they recruited from Syria, Egypt, or any other major Roman military hub were at least partly comprised of the sons of Roman soldiers born in those places during their fathers' service. This was a very common practice.

Just because a Roman citizen was from Gaul, Spain, Britannia, or Egypt didn't make them any less of a Roman citizen. It can be reasonably asserted that any member of the legionnaires, regardless of their place of birth, was a patriotic citizen who was very proud of that citizenship and would almost surely identify himself as a Roman.

In addition, the six legions that took part in the Jewish war were stationed in a variety of places, not just the Middle East, including those who came from a large military base in the Balkans (modern day Romania and Bulgaria).

It would be one thing if the Bible contained a clue that in this particular case (the only case in the Bible that I know of), we were to assume that the people of a kingdom should not be identified with the king or kingdom that they were obviously a part of but instead we are to look through very incomplete and inconclusive records about the ethnicity of each individual soldier in that army to determine what nation is being referred to in the Bible. I suggest that this theory is grasping at straws and that Roman soldiers are simply Roman soldiers.

I should mention another theory about this passage that, if true, means this verse is not giving us any information whatsoever about the nationality of the Antichrist.

When this verse says "the people of the prince who is to come shall destroy the city and the sanctuary," it may simply be saying it was not Titus who ordered the destruction of the temple, but rather his people who disobeyed his orders and destroyed the temple and city. In almost any other conquest by the Romans, there would be no need to make this distinction. After all, if Titus or any other general ordered the destruction of something, he would be responsible for it, and it would be right for Scripture to put the blame on him. But the events of that day made it necessary to describe the destruction of the temple and city as not being by Titus, but instead by his people.

Josephus who was actually present at the battle with Titus, made it very clear that Titus did not order the destruction of the temple and city. In fact he went to great lengths to stop it from happening, but it happened anyway.

For example, Josephus quotes Titus in a meeting with his generals about what to do with the temple. This was because the Jews were using the temple as a citadel for a kind of last stand. Josephus says:

> "But Titus said, that 'although the Jews should get upon that holy house, and fight us thence, yet ought we not to revenge ourselves on things that are inanimate, instead of the men themselves': and that he was not in any case for burning down so vast a work as that was, because this would be a mischief to the Romans themselves, as it would be an ornament to their government while it continued."

Then, after Titus was informed that, despite his orders, the soldiers set fire to the temple, Josephus describes the following scene:

"And now a certain person came running to Titus, and told him of this fire, as he was resting himself in his tent after the last battle; whereupon he rose up in great haste, and, as he was, ran to the holy house, in order to have a stop put to the fire.... Then did Caesar, both by calling to the soldiers that were fighting, with a loud voice, and by giving a signal to them with his right hand, order them to quench the fire. But they did not hear what he said, though he spake so loud, having their ears already dimmed by a greater noise another way; nor did they attend to the signal he made with his hand neither, as still some of them were distracted with fighting, and others with passion. But as for the legions that came running thither, neither any persuasions nor any threatenings could restrain their violence, but each one's own passion was his commander at this time."

Josephus offers still more descriptions of the events of that day:

"Moreover, the hope of plunder induced many to go on, as having this opinion, that all the places within were full of money, and as seeing that all round about it was made of gold.... And thus was the holy house burnt down, without Caesar's approbation."

If the Scripture had said that the prince— that is, Titus in this view—destroyed the temple, it would have been factually inaccurate. Instead, it says "the people of the prince" destroyed it. You can see why this would be an important distinction to make given the circumstances, and I should point out that this view reveals this verse to be a very accurate prophecy by Daniel.

The "to come," as in "the people of the prince who is to come," is therefore from Daniel's perspective, as this prince (Titus) was almost five hundred years in the future at the time Daniel wrote. But for us looking back, that prince to come has already come.

This in no way conflicts with the rest of this prophecy requiring a future fulfillment, as it is clear that the next verse (Daniel 9:27) is talking about the future actions of the Antichrist. I discuss this in much greater detail in my book *False Christ*.

In conclusion, there is no way to confirm where the Roman citizens who made up 90 percent of the forces that day were born, but to suggest that they were all products of the base in which they were stationed at the time is just wishful thinking on the part of the Islamic Antichrist proponents. Even if it were the case, why should we believe that those Roman soldiers are not to be understood as Romans in this case simply because they came from various ethnic backgrounds? What if we applied this method of interpretation to other empires in the Bible? For example, after the Assyrian Empire conquered a country, they simply forced people to fight in their army or die, but when we hear about Assyrian armies in Scripture, we do not have to stop and think, "Well, where were the Assyrian soldiers in this particular battle stolen from originally?" No, we simply accept that Assyrian soldiers are part of the Assyrian Empire regardless of where they were born.

I believe that for futurists like myself, there are only two possibilities to the reference, "the people of the prince who is to come shall destroy the city and the sanctuary." Either the prince is referring to the Antichrist, in which case the reference to the "people" is to the Romans who destroyed the temple. Or it is talking about how Titus didn't want the temple destroyed but his people did it anyway, in which case this verse was never intended to tell us where the Antichrist comes from.

Chapter 4
Types of the Antichrist

A number of arguments for the Islamic Antichrist theory center around what are sometimes called "types" of the Antichrist. A type can be defined as "a preordained representative relation in which certain persons, events, or institutions in the Old Testament correspond to persons, events, or institutions in the New Testament."[4] For example Moses, in his role of prophet, leader, and mediator for God's people, was a type of Christ.

There are also many types of the Antichrist in Scripture; one of the more prominent and obvious types of Antichrist was Antiochus Epiphanies. The arguments that Islamic Antichrist theorists make in this case center around the idea that since Antiochus, who ruled in Syria, was such a major type of Antichrist that we should expect the Antichrist to be from Syria as well. Alternatively they might make general statements about how most of the types of Antichrist were Middle Eastern, even if not from Syria itself, so the Antichrist will be Middle Eastern as well.

The problem with this is idea is that even if we are relatively selective

---

[4] Jackson, Wayne. "A Study of Biblical Typology." *Christian Courier*. N.p., n.d. Web. 15 Jan. 2015.

with what we decide is a type of Antichrist in Scripture, we find that these types are from different places and include both Jews and Gentiles.

- Pharaoh, king of Egypt
- Antiochus of Greece/Syria
- The king of Tyre
- The king of Babylon
- Herod of Israel
- Saul of Israel
- Absalom of Israel

The obvious problem with deciding a certain type of Antichrist will give us information about where the Antichrist comes from is if you do that, you will have several mutually exclusive answers to that question. Using typology in this way is simply not a sound method of interpretation.

Even the people who want to focus in on Antiochus sometimes overlook the fact that, although he ruled in Syria, he was a Greek man ruling a Hellenistic empire and worshipping Greek gods. Calling him a prefiguration of a Muslim ruler would be like calling Julius Caesar a Muslim king because Rome ruled over Egypt.

To conclude this point, types of Antichrist are not clues to the country of origin of the Antichrist, not simply because the Bible never gives us the impression that we are to understand types in this way, but because by applying this idea you come up with multiple contradictory origins for the Antichrist. Even the types of Antichrist that people hold in high regard, such as Antiochus, would have to be considered more Greek than anything else.

Chapter 5
The Assyrian in Isaiah and Micah

An increasingly popular view is that the Antichrist will be an Assyrian. This conclusion is arrived at by a citing few passages in Isaiah, primarily Isaiah 10, and one passage in the book of Micah. I want to look closely at these passages, as well as what the proponents of this view say about them, to show you why I think this view is artificially contrived.

Isaiah

Let's first look at the passages used to support the Assyrian Antichrist view from the book of Isaiah. The context of Isaiah is extremely important for our discussion, so I will spend a few moments describing the issues the prophet was dealing with and writing about in his day.

Isaiah wrote when Israel was being threatened with destruction from Assyria. Isaiah warns that the Assyrian king, whom the prophet occasionally refers to as "the Assyrian," will capture and carry off the ten northern tribes in addition to many cities in the Southern Kingdom, but the city of Jerusalem would not fall to the Assyrians and God would come to His people's aid. All of this happens within the book of Isaiah: The Assyrians do indeed conquer the Northern Kingdom, as well as many cities in the Southern Kingdom. The Assyrian king Sennacherib even sets up a siege of the city of Jerusalem. But, as promised, God protects the city by sending an angel who destroys 185,000 Assyrian soldiers surrounding the city and causes the rest of the army to flee, never to threaten Israel again.

In addition to relating this judgment of Assyria, Isaiah also tells us that, later, Sennacherib is killed by his own sons. The Assyrian Empire goes into sharp decline shortly after that and is eventually conquered by Neo-Babylon. The rest of the book of Isaiah is focused on warning Judah, in the Southern Kingdom, that although it was spared from the Assyrians, it would in fact be captured by the empire that would come after the Assyrians—the Babylonians.

In *Mideast Beast*, Joel Richardson, repeatedly tells his readers that the book of Isaiah says the Messiah will defeat "the Assyrian":

> "God's promise was that a military leader would be born from the line of David who would deliver all of God's people from 'the Assyrian.' The problem, however, is that this never occurred in history."

> "This passage declares that the Messiah will deliver Israel from the Assyrian."

> "So despite the numerous references throughout Isaiah to the Messiah destroying the king of Assyria in the land of Israel, historically this deliverance never occurred."

Clearly Richardson believes there are prophecies in the book of Isaiah that say the Messiah will defeat "the Assyrian," and since this obviously has never happened, he believes these passages must refer to the end times and that the references to the Assyrian must apply to the Antichrist, as well as to the Assyrian king Sennacherib.

If there were such prophecies in Isaiah stating that the Messiah would defeat the Assyrian, I would have to agree with Richardson that there must be an Assyrian component to the Antichrist. But, as we will see, there isn't a single verse in all of Isaiah that says the Messiah will defeat the Assyrian. Richardson and others come to this conclusion in an extremely roundabout way.

The first thing Richardson does to explain what he means by saying the Messiah is said to destroy the Assyrian is point to Isaiah 7:14–20.He uses this passage to establish that there is a dual prophecy in certain sections of Isaiah that deal with the Assyrian. That passage begins with words that are familiar to Christians as partially a prophecy of Jesus' birth. But, as Richardson correctly points out, in the original context, these words are also a prophecy of a child in Isaiah's day that was to be a sign that the Assyrians were going to destroy much of Israel.

> "Therefore the Lord Himself will give you a sign: Behold, the virgin shall conceive and bear a Son, and shall call His name Immanuel. Curds and honey He shall eat, that He may know to refuse the evil and choose the good. For before the Child shall know to refuse the evil and choose the good, the land that you dread will be forsaken by both her kings. The Lord will bring the king of Assyria upon you and your people and your father's house— days that have not come since the day that Ephraim departed from Judah." (Isaiah 7:14–20)

The idea that this prophecy, in addition to being about the birth of Jesus, is also about a child in Isaiah's day who was to be a sign of Israel's impending destruction is more clearly described in the next chapter.

> "For before the child knows how to cry out, 'My father' or 'My mother,' the wealth of Damascus and the plunder of Samaria will be carried off by the king of Assyria." (Isaiah 8:4)

Richardson wants to apply all of this prophecy, not just the virgin birth idea (7:14), to the Messiah in order to have a basis for saying that the Messiah will have some application to the Assyrian. He would not deny that the passage was fulfilled historically, but he would also say that it is a prophecy of future events as well. There are a number of problems with this, however. The first is even if we allowed that every word of this prophecy was to be applied to Jesus in the end times, it is still not saying anything about the child defeating the Assyrian. In fact, it is quite clearly saying the opposite, that the Assyrian Empire will be victorious over the northern tribes. The child in this prophecy is doing nothing but acting as a sign that the destruction of Israel is imminent. There isn't a single aspect of this prophecy that gives the reader the idea that the child is to defeat the Assyrians. Yet, Richardson says of this passage:

> "The fuller context is the coming of the Messiah to break the Assyrian."

How can a prophecy that a child will be a sign of the destruction of Israel by the Assyrians be evidence that the child will destroy the Assyrians? The point of this passage is that the Assyrian armies are a judgment from God and they will be victorious, not defeated.

Setting aside the fact that this verse is saying the opposite of what Richardson says it is saying, let's look at the limits of the prophecy of the virgin birth in verse 14, since that seems to be the reason Richardson is suggesting it is okay to treat this entire section as a prophecy of the end times.

It is notable that to even make this erroneous claim Richardson must assert that most of the prophecy in Isaiah 7 is about Jesus, not just the virgin birth idea, which in itself is a problematic claim. The problem with assuming the rest of the prophecy is about Jesus is that the destruction of the northern tribes of Israel was to occur before this child was able to talk (Isaiah 8:4). Obviously, there is danger in applying too much of this prophecy to Jesus because there is nothing even remotely close to a fulfillment of this in the days after Jesus' birth. There was no attack by the long-dead Assyrian Empire on the northern tribes before He was able to talk. Such a preposterous notion forces us to recognize what scholars have long known: The prophecy of the virgin birth in Isaiah 7:14, like so many other prophecies of the Messiah that have an original context, have a limit as to how much of that context we can apply to Jesus.

For example, Matthew 2:14–15 states that when Joseph, Mary, and the infant Jesus came back to Israel from Egypt, where they had fled to escape Herod, it was a fulfillment of Hosea 11:1:

> "When Israel was a child, I loved him, And out of Egypt I called My son." (Hosea 11:1)

Here, the original context is speaking about Israel, but Matthew tells us it is also a picture of Jesus. We know to stop short at that verse and not apply the rest of Hosea 11 to Jesus, because the next verse begins:

> "As they called them, So they went from them; They sacrificed to the Baals, And burned incense to carved images." (Hosea 11:2).

Unless we are willing to say that Jesus made sacrifices to Baal, we would have to admit that there is a limit to how much of a messianic prophecy found in another context can apply to Jesus.

To conclude my main point, there is no mention of the Messiah defeating the Assyrian in Isaiah 7–8. It doesn't matter if you think that some or all of this prophecy has a future fulfillment. The fact is that the child in this prophecy does not defeat the Assyrian.

Let's move on to other evidence Richardson offers to support this most important claim that the Messiah is said to defeat the Assyrian. He quotes an obvious messianic prophecy in Isaiah 9:

> "But there will be no gloom for her who was in anguish. In the former time he brought into contempt the land of Zebulun and the land of Naphtali, but in the latter time he has made glorious the way of the sea, the land beyond the Jordan, Galilee of the nations. The people who walked in darkness have seen a great light; those who dwelt in a land of deep darkness, on them has light shined....For the yoke of his burden, and the staff for his shoulder, the rod of his oppressor, you have broken as on the day of Midian. For every boot of the tramping warrior in battle

tumult and every garment rolled in blood will be burned as fuel for the fire. For to us a child is born, to us a son is given; and the government shall be upon his shoulder, and his name shall be called Wonderful Counselor, Mighty God, Everlasting Father, Prince of Peace. Of the increase of his government and of peace there will be no end, on the throne of David and over his kingdom, to establish it and to uphold it with justice and with righteousness from this time forth and forevermore. The zeal of the Lord of hosts will do this." (Isaiah 9:1–7)

Richardson writes the following about this prophecy:

"This passage declares that the Messiah will deliver Israel from the Assyrian in the same manner that Gideon in Judges 8 delivered Israel from the Midianite armies."

That's quite a claim! Is this really telling us that Jesus will destroy the Assyrian? There is obviously no mention of the Assyrian or even Assyria in this passage, so how is Richardson coming to this conclusion?

Before I answer that, let's consider this passage in context. As I have pointed out, it was pretty horrible news that the prophet Isaiah was told to deliver. God asked him to tell Israel that He was mad at them and He was going to send the Assyrians to wipe out the Northern Kingdom. The prophecy we just read tells of a future Israel in which the Messiah will rule with strength and justice. There will be no more conquering of Israel by its enemies when the Messiah begins His reign. This prophecy is clearly meant to be an encouragement to Israel in light of the fact that God is saying through Isaiah that it is about to be conquered.

Richardson is essentially saying since this prophecy about hope for a future peace comes in close proximity to other chapters warning of Israel's destruction by Assyria, that this is a prophecy of the Messiah defeating Assyria when He comes, despite no mention whatsoever of the Messiah defeating Assyria. This same method of interpreting Scripture is applied to Isaiah 10 in order to come to the Assyrian Antichrist view. Here is how another author describes the basis for the idea that the

Antichrist will be an Assyrian based on Isaiah 10:

> "But there is a catch! Immediately after the Assyrian invades Israel in Isaiah chapter 10 we are introduced to the Messiah on earth! [in the next chapter] That is to say, Jesus Christ sets up his everlasting throne in Jerusalem. In other words this passage also predicts a future event. The Assyrian will once again invade Israel, and then Jesus Christ will come back to earth to defeat the Assyrian and to rule forever!"[5]

We can see from these words that the mere proximity of a chapter about the Assyrian to another chapter about the messianic kingdom is proof to him that the Messiah will destroy the Assyrian, despite no evidence in the text to support such a scenario. This fits the definition of *eisegesis* (reading one's own ideas into the text). There is simply no mention of the Messiah defeating the Assyrian in Isaiah 9:1–7.

If we were to apply this method of interpretation to other passages, we would have many contradictory proof texts for the origin of the Antichrist in Scripture. For example, later on in the book of Isaiah, when Assyria is out of the picture and Babylon is the main threat, we find similar prophecies of hope about the future messianic kingdom that directly follow warnings of Judah's destruction by the king of Babylon. If we applied Richardson's view here, we would have to assume that Antichrist would be Babylonian. The same thing can be done to "prove" the Antichrist will be Egyptian. Warnings of impending destruction followed by prophecies of the redemption of Israel are among the most common motifs in the Bible. Unless the text offers an actual reason for us to think we are to apply wholesale the immediate context of one chapter to the prophecy of the Millennium that follows, we shouldn't do it unless we don't mind the myriad contradictions it creates.

---

[5] White, Craig C. "The Assyrian Is the Antichrist!" *High Time to Awake*. N.p., n.d. Web. 16 Jan. 2015.

Richardson also appeals to Isaiah 10 to try to show evidence of the Messiah defeating the Assyrian. In this chapter, God tells His people that after He has used Sennacherib to destroy the Northern Kingdom and humble those in Jerusalem with famine, He will destroy Sennacherib.

> "Then, after the Lord has finished His redeeming work of chastisement toward His people. He will punish the Assyrian: 'When the Lord has finished all his work against Mount Zion and Jerusalem, he will say, "I will punish the king of Assyria for the willful pride of his heart and the haughty look in his eyes."'" (Isaiah 10:12.

Twenty-six chapters later, the book of Isaiah gives us a picture of this judgment of the Assyrian:

> "Then the angel of the Lord went out, and killed in the camp of the Assyrians one hundred and eighty-five thousand; and when people arose early in the morning, there were the corpses all dead. So Sennacherib king of Assyria departed and went away, returned home, and remained at Nineveh. Now it came to pass, as he was worshiping in the house of Nisroch his god that his sons Adrammelech and Sharezer struck him down with the sword; and they escaped into the land of Ararat. Then Esarhaddon his son reigned in his place." (Isaiah 37: 36–38)

Proponents of the Assyrian Antichrist view try to make the case that this judgment of Assyria is not yet complete. But, from a Biblical perspective, there is no doubt that the destruction of the 185,000 Assyrian soldiers and the murder of Sennacherib by his sons, as well as the eventual desolation of the Assyrian Empire, are considered God's judgment against "the Assyrian" because Jeremiah refers to God's judgment of the Assyrian as a past-tense event in his day:

> "Therefore thus says the Lord of hosts, the God of Israel: 'Behold, I will punish the king of Babylon and his land, **As I have punished the king of Assyria.**'" (Jeremiah 50:18)

Richardson makes the case that, despite Jeremiah and Ezekiel[6] saying the judgment of the king of Assyria prophesied in Isaiah 10 is complete, it can't be fulfilled because Isaiah 14 says:

> "I will break the Assyrian in **My land,** And **on My mountains** tread him underfoot. Then his yoke shall be removed from them, and his burden removed from their shoulders." (Isaiah 14:25)

He says that since Sennacherib wasn't killed in Israel, but back home in Assyria by his sons, there must be a future fulfillment in which some other Assyrian man is killed, but this time in Jerusalem.

This is answered with a simple study of the grammar of the passage. This is not a reference to the king of Assyria being "broken," but rather to the fact that the "burden" of the Assyrian yoke was forever broken on the day that God killed 185,000 Assyrians and they left Israel for good.

The NET Bible translates the passage this way:

> "I will break **Assyria** in my land, I will trample **them** underfoot on my hills. **Their yoke** will be removed from my people, the burden will be lifted from their shoulders." (Isaiah 14:25, emphasis added)

The footnotes in the NET Bible explain that the pronouns are collective singular, meaning they likely refer to the nation and not the king. The actual Hebrew word sometimes translated "the Assyrian" is simply *Ashshuwr*, which is ambiguous because it can mean Assyria or Assyrian. Because of the collective singular pronouns, as well as the context which suggests this prophecy is about the nations yoke, or burden, being removed, the most likely translation of *Ashshuwr* here is Assyria, not Assyrian

Since the Assyrian yoke was in fact destroyed on the "mountains of Israel" when the angel destroyed the Assyrian troops surrounding

---

[6] Ezekiel 31:3– 17

Jerusalem, this is not a reason to deny that God has fulfilled His judgment on the Assyrian nation. It should also be noted that the prophecies of Assyria's past-tense judgment are spoken of in Ezekiel 31: 3–17, which reiterates the very elements described in Isaiah 10, further enforcing the idea that the Bible considers this particular judgment having been fulfilled when God destroyed the Assyrian yoke forever by killing 185,000 soldiers in Israel and forcing the Assyrians to abandon military actions against Israel for good.

Micah 5:5

Micah 5:5 provides the best hope for anyone wanting to say the Antichrist is an Assyrian. But, as I plan to show, it is a false hope. It is no surprise that Micah mentions "the Assyrian," since he wrote at the exact same time as Isaiah, during the period when Assyria was threatening Israel. Sennacherib was public enemy number one in Micah's day, and this fact is evident throughout his writings. The passage in question is another prophecy of the Millennium, encouragement to the people of Israel that one day they would not have to deal with being continually conquered and the Messiah would rule Israel with peace and justice. The difference between this passage and the others we looked at in Isaiah is that Micah actually mentions the phrase "the Assyrian" within the millennial context. In other words, the phrase "the Assyrian" is not just near a chapter about the Messiah; it's actually in the same chapter and context.

The passage reads as follows:

> "But you, Bethlehem Ephrathah, Though you are little among the thousands of Judah, Yet out of you shall come forth to Me The One to be Ruler in Israel, Whose goings forth are from of old, From everlasting. Therefore He shall give them up, Until the time that she who is in labor has given birth; Then the remnant of His brethren Shall return to the children of Israel. And He shall stand and feed His flock In the strength of the Lord, In the majesty of the name of the Lord His God; And they shall abide,

For now He shall be great To the ends of the earth; And this One shall be peace. When the Assyrian comes into our land, And when he treads in our palaces, Then we will raise against him Seven shepherds and eight princely men. They shall waste with the sword the land of Assyria, And the land of Nimrod at its entrances; Thus He shall deliver us from the Assyrian, When he comes into our land And when he treads within our borders." (Micah 5:2–9)

The Assyrian Antichrist proponents would say the fact that Micah mentioned the Assyrian in the context of the Millennium is clearly proof that Messiah will defeat "the Assyrian" in the end times and the Antichrist is an Assyrian. However, there are quite a few problems with this interpretation.

The first problem for this theory is that it is almost certainly not Micah's intention to give a prophecy of a future attack by an Assyrian in the Millennium. Rather, he is essentially saying, "Yes, it's really terrible for us right now, being attacked by the Assyrians, but keep in mind that when the Messiah comes, everything will be different, and **should** the Assyrians try to invade our land at that time, we would prevail over them." This interpretation is not wishful thinking on my part. The NET Bible, as well as other Bible translations of this passage, highlights Micah's hypothetical intention:

> "He will give us peace. **Should** the Assyrians try to invade our land and attempt to set foot in our fortresses, we will send against them seven shepherd-rulers, make that eight commanders. They will rule the land of Assyria with the sword, the land of Nimrod with a drawn sword. Our king will rescue us from the Assyrians **should** they attempt to invade our land and try to set foot in our territory." (Micah 5:5–6, 49 NET, emphasis added)

The reason the NET Bible and others translate this as a hypothetical scenario is because each of the instances in question are initiated by the Hebrew particle (*ki*).

This particle has many different uses. It can be related to time, such as when, as in "when the Assyrian"; or it can be conditional, as in "if the Assyrian." The choice depends completely on context and the translator's exegesis. In this case at least one contextual reason to suggest the particle should be translated in its conditional form—as it is 170 other times in the Old Testament—is because of the next problem we will look at, the theological impossibility of putting an Assyrian threat in the middle of the millennial reign when Jesus is ruling with strength and power.

Micah 5:5 is most likely a kind of boast, not a prophecy. It is a hypothetical example to illustrate the security that Israel will finally have in the days of Messiah's millennial rule. The reason Micah uses the Assyrians as an example of people who wouldn't be able to attack Israel when the Messiah comes is tied to the reason this message of hope was given in the first place. The people of Israel were being so terribly destroyed by the Assyrians in Micah's day, it seemed that the promises of God would never come true. This is like saying, "Yeah, the Assyrians are hurting us now, but I'd like to see them try this when the Messiah finally rules Israel."

The second problem with this theory is that this is clearly a reference to events within the millennial reign itself. Not just before the millennial reign, or after, but during the 1000-year period, which would preclude this having anything to do with the Antichrist who is thrown into the lake of fire before the Millennium begins, never to come out again (Revelation 19:20; 20:10). Since the Antichrist's destruction occurs before the Millennium begins, it is impossible for this to refer to the Antichrist. By contrast, Satan is thrown into the "bottomless pit" at the beginning of the Millennium and is let out at the end for one last deception, in which he gathers people and nations to march on the beloved city in a very unsuccessful campaign. After that, Satan is thrown into the lake of fire, the place where the Antichrist has apparently been the whole time (Revelation 20:1– 10; 19:20). If we absolutely had to link the reference to an Assyrian in Micah 5:5 to a future event, we would be limited to it being a reference to Satan or one of the people he recruits to march on Jerusalem at the end of the Millennium. There is no theological scenario that allows for the Antichrist to cause problems during the Millennium; therefore, there is no possibility that the Assyrian in Micah 5:5 refers to the Antichrist.

In conclusion on this point, the references to the "Assyrian" in Isaiah are clearly referring to the Assyrian king of the day, most notably Sennacherib. There is no reason for anything said about him to require a double fulfillment in the last days, since all the things God said He would do to Sennacherib were accomplished within the book of Isaiah and the later prophets testify that his judgment is complete. In the case of Micah 5:5 the references are almost certainly to be seen as a hypothetical scenario, based on the grammar and context. Even if it isn't, the references still can't be about the Antichrist because the Antichrist will be in the Lake of Fire during the events in Micah 5:5.

Chapter 6
The Seven-Headed Beast

In the book of Revelation we are told of a monstrous beast with seven heads and ten horns. In the last days one of the heads of this beast is said to persecute the saints, force everyone to worship him and his image, and force people to receive some kind of mark on their forehead or right hand to show their allegiance to him. This seven-headed beast is almost universally believed by premillennial scholars to be the Antichrist, the Antichrist's kingdom, or both.

Though I will have much to say about the interpretation of this beast by those who subscribe to the Islamic Antichrist theory, I will start with a particular passage in Revelation 17. This passage is primarily used by proponents of that viewpoint as evidence that the seventh head of this beast refers to an Islamic Empire.

In Revelation 17 John has a vision of a strange woman sitting on top of the same seven-headed beast that was first introduced five chapters earlier in Revelation 13. This woman, who we are told represents a city (Revelation 17:18), is riding on top of the Antichrist, seemingly endorsing and promoting the beast and his doctrine. Around verse 7 of this chapter, an angel begins to explain to John the meaning of this particular vision, and in verses 9-11 the angel tells John the meaning of the beast's seven heads. It is this section about the heads of the beast that is so important to the Islamic Antichrist theory.

> "(This requires a mind that has wisdom.) The seven heads are seven mountains the woman sits on. They are also seven kings: five have fallen; one is, and the other has not yet come, but whenever he does come, he must remain for only a brief time. The beast that was, and is not, is himself an eighth king and yet is one of the seven, and is going to destruction." (Revelation 17:9–11 NET)

Before I begin discussing the Islamic Antichrist theorists' interpretation of this passage, it would be helpful to describe some of the more traditional interpretations.

The early reformers who tended to view the Antichrist and his kingdom as the Roman Catholic Church taught that the seven "mountains" were a reference to the seven hills in Rome. On the surface this sounds plausible, but an examination of the original Greek in this passage will reveal that the seven mountains are *also* "seven kings." They are not just mountains. One of those kings seems to come back to life, demand worship, and speak blasphemies. All of this makes it very unlikely that this is a reference to a few hills in Rome —a hill in Rome simply cannot speak, demand worship, or come back to life in any sense. In addition there is a clear reference to five of these mountains/kings having "fallen away" in John's day; it also says "that one is, and one is yet to come." This then simply cannot refer to physical hills in Rome based on the fact that it cannot be said that five of the hills in Rome had "fallen away" in John's day and only one hill remained, while yet another would show up later. This view that the seven heads of the beast are seven hills in Rome, which was widely believed and taught in the past few centuries, is no longer considered a viable interpretation by the majority of premillennial scholars, because of the underlying Greek and the logical inconsistencies.

Most of the other interpretations of this passage tend to see the seven heads/mountains/kings as being aspects of the Antichrist and/or his kingdom over the centuries. For example, they would see the five fallen kings as historical kings or kingdoms that Satan influenced to do his bidding in the past. A typical list of the five fallen kings or kingdoms might look something like this:

1.) Egypt (Pharaoh)
2.) Assyria (Sennecherib)
3.) Babylon (Nebuchadnezzar)
4.) Medo-Persia (Ahasuerus)
5.) Greece (Antiochus Epiphanies)

When the angel says, "one is," it usually is taken to mean that one of these kings or kingdoms existed at the time John was writing. So the sixth kingdom would be Rome with Nero or Domitian being the king in view, depending on when the book was written.

The seventh king is the one we are told is "not yet come." This is the one that is typically seen as the future Antichrist the one that the Bible has so much to say about. Of this final head/mountain/king, it says, "The beast that was, and is not, is himself an eighth king and yet is one of the seven." I know this is a bit confusing, but it seems that the idea here is that the seventh king experiences a kind of death and resurrection which is described in other places in the book. In effect this seventh head rules twice, making it eight kings that rule in one sense, but since the seventh king is the same as the eighth, the angel emphasizes that there really are only seven in total.

Although there are a huge variety of interpretations of Revelation 17:9-11, many follow the basic premise I have outlined: Five kings or kingdoms have fallen in the past, one was at the time John wrote, and the seventh and final head would experience some kind of resurrection. Some interpreters may see different kings or kingdoms than the ones I have listed, or they may see the heads of the beast as only a reference to kingdoms or nations and not at all to people or kings, but they do tend to agree with the basic premise I have described.

With that background in mind we can now fully understand the arguments that Islamic Antichrist proponents like Joel Richardson make with regard to Revelation 17:9-11. They follow the basic pattern as above (5 past fallen heads, one in John's day, and one yet to come who will rule twice after some kind of resurrection). Richardson begins by making a case that the heads/mountains/kings should only be viewed as kingdoms and not as actual kings, a point I will discuss at length later. After making his case that only kingdoms and not kings are in view, he presents the following list of the seven heads of Revelation 17:9-11:

1.) Egypt
2.) Assyria
3.) Babylon
4.) Medo-Persia
5.) Greece
6.) Rome
7.) Islamic Empire
8.) Revived Islamic Empire

The first six kingdoms are in line with what many scholars believe; however, the final head which, as we have discussed, is the seventh as well as the eighth, he insists is the Islamic Caliphate. His main argument for this is the Islamic Empire was the next major empire to follow the Roman Empire, so it should be listed as the seventh. He then applies the traditional views of the dying and resurrecting seventh head to envision a revival of the Islamic Empire in the last days as the embodiment of the eighth head.

At first glance this is not a bad argument. The strength of this interpretation is the Islamic Empire is chronologically the next great empire to appear after Rome's demise. It also seems to correctly understand that the seventh head, the one that resurrects and becomes the eighth head, is not necessarily the same as the sixth head, which is clearly Rome. As Richardson notes in his book, many scholars try to make this passage a reference to the "Revived Roman Empire," but that would require putting Rome as the sixth, seventh, and eighth heads in this list, essentially reviving Rome twice in addition to the historical Rome. This seems forced because it conflicts with the description of timing of the resurrection in verses 9-11, as well as the order of the heads. That being said, I will try to show you why, although I think it is a better interpretation than some, I believe the Islamic Antichrist view of the seven heads of Revelation 17 is fatally flawed.

Richardson believes he has identified the seventh/eighth kingdom as the Islamic Caliphate based solely on the idea that the Islamic Empire directly followed the Roman Empire chronologically. While it is true that the Islamic Empire followed the Roman Empire chronologically, there is nothing whatsoever in the text of Revelation 17 that says the seventh/eighth head is supposed to follow directly after the sixth kingdom (Roman Empire), or that no other empires will precede the seventh head's coming. All it says with regard to the seventh head's chronology are the words "the other has not yet come, but whenever he does come…" This certainly is not telling us to simply look for the next empire to come on the scene after Rome and declare it to be the final head. It is basically saying that it will come at some point in the future. The strength of Richardson's view here is the other empires on this list, Egypt, Assyria etc., did appear more or less chronologically, and so, if there is supposed to be any kind of chronological pattern, then the Islamic Empire would be the logical choice for the seventh head.

The problem with this is there seems to have been a kind of prophetic pause button pressed after 70 AD when the Romans destroyed the Jewish temple. This period of dispensation and waiting has lasted over 2000 years so far, and there is little reason to try to figure in all the empires that have come and gone during that time into the prophetic equation. For example, very few people are attempting to factor the British Empire into this system of ruling empires. Scripture seems to disregard world politics from the time of the destruction of the temple in 70 AD until the future Antichrist appears on the scene. This is the basic dispensationalist understanding of the so-called 70th Week of Daniel, in which there is a kind of prophetic gap, ending with the destruction of the temple by the Romans and beginning again when the Antichrist makes a covenant with Israel (Daniel 9:27). This is why when the angel says, "the other has not yet come, but whenever he does come…" It is quite natural to assume that the advent of the seventh head, which we know as the Antichrist, will make its first appearance with the start of the 70th week of Daniel, which is a future event. There is no reason to go hunting for empires that existed in the last 2000 years during this prophetic no-mans-land for a fulfillment of this seventh kingdom.

The best argument Richardson and other Islamic Antichrist proponents make here—that the Islamic Empire came after the Roman Empire chronologically and should thus be considered the seventh/eighth kingdom—is nullified by the fact that Scripture in no way tells us that the seventh/eighth kingdom is supposed to be the next empire that shows up after Rome. It is far more likely, perhaps even obvious, that the first appearance of the seventh kingdom of the Antichrist coincides with the beginning of the 70th week of Daniel, and, therefore, we can easily disregard empires like the Islamic Empire which appears almost 600 years after 70 AD, as well as empires like the British Empire which came after it. These empires are just not significant to prophecy and are totally overlooked in terms of Daniel's ⁻seventy-week prophetic timetable.

The second problem with this interpretation is that one of the only descriptive details the angel gives us about the seventh head, besides the fact it will seem to resurrect, is it only remains a "brief time."

> "Five have fallen; one is, and the other has not yet come, but whenever he does come, he must remain for only a brief time."
> (Revelation 17:11)

In another place in his book,[7] Joel Richardson tells us the Islamic Empire lasted from 632AD to 1923AD, almost 1300 years. To put that in perspective, the Islamic Empire lasted longer than the Babylonian, Assyrian, Medo-Persian, and Grecian Empires combined! Why would the angel describe the Islamic Empire as only lasting a "brief time," when it's one of the longest lasting empires in the history of the world?

---

[7] Richardson, Joel (2012-06-08). *Mideast Beast: The Scriptural Case for an Islamic Antichrist* (p. 57). Joel Richardson. Kindle Edition.

I can imagine that Richardson and others would say they believe this "brief time" description is only referring to the second manifestation, or the "revived" version of the Islamic Empire in the last days. But all it takes is a simple reading of verse 11 to see that both the context and grammar of the passage demand that the angel is referring to the seventh head, or possibly even to the combined seventh and eighth reigns as being short, but it does *not* seem possible to see this as skipping the seventh head altogether and only referring to the second manifestation of the final, or eighth king. There is an unbroken chronology being laid out in verse 11 that requires us to apply the "brief time" description to the seventh head and, therefore, cannot logically be a reference to the incredibly long lasting Islamic Empire.

> Five have fallen; one [the sixth] is, and the other [the seventh] has not yet come, but whenever he [the seventh] does come, he [the seventh] must remain for only a brief time.

Some might argue that the Bible speaks of things from a larger perspective and so it is okay for it to describe the Islamic Empire as lasting only a short time, since in the grand scheme of world history 1300 years is not that long of a time. I suppose I would agree with this if it weren't for the fact that this kingdom/king is found in a list of six other kingdoms that were not described as being short. The angel only singles out the seventh as being short. It stands to reason that the one kingdom in this list that was described as being short should at least be one of the shorter ones on the list, if not the shortest. But as I have already mentioned the Islamic Empire lasted longer than the combined length of four other kingdoms on the list and is easily one of the longest lasting empires on the list.

There is a very good reason for the angel saying the seventh kingdom only remains a short time and it actually includes the eighth manifestation of the seventh head in that calculation. In other words the combined seventh and eighth reigns of the Antichrist are collectively considered to be "brief," but to understand this, you need to be willing to see the kings in Revelation 17 as kings and not just kingdoms. This shouldn't be too hard since "kings" is exactly what the angel says they are—but more on that later.

The description of the seventh head lasting only a short time, and the fact that the Islamic Empire was unusually long lasting, and there is no good reason given in the text to necessitate the seventh head directly following Rome, combine to form good reasons to doubt Richardson's interpretation of Revelation 17: 9-11. But there is another reason that I think is even better.

As I mentioned earlier Richardson holds the position that the seven heads/mountains should only be seen as nations or kingdoms and not as people or kings. As far as I can tell from his books and blogs, he does not allow for this possibility, which I suppose is good for him because if he did, it would throw a major monkey wrench into his understanding of Revelation 17: 9–11. It would mean there is absolutely no reason to see the seventh king as having anything to do with Islam.

Explaining why this is so will take some time, and it may seem like I am getting off topic during the rest of this chapter, but the following discussion will prove to be significant to the point that the seventh head cannot possibly be the Islamic Empire.

Richardson makes the point that since "mountains" *can* mean empires or kingdoms in other places in Scripture, the heads are referring to nations and not kings. However his interpretation is very strained due to the angel further describing these mountains as "kings" and not kingdoms.

> "(This requires a mind that has wisdom.) The seven heads are seven mountains the woman sits on. **They are also seven kings.**" (Revelation 17:9, emphasis added)

In addition, of the seventeen Bible translations I checked, every single one of them gives the pronoun "he" or "himself" to the actions of the seventh king, suggesting it is a person and not just a kingdom.

> "Five have fallen; one is, and the other has not yet come, but

whenever **he** does come, **he** must remain for only a brief time. The beast that was, and is not, is **himself** an eighth king and yet is one of the seven, and is going to destruction." (Revelation 17:10–11, emphasis added)

I should point out here that many other interpreters and scholars also understand the seven heads/mountains as kingdoms, too. It is true that the Bible often uses the term interchangeably, in part because the actions of a king and his kingdom are usually one and the same thing when dealing with matters of state. But these other scholars, when interpreting Revelation 17:9–11 also allow that the heads/mountains/kings are referring to human kings in addition to kingdoms. Take for example this quote from John Walvoord in his commentary on Revelation 17:9–11:

> "The reference here is to kings, to mountains of temporal dominion, to empires. It must therefore take in all of them."[8]

The reason they can be sure that we must also see the seventh head of the beast as a physical human king as well as a kingdom is not just because the grammar and context of Revelation 17:9-11 seems to demand it, but because we see the exact same seven- headed, ten-horned beast in Revelation 13. In that chapter it is very clear that the head of the beast in question is speaking of the person, not just the kingdom of the Antichrist.

In case there is any doubt that we are dealing with the same beast in Revelation 17 as the one in Revelation 13, take a look at just a few of the characteristics that they both share.

- They both had seven heads, ten horns.
- They both had names of blasphemy on their heads.
- They both were referred to as having been killed yet living.
- They both have the "earth dwellers" "wonder" at them when they see their apparent resurrection.

---

[8] Walvoord, John. *The Revelation of Jesus Christ*. Chicago: Moody Bible Institute of Chicago, 1966

- They both are worshiped by people whose names were not written in the book of life.

Now consider that in Revelation 13 the head of the beast with the mortal head wound is the same one who has an image of himself set up, has people accept a mark that is the number of his name, persecutes the saints, and more, We cannot say that the head in question is simply a kingdom, unless we are also willing to say there really won't be a man who does any of the things we have typically understood the Antichrist will do, since without the details in Revelation 13 we would know very little about the actions of the Antichrist. Joel Richardson himself would have very little to talk about in his books if he did not also believe the head of the beast in Revelation 13 was a man, not just a kingdom.

As I said many other scholars and writers believe the seven heads are kingdoms, but they also are forced to agree that they must also be a reference to human kings. I say they are forced because many writers and scholars, though they see the necessity of such an admission, do not like the theological implications that arise if they accept that the seventh head of the beast in Revelation 17 is referring to an actual person. i.e. the Antichrist. They tend to downplay the human king aspect of the heads and focus only on the "mountains" or kingdoms aspect because focusing on the human king aspect of the final head would mean that the person of the Antichrist is said to physically die and resurrect (Revelation 13:3, 13:12, 13:14, 17:8, 17:11). They rightly see this as a conflict with the idea that only God can raise the dead. So instead, many of them act as if the heads of the beast are only about kingdoms because it is theologically more palatable to say a nation will die and resurrect, even though most of them, if pressed, would admit that this must also have something to do with the Antichrist himself resurrecting. The typical idea they propose is that the

Antichrist doesn't actually die but only seems to, and his resurrection is therefore a fake or counterfeit.

An interesting way to demonstrate this problem is by citing an article put together by Nathan Jones of www.LambLion.us.[9] Jones asked eleven Bible prophecy experts the question: Will the Antichrist be killed and resurrected from the dead? Of the eleven polled, only two, Arnold Fruchtenbaum and Mark Hitchcock, said yes without reservation. One was undecided and the other eight said no. This would seem to suggest that the majority of experts, at least the ones polled, do not believe the heads of the beast are kings, but only kingdoms. However, on closer inspection of the statements of the eight who answered "no," it emerges that they do in fact believe the Antichrist himself will fulfill this prophecy of resurrection in some sense, but that he will only *seem* to die, or his resurrection will be a fake. When you look at it this way, there are really only two people in this poll who believe that the seven heads of the beast have nothing to do with the person of the Antichrist but only his kingdom, and one of those two has clearly been influenced by Joel Richardson.

Typically, Bible teachers are deliberately wishy-washy on this subject. They usually state their belief about the heads being kingdoms with a caveat that if it is talking about the Antichrist, then they believe it has to be a fake resurrection. Take for example this quote from David Reagan

> "I side with those who believe the Antichrist will not be killed and resurrected from the dead. I think the passage is speaking of the Roman Empire rising from the dead and not the Antichrist. **But, if it is speaking of the Antichrist**, I do not believe he will be resurrected from the dead. Instead, I believe his death and resurrection will be a deception using

modern technology."[9]

Others, like John Walvoord, confidently state when commenting on Revelation 13:3 that the deadly wound that was healed on the beast's head is simply a reference to the "Revived Roman Empire" and not to the Antichrist himself. Yet he continues his commentary, referring to the same wounded and healed head as the person of the Antichrist, seemingly oblivious of the contradiction that is inherent in his teaching. As far as I know, he never attempts to explain why the same head is a nation in every verse that talks about it having a deadly wound and a person in every other verse.

I believe there is a simple solution to this problem. In Appendix 2 of this book, I include a detailed explanation of this issue, but I will include a summary of it here. I will also recommend a paper by Gregory Harris professor of Bible Exposition at the Masters Seminary, called "Can Satan Raise the Dead - Toward a Biblical View of the Beast's Wound."

In essence, the idea that whether the Antichrist really dies or only gets a severe wound that would have caused death if he had not been miraculously healed is open to some debate, but when you consider all five verses in Revelation that speak of this wound and its healing, it seems he really does die and really is brought back to life. This, however, poses no theological problem because, based on 2 Thessalonians 2:9–12, it is God, not Satan, who sends the "strong delusion" that eventually causes the world to worship the beast.

> "The coming of the lawless one is according to the working of Satan, with all power, signs, and lying wonders, and with

---

[9] Ibid.

all unrighteous deception among those who perish, because they did not receive the love of the truth, that they might be saved. And for this reason **God will send them strong delusion, that they should believe the lie, that they all may be condemned** who did not believe the truth but had pleasure in unrighteousness." (2 Thessalonians 2:9–12).

When you cross reference this idea with the verses that speak of the beast's wound being healed in Revelation, you find that the reason the world ultimately gives their allegiance to the beast, and thus damn themselves for eternity, is because of the beast's wound being healed, i.e. the strong delusion (Revelation 13:2–4, 17:8). The healing of the beast's wound seems to be the pivotal moment when the world begins to follow the beast and worship him, and that is why I believe Paul in 2 Thessalonians speaks of the "strong delusion" that God Himself sends, the same way.

Now we have come full circle, and as promised I will attempt to quickly explain how this fits into Revelation 17:9–11, and why it is a strong argument against the Islamic Antichrist theorists'' understanding of the passage.

I will quote it again here so you won't have to flip back to the previous page to get the context.

"(This requires a mind that has wisdom.) The seven heads are seven mountains the woman sits on. They are also seven kings: five have fallen; one is, and the other has not yet come, but whenever he does come, he must remain for only a brief time. The beast that was, and is not, is himself an eighth king and yet is one of the seven, and is going to destruction." (Revelation 17:9–11 NET)

When verse 9 says, "The beast that was, and is not," it is actually a reference to the verse 8 before it:

> "The beast you saw was, and is not, but is about to come up
> from the abyss and then go to destruction. The inhabitants
> of the earth—all those whose names have not been written
> in the book of life since the foundation of the world—will
> be astounded when they see that the beast was, and is not,
> but is to come." (Revelation 17:8)

The phrases in this verse, "The beast you saw was, and is not, but
is about to come up from the abyss and then go to destruction." and
"the beast was, and is not, but is about to come" are another way to
say that this beast lives, dies, seems to rise again, and will
ultimately go to destruction or perdition. It's sort of a chronology
of the Antichrist's entire career on earth. This aspect of the
Antichrist functions as a title on several occasions in the book of
Revelation, such as in 13:12,14, but by Revelation 17 this idea of
him living, dying, coming back to life, and going to destruction is a
very firm title of the Antichrist. Even the idea of his coming up
from the "abyss" is a reference to his resurrection, which can be
demonstrated by showing how Jesus' resurrection is described as
coming up from the abyss as well   (Romans 10:6–7). See
Appendix 2 for more on this.

By the time we get to verse 11 which says, "The beast that was,
and is not, is himself an eighth king and yet is one of the seven,
and is going to destruction..." We can see that, when it says "The
beast that was, and is not..." it is an established title of the
Antichrist that refers to his apparent death and resurrection.

First this shows us that the reason for describing the Antichrist as
the seventh and eighth kings is because he essentially has two
aspects of his reign, one before he dies and one after he is
resurrected. One aspect probably begins when he makes a covenant
at the start of the last seven years of the 70th week of Daniel, and

the other aspect of his reign, i.e. the eighth king aspect, occurs at the midpoint. One can assume that the boundaries and nature of his kingdom after the midpoint will be substantially different as well.

This also means that we can make sense of the grammar and context of Revelation 17:9–11 when it seems to suggest that the combined seventh and eighth rule of the Antichrist is short or "brief" because, at only seven years total (three and a half for each), it is by far one of the shortest empires of all time, certainly the shortest of the other six kings/kingdoms on the list.

The third thing this means for us is there is absolutely no reason to see the seventh king/kingdom as being a previously existing kingdom because both the seventh and eighth aspects of the final head, who we are told are actually the same person, have not come on the scene yet, so the idea that this is a the Islamic Empire or any other ancient empire is unnecessary.

I have given several reasons in this chapter as to why the seventh head of the beast in Revelation 17:9–11 is not the Islamic Empire:

- The text is not telling us to simply look for the next empire after Rome.
- The Islamic Empire is one of the longest lasting Empires in history and, therefore, would not be described by the angel as lasting only a "short time."
- Identifying the seventh head as the one yet to come is not just more grammatically and contextually accurate; it is also what one would expect based on the usual understanding of the 70th week of Daniel.
- By limiting the mountains/heads/kings of Revelation 17 to only kingdoms, despite Scripture clearly telling us that "kings" are in view, Richardson contradicts himself and

makes it impossible to see that the seventh and eighth kings are speaking of the Antichrist himself. This means there is no reason to understand the seventh king as the Islamic Empire.

Chapter 7
Mystery Babylon in Saudi Arabia / Mecca

In this chapter I will focus mainly on the claims about Mystery Babylon from Walid Shoebat in his book *God's War on Terror*. It should be noted that Joel Richardson was the co-author of this book, and he seems to agree with this view as well.

Shoebat believes that Mystery Babylon in Revelation 17 and 18 is a reference to Saudi Arabia where the infamous city of Mecca is located. Based on his argumentation, it would not be proper to say Shoebat believes that Mystery Babylon is the city of Mecca but rather the entirety of Saudi Arabia. That being said, it should be noted that in some of his articles for *World Net Daily*, he claims that Mystery Babylon is the city of Mecca in the title of the article, even though the argumentation within the article itself is the same argumentation in his books that Mystery Babylon is Saudi Arabia in general. Because I can't be exactly sure where Shoebat stands on this issue I will make arguments against both positions.

Most of Shoebat's arguments center around the references to the destruction of Babylon in the Old Testament. Because of that, it is important for us to first take a step back and refresh our memories on a few subjects.

In the book of Revelation chapters 17 and 18, we hear of the infamous Mystery Babylon. John describes her as a woman who is riding the seven-headed, ten-horned beast. Later the angel gives us the interpretation of this vision describing the woman as a "city" which is causing the world to sin, especially in relationship to the Antichrist beast that she is riding. It is not clear from the text of Revelation 17 and 18 if we are to see the title of Mystery Babylon as referring to the ancient city of Babylon revived, or if the title "Mystery" is suggesting that there is another, entirely different city in view that is acting like Babylon of old. There are many good scholars on both sides of that issue.

There are also many references to the destruction of Babylon in the Old Testament, notably in Isaiah and Jeremiah. There can be no question that at least some of the Old Testament prophecies were predicting the demise of the historical Babylon both by Cyrus the great when he walked unchallenged into the city of Babylon, thereby ending the Babylonian Empire, and by the Assyrian king Sennacherib when he completely destroyed the city of Babylon in an effort to put down a rebellion. At the same time many phrases found in the Old Testament prophecies about the destruction of Babylon are reused by John in the book of Revelation. These phrases, such as "Babylon is fallen, fallen," are very interesting; clearly there is some kind of association that readers of the Mystery Babylon passages in Revelation are supposed to make with Old Testament prophecies of the destruction of Babylon. In addition, certain prophecies about the destruction of Babylon in the Old Testament, such as the one found in Isaiah 13, clearly use imagery associated with the Day of the Lord and the end times. This has led to speculation as to how much of the Old Testament prophecies about the destruction of Babylon were historical and how much of them should be seen as prophecies that will ultimately be fulfilled in the future.

It is difficult to talk of a general consensus among scholars on this issue, but it seems that most of the premillennial prophecy experts see the Old Testament prophecies about the destruction of Babylon much like they see prophecies about the Greek king Antiochus Epiphanies or the destruction of the Temple in 70 AD. That is, they see these prophecies as having both a near and far fulfillment in which certain aspects of the prophecy have been fulfilled while other aspects of the same prophecy await a future fulfillment. Perhaps another way to say this is that though these prophecy experts tend to see the Old Testament prophecies about the destruction of the historical city of Babylon as being fulfilled in the past, they understand that Scripture is using that historical event as a picture or type of the future destruction of the so called Mystery Babylon in Revelation 17 and 18.

With all that in mind I am going to try to take each claim that Shoebat makes about Mystery Babylon in Revelation or the Old Testament prophecies about the destruction of Babylon on a case-by-case basis. I'll try not to assume too much about how the prophecies in the Old Testament about Babylon and the prophecies in the New Testament about Mystery Babylon are related. I will say, however, that Shoebat's method of interpreting these prophecies is extremely unorthodox, and while that is not always a bad thing, it should be noted that very few people, if any, in the history of the church would apply the methods of interpretation that he does.

The centerpiece of Shoebat's argument that Mystery Babylon is Saudi Arabia is found in Isaiah 21 in which Isaiah predicts the fall of Babylon. I will quote the entire chapter here for your reference.

"The burden of the desert of the sea. As whirlwinds in the South pass through; so it cometh from the desert, from a terrible land. A grievous vision is declared unto me; the treacherous dealer deals treacherously, and the spoiler spoils. Go up, O Elam: besiege, O Media; all the sighing thereof have I made to cease. Therefore are my loins filled with pain: pangs have taken hold upon me, as the pangs of a woman that travails: I was bowed down at the hearing of it; I was dismayed at the seeing of it. My heart panted, fearfulness affrighted me: the night of my pleasure hath he turned into fear unto me. Prepare the table, watch in the watchtower, eat, drink: arise, ye princes, and anoint the shield. For thus hath the LORD said unto me, Go, set a watchman, let him declare what he sees. And he saw a chariot with a couple of horsemen, a chariot of asses, and a chariot of camels; and he hearkened diligently with much heed: And he cried, A lion: My lord, I stand continually upon the watchtower in the daytime, and I am set in my ward whole nights: And, behold, here cometh a chariot of men, with a couple of horsemen. And he answered and said, Babylon is fallen, is fallen; and all the graven images of her gods he hath broken unto the ground. O my threshing, and the corn of my floor: that which I have heard of the LORD of Hosts, the God of Israel, have I declared unto you.

"The burden of Dumah. He calls to me out of Seir, watchman, what of the night? Watchman, what of the night? The watchman said, The morning cometh, and also the night: if ye will enquire, enquire ye: return, come.

"The burden upon Arabia. In the forest in Arabia shall ye lodge, O ye traveling companies of Dedanim. The inhabitants of the land of Tema brought water to him that was thirsty; they prevented with their bread him that fled. For they fled from the swords, from the drawn sword, and from the bent bow, and from the grievousness of war. For thus hath the LORD said unto me, Within a year, according to the years of an hireling, and all the glory of Kedar shall fail: And the residue of the number of archers, the mighty men of the children of Kedar, shall be diminished: for the LORD God of Israel hath spoken it." (Isaiah 21)

Shoebat's main point is that this chapter contains numerous references to cities he believes are in Arabia, such as Duma, Tema and Kedar. Here are a few quotes from his book that highlight his position.

> "Some might argue that the context of Isaiah 21 is only historical. But it is difficult to ignore the multiple references throughout the Book of Isaiah to Kedar, Tema, Dedan and Dumah. Dumah is in Saudi Arabia near Yathrib (Medina), and today is known as "Dumat el-Jandal."[10]

---

[10] Shoebat, Walid; Richardson, Joel (2008-07-21). *God's War on Terror: Islam, Prophecy and the Bible* (p. 397). Top Executive Media. Kindle Edition.

"Contenders to this interpretation would have a difficult time refuting the very direct Biblical references. The names used in these passages make it clear that the reference is not to Rome or literal Babylon on the Euphrates River. Not once do they speak of Rome, Nineveh, Ur, Babel, Erech, Accad, Sumer, Assur, Calneh, Mari, Karana, Ellpi, Eridu, Kish, or Tikrit. All of these literal locations are in Arabia, which was part of the ancient Babylonian Empire."[11]

We can begin to see his position is that Isaiah 21 is not a prophecy of the destruction of historical Babylon but is instead solely a prophecy of the future destruction of Mystery Babylon. Further he believes that this prophecy is not even referencing the geographical area of Babylon in Mesopotamia but rather a reference to Saudi Arabia. In verse 9, which clearly tells us that "Babylon" is in view in this prophecy, he seems to disregard it as a metaphorical reference to Saudi Arabia.

There are so many problems with this interpretation that it is difficult to know where to begin, but I think it would be helpful to try to put this chapter in its historical context first because doing so almost debunks Shoebat's argument by itself.

At the time Isaiah was writing, the main empire of the day was Assyria. Babylon at this time was a major city in the Assyrian Empire, even though the Assyrians had a difficult time controlling Babylon because the citizens of the city were constantly rebelling against Assyrian rule.

Throughout the book of Isaiah, Israel is decimated by the Assyrian Empire. Not only did the Assyrians destroy and capture the entire northern part of Israel, but they also laid siege to Jerusalem and destroyed all the towns and villages in Judah that were not protected by

[11] Shoebat, Walid; Richardson, Joel (2008-07-21). *God's War on Terror: Islam, Prophecy and the Bible* (p. 396). Top Executive Media. Kindle Edition.

the walls of Jerusalem. In other words, Israel had very good reason to hate and fear the Assyrians at this time.

At some point a number of countries in the area decided to rebel against the Assyrians. They thought that if they got enough people together, they would be able to defeat the Assyrian Empire and throw off its yolk. This rebellion was led in part by a man from Babylon named Merodach-Baladan. Keep in mind that at this point it would still be another 100 years or so before Babylon would actually defeat the Assyrians. Merodach-Baladan was nothing more than a rebel leader who seized the city of Babylon and proclaimed himself king, even though the Assyrians still technically controlled Babylon.

Both the Bible and ancient inscriptions tell us that the king of Judah, Hezekiah, decided to make political alliances with Merodach-Baladan in Babylon as well as with Egypt. Hezekiah's plan was to join this rebellion against Assyria in hopes of gaining independence from Assyria, even though by doing so he would be essentially joining up with his sworn enemies. The old adage "the enemy of my enemy is my friend" probably describes his position fairly well. This was a very dangerous move on Hezekiah's part because if their rebellion, led by Babylon, was defeated by Assyria, there would be nothing in the way of Assyria expanding its empire to an unprecedented size.

There are several occasions in the Bible where the prophet Isaiah warns Hezekiah and the people of Judah that making these political alliances is not just foolish, but against the will of God. Despite Isaiah's warnings, Hezekiah joined Judah to the rebels and rolled the dice, putting all his hopes on Babylon and the rebel leader Merodach-Baladan's ability to defeat the Assyrians.

The battle, when it finally came, was devastating for the rebel alliance. The Assyrian king Sennacherib, who by this time was totally fed up with all the trouble that the city of Babylon was causing Assyria, completely destroyed the city. The complete destruction of Babylon and its temples, down to the foundations, is attested to in the historical inscriptions of the time as well as by modern archeologists. The destruction of Babylon shocked the world, mainly because temples in the city, which were considered very holy by many in the area, were also destroyed. Later when Sennacherib's sons assassinated him, they seemed to suggest it was in retaliation for his completely destroying Babylon and its temples. Eight years later, the Assyrians began rebuilding the city from scratch. This marks the only time in history that the city of Babylon was completely destroyed.

After the Babylonian rebellion was crushed, the Assyrian Empire expanded significantly to the east and to the south. They finally conquered Egypt as well as the areas in northern Arabia that were specifically mentioned by Isaiah in chapter 21.

I will now begin making the case that Isaiah 21 should be viewed as prophecy describing the events I have just discussed; the references to the places in Arabia can easily be explained in this context.

Before I begin, I want to assure the reader that I have no trouble with understanding certain prophecies as having both a near and far fulfillment. I see other prophecies about Babylon in Isaiah as requiring us to understand them with that near/far concept in mind. At the same time, I do not see in Isaiah 21 the same "Day of the Lord" language as I see in Isaiah 13 and, therefore, see no reason in the text that demands chapter 21 should be seen as having a near and far fulfillment, let alone as having *only* a future fulfillment, as Shoebat claims.

I would also like to point out that many commentators, especially those of the previous centuries, have seen Isaiah 21 as a reference to Cyrus the Great's conquest of the city of Babylon in 539 BC, which is pictured in Daniel 5, despite the fact that neither the city nor the temples were destroyed at that time. However, as more archeological evidence has become available in the last century, giving us specific details of the events Isaiah lived through and wrote about, we now can see a perfect match with the events described in Isaiah 21 and Sennacherib's destruction of the Babylonian rebellion in 689 BC. As we will see, this not only explains many of the details of Isaiah 21 that were previously a mystery, but it also connects us to the very issues that Isaiah was writing about, such as the foolishness of Hezekiah making alliances with Babylon and Egypt. Thus it is a great theological lesson about failing to trust God that would be difficult to reconcile with any other interpretations.

This is not to say that I believe all references to the destruction of Babylon in Isaiah or Jeremiah refer to the 689 BC event; neither does it mean that I think every prophecy of Babylon's destruction in the Old Testament is purely historical. Rather, I think each prophecy should be examined on a case-by-case basis, and in this case, I think Isaiah 21 is primarily a reference to the destruction of Babylon by Sennacherib in 689 BC.

Why is Isaiah 21 Historical?

One question that seems impossible to explain, if Shoebat's interpretation of Isaiah 21 is correct, is why Isaiah, who sees himself as a "watchman" in this passage, is so upset when he hears the news of Babylon's destruction in verse 9. He is "fearful," "dismayed," and his "pleasure has turned into fear" upon hearing the news that Babylon is fallen. It's not as though this watchman can be seen as a pagan who is upset at Babylon being destroyed, because in verse 10 he tells us he is a servant of "the LORD of Hosts, the God of Israel."

This makes sense only if you understand the context of the rest of the book of Isaiah, in which the prophet has warned Hezekiah of making alliances with Babylon and Egypt against Assyria. Upon hearing the news that Babylon, in whom Hezekiah has put his hopes of salvation, has fallen, there will be no one to stop the expansion of Assyria and thus is terrible news for Israel.

What about all the references to Arabian cities in the chapter? It is because of these references that Shoebat claims that Mystery Babylon is in Arabia, so we need to look closely at each reference to one of these cities.

Dumah

> "The burden of Dumah. He calls to me out of Seir, watchman, what of the night? Watchman, what of the night? The watchman said, The morning cometh, and also the night: if ye will enquire, enquire ye: return, come." (Isaiah 21:11–12)

This little prophecy comes directly after the section about the fall of Babylon and is pretty vague. It pictures the watchman being asked by a passerby "what of the night" and the watchman basically tells him that the morning is coming but also the night"

Dumah was a town located halfway between Israel and Babylon in Northern Arabia. It was the principal city of the Kedarites (a fact that will be important later). Because Dumah lay halfway between Babylon and Israel on a major trade route, it would be natural to inquire of the watchman for news of the events in Babylon. When we look at this in context, we see a man asking the watchman for news of the battle that was described earlier in the chapter, the one where Babylon rebelled against Assyria. The watchman essentially tells the person that there will be a kind of calm before the storm. He essentially says, "Yes, morning is about to come, but night is coming after that." This is a particularly important prophecy when you consider the historical context. Dumah had a particular interest in the outcome of Babylon's rebellion against Assyria since they too had thrown their lot in with the Babylonians in previous rebellions against Assyria.[12][13] A year before the fall of Babylon to the Assyrians, Dumah was captured by the Assyrians and the Kedarite queen Te'elkhunu, who ruled from Dumah, was taken captive back to Assyria. The people in Dumah were devastated and were hoping the rebellion against Assyria by Babylon would be successful. However, as

---

[12] Boardman, John; Bury, John Bagnell; Cook, Stanley Arthur; Adcock, Frank E.; Hammond, N. G. L.; Charlesworth, Martin Percival; Lewis, D. M.; Baynes, Norman Hepburn et al, (1988), p.34. *The Cambridge Ancient History IV: Persia, Greece and the Western Mediterranean c.525–479 B.C.* (2nd, illustrated, reprint, revised ed.), Cambridge University Press.
[13] Leslie (1999), p. 249. Students' aid to pre-modern Middle Eastern studies, Pentland.

we know the rebellion was not successful and there would be no escape for the people of Dumah from the Assyrians. The people of Dumah, although now firmly under the Assyrian yoke, continued to rebel against Assyria in the years that followed but were defeated each time.

Walid Shoebat attempts to convince his readers that the mere mention of Dumah in Isaiah 21 means that Arabia is in view when the watchman speaks of "Babylon." Shoebat doesn't even attempt to explain the context of the passage or why Dumah is mentioned by the prophet. He simply makes the case that since the word Dumah appears in Isaiah 21 and that Dumah is in Arabia, Babylon really means Arabia.

One of the interesting patterns we will see is Shoebat trying his best to make it seem as if these place names are much further south in Arabia. Saying things like "Dumah is in Saudi Arabia near Medina." In reality Dumah is closer to Israel or Babylon than it is Medina. The point here is that though these cities are technically in Arabia, they are all in the very north of Arabia, the only part of Arabia that would fall under Assyrian control. In addition, these cities all have something very important in common; they all had an interest in the Babylonian rebellion against Assyria and as a result of the fall of Babylon, every one of them would soon be swallowed up by the unchecked power of the Assyrian Empire.

Kedar

The next place name in Isaiah 21 mentioned by Shoebat is Kedar. He makes the following statement about Kedar in his book.

> "It is likely that Mecca is the 'glory of Kedar' mentioned in verse 16."[14]

Shoebat gives his readers no clue as to why Kedar is "likely" to be a

---

[14] Shoebat, Walid; Richardson, Joel (2008-07-21). *God's War on Terror: Islam, Prophecy and the Bible* (p. 397). Top Executive Media. Kindle Edition.

reference to Mecca; he simply states this as if it were true and then moves on. To be blunt, there is not a shred of evidence to back up this statement and quite a lot of reasons to refute it.

The Kedarites were a nomadic people who lived in parts of Transjordan and Northern Arabia We know quite a bit about where they lived from various historical records. For example, eighth century BC Assyrian inscriptions place the Kedarites as living in the area to the east of the western border of Babylon. They moved further east into areas of the Transjordan and southern Syria in the seventh century BC, and by the fifth century BC they had spread into the Sinai and as far as the Nile Delta.

By all accounts the Kedarites never extended anywhere near Mecca; at any given time in their history they were hundreds of miles north of Mecca. How could the "glory of Kedar" be a reference to Mecca when they never even came close to the city? We may never know since Shoebat never elaborates on this point.

The principal cities of the Kedarites were Tema, Dedan, and Dumah, all of which are mentioned in Isaiah 21. Dumah, which we have already mentioned, was the capital of the Kedarites. It was a very important religious and political center for them as it was strategically placed on an important trade route, making it sought after by the Assyrians and Babylonians.

Let's look at what Isaiah says about Kedar to learn whether there are good reasons to see this as having any kind of historical fulfillment.

> "The burden against Arabia. In the forest in Arabia you will lodge, O you traveling companies of Dedanites. O inhabitants of the land of Tema, Bring water to him who is thirsty; With their bread they met him who fled. For they fled from the swords, from the drawn sword, From the bent bow, and from the distress of war. For thus the Lord has said to me: 'Within a year, according to the year of a hired man, all the glory of Kedar will fail; and the remainder of the number of archers, the mighty men

of the people of Kedar, will be diminished; for the Lord God of Israel has spoken it.'" (Isaiah 21:13-17)

The Kedarites were considered to be synonymous with "Arabs." This can be seen clearly in several ways, both in the Bible,[15] as well as in historical inscriptions.

Geoffrey W. Bromiley points out[16]:

> "Statements about the Qedarites in the annals of the Assyrian kings of Ashurbanipal and his son Esarhaddon indicate that the term Kedar was almost synonymous with Arabia. Hazael, who ruled c. 690–676 BC, is described as a Qedarite king by Ashurbanipal and 'king of the Arabs' by Esarhaddon."

Thus, though it should be obvious from the context, the "burden against Arabia" in verse 13 is a burden against the Kedarites who are considered the kings of Arabia. This is made even more obvious because the three cities listed in the passage are the three principal cities of Kedar.

The rest of this prophecy is a picture of refugees fleeing. It seems contextually as though these refugees are fleeing from the battle with Assyria since the aforementioned trade route that goes out of Babylon leads strait to Dumah and the other Kedarite cities where the refugees would seek food and shelter.

The last two verses seem to be telling Kedar to give this aid to the refugees fleeing Babylon because in a short time it will be they who will conquered by Assyria, just like the refugees they are told to help.

> "Within a year, according to the year of a hired man, all the glory of Kedar will fail; and the remainder of the number of archers, the mighty men of the people of Kedar, will be diminished." (Isaiah 21:16)

---

[15] Jer 25:23-24; Ezek 27:20-21, Isa 21:13-17.
[16] Bromiley, Geoffrey W. (1994), p. 5, *International Standard Bible Encyclopedia: K-P* (Revised ed.), Wm. B. Eerdmans Publishing.

The prophet says this will happen "within a year." I believe that this is most properly to be understood as a year after this prophecy was given to them by the prophet Isaiah or perhaps a year after the refugees flee. In either case the prophecy seems to be accurate. I believe it is speaking of when they heard this prophecy, and thus determining when the prophet delivered this message is of some importance.

Although it is difficult to determine exactly when this section of Isaiah was written, we can get a pretty good idea. We know that Isaiah lived between 739-681 BC and most scholars think chapters one through thirty-nine were written somewhere around 700 BC, though finding the exact date for each prophecy within those chapters is difficult if not impossible. We know the Kedarites were conquered by the Assyrians in 690 BC, so just based on the most basic assumptions, we at least know that this prophecy of the Kedarites being conquered was fulfilled nine years before Isaiah died. In other words, he lived through the fulfillment of this prophecy; therefore, it is not hard to believe that he really did give them this message exactly one year before it happened.

The "glory of Kedar" could either be a symbolic reference to the good things of Kedar or it could be a reference to the fall of its capital city, Dumah. I believe the latter is the more likely option. When the Assyrians captured Dumah in 690 BC the Kedarite queen was taken captive and Assyrian rule was established. Dumah was by far the most glorious city of the Kedarites, and it contained the principal temple to the goddess Ishtar.

Elam and Media

Shoebat doesn't discuss in his book the references to Elam and Media in Isaiah 21:2, probably because they could never be said to live in Arabia, but I will make a brief mention of them and the most likely reason they are mentioned by the prophet.

Elam and Media were both long-time enemies of Assyria and long-time allies with one another. In fact, they formed the core of the Medo-Persian Empire that would come much later. They both joined several rebellions against the Assyrians around this time, and Elam played a major role in Merodach-Baladan's rebel coalition, which resulted in the destruction of Babylon. Like all the other nations listed in this chapter, they had a lot to lose if the rebellion against Assyria failed. Indeed after Sennacherib destroyed Babylon, the Assyrians were able to spread their influence much further into Elam and Media, and though Elam and the Medes still rebelled from time to time, they would remain firmly under the Assyrian yoke after the fall of Babylon. Therefore, "Go up, O Elam: besiege, O Media" is a reference to Elam and Media's participation in the rebellion against Assyria. In the *New America Commentary*, Larry Walker agrees with this when he says of the participation of Elam and the Medes:

> "This probably relates to the Assyrian attack on Babylon around 689 BC. Babylon's neighbors are being encouraged to attack the Assyrian invading forces."[17]

The Desert of/by the Sea

To make his case that Babylon is not in view but rather Mystery Babylon, which he says is Arabia, Shoebat points to the first verse in Isaiah 21:

> "The burden of the desert of the sea." (Isaiah 21:1)

He argues that this can't be about Babylon in Mesopotamia since Babylon is neither "of" nor "by" the sea (both translations are possible). He says that Saudi Arabia is in view because it is bordered by the Red Sea on the west and the Persian Gulf on the east. Typically Bible scholars see this "desert of the sea" phrase as a reference to Babylon

---

[17] Walker, Larry (2007-06-15). *The New American Commentary* - Volume 15A - Isaiah 1-39 (p. 371). B&H Publishing. Kindle Edition.

sitting between two rivers, the Tigris and the Euphrates, and to the marshy conditions that surrounded the city. If this were the case, we would be encouraged that the same word for "sea" was used in other places to describe rivers that formed marshlands, such as the Nile delta (Isaiah 11:15).

The problem for Shoebat here is that verse 9 tells us bluntly that this burden is about "Babylon" and, whether we like it or not, we must, therefore, understand the "desert of/by the sea" as a poetic term that refers to Babylon. Such an understanding is made much easier when you find other instances of God referring to the rivers of Babylon as a "sea." For example, when Jeremiah is referring to the destruction of Babylon he says:

> "Therefore thus says the Lord: 'Behold, I will plead your case and take vengeance for you. I will dry up her [Babylon's] sea and make her springs dry.'" (Jeremiah 51:36)

We have taken a look at the centerpiece of Shoebat's argument that Mystery Babylon is Saudi Arabia, which is found in Isaiah 21. As we have seen, his argument that there is no historical fulfillment of the events of Isaiah 21 is simply not true. There seems to be a perfect fulfillment in history with the complete destruction of Babylon in 689 BC by Sennacherib. We have also seen that the Arabian cities mentioned in Isaiah 21 which play such an important role in Shoebat's view, have a very natural reason for appearing in the context of a prophecy about the geopolitical fallout that occurs after the destruction of Babylon in 689 BC and the expansion of the Assyrian Empire. There is no reason to suggest the mere appearance of these cities in the text gives us a license to suggest that "Babylon" in verse 9 should be understood as "Saudi Arabia."

We will now move on to some of the other arguments that Shoebat makes in his attempt to equate Mystery Babylon of Revelation 17-18 with Saudi Arabia.

The Merchants and the Red Sea

Revelation 18 describes how sea merchants will lament at the destruction of Mystery Babylon because they will no longer be able to sell the city their merchandise. Verse 9 says that these people will be able to see the smoke that arises from Mystery Babylon from far off. Walid Shoebat makes the following claim about this event in his book, *God's War on Terror*:

> "Where are these sea captains when they hear and view this destruction? Jeremiah tells us they will be in the Red Sea: 'The earth is moved at the noise of their fall, at the cry the noise thereof was heard in the Red Sea'" (Jeremiah 49:21).[18]

Let's examine Jeremiah 49:21 in context to see if this verse is really telling us that the merchants who see Mystery Babylon's smoke in Revelation 18:9 are seeing that smoke from the Red Sea.

> "Therefore hear the counsel of the Lord that He has taken against Edom,
> And His purposes that He has proposed against the inhabitants of Teman:
> Surely the least of the flock shall draw them out;
> Surely He shall make their dwelling places desolate with them.
> The earth shakes at the noise of their fall;
> At the cry its noise is heard at the Red Sea." (Jeremiah 49:20-21)

The first thing you might notice is that this prophecy isn't even about historical Babylon at all; it's about Edom. I would consider it bad form just to apply prophecies of historical Babylon directly to Mystery Babylon, but here Shoebat is going one step further by applying historical prophecies that have nothing to do with Babylon to Mystery Babylon!

---

[18] Shoebat, Walid; Richardson, Joel (2008-07-21). *God's War on Terror: Islam, Prophecy and the Bible* (p. 398). Top Executive Media. Kindle Edition.

In another place, Shoebat tells his readers that is OK for him to use prophecies about Edom and apply them to Mystery Babylon because small parts of Edom were located in modern day Saudi Arabia (very small parts), and since he believes Saudi Arabia is Mystery Babylon, he deems this to be an acceptable way to interpret Scripture when in fact it is nothing more than circular reasoning.

One more reason Shoebat believes it's OK to treat prophecies of Edom as prophecies of the future Mystery Babylon is that he believes Psalm 137:7–8 says that Edom is the "Daughter of Babylon."

> "The Psalms even give us a literal reference to Edom being the daughter of Babylon (born of Babylon): 'Remember, O Lord, against the sons of Edom the day of Jerusalem, who said, "Raze it, raze it, to its very foundation! O daughter of Babylon, who are to be destroyed"' (Psalm 137:7–8)."[19]

Let's take a closer look to see why this verse isn't saying that Edom is the "daughter of Babylon" at all.

In Psalm 137 we have a lament about the Israelites in bondage in Babylon. They are sad because they are being forced to sing happy songs by their Babylonian captors even though they quite naturally don't feel happy at all. In verse 7 the psalmist is remembering that when the Babylonians destroyed the city of Jerusalem, their neighbors, the Edomites, rejoiced and even encouraged the Babylonian soldiers. This Edomite encouragement of the Babylonians soldiers can be seen in other places in Scripture (see Lamentations 4:21–22; Ezekiel 25:12; Ezekiel 35:5; Obadiah 1:10–14).

The issue, however, is with the next two verses in the psalm:

---

[19] Shoebat, Walid; Richardson, Joel (2008-07-21). *God's War on Terror: Islam, Prophecy and the Bible* (p. 398). Top Executive Media. Kindle Edition.

"O daughter of Babylon, who are to be destroyed,
Happy the one who repays you as you have served us!
Happy the one who takes and dashes
Your little ones against the rock!" (Psalm 137:8–9)

This is talking about Babylon, not Edom! The Psalmist has at this point resumed speaking against Babylon and is reminding Babylon of their ultimate destruction. The term "Daughter of Babylon" is used in several places to describe the people of Babylon (Isaiah 47:1, Jeremiah 50:42, Jeremiah 51:33, Zechariah 2:7). The word *Edom* doesn't even appear in any of those chapters. Referring to the "daughter" of a city is a very common biblical motif that refers to the people of that city.

I have read ten commentaries on this passage so far, and every single one of them understands "the daughter of Babylon" in Psalm 137:8 to be a reference to Babylon and not Edom. Walid Shoebat seems to be alone in his understanding of Psalm 137:8, which wouldn't be such a bad thing if he weren't using this interpretation to justify another interpretation, that is its OK to see references to biblical Edom as references to Mystery Babylon.

Getting back to his original claim, let's try to overlook the fact that he is actually using a reference to Edom and telling his readers it's about Mystery Babylon. Let's test the merits of this interpretation using other criteria.

Remember, he said that Jeremiah 49 tells us the sea in which the merchants see the smoke of Mystery Babylon's burning is the Red Sea. However, the verse he is referring to only says "the cry its noise is heard at the Red Sea." This is talking about when Edom falls, people will be able to hear the noise as far as the Red Sea. This isn't saying anything about merchants seeing smoke at all. In addition it's totally logical to speak of the noise of Edom's fall being heard at the Red Sea because Edom is touched by the Red Sea on its southwestern border.

To sum up this point, Shoebat's claim that Jeremiah 49 tells us the merchants who see the smoke of Mystery Babylon's burning in

Revelation 18:9 are in the Red Sea is incompetent at best, and dishonest at worst. There is no mention of anyone seeing smoke or anything else in Jeremiah 49, nor are merchants mentioned at all. The fact that he uses a prophecy of Edom's destruction in Jeremiah 49 and calls it a prophecy about Mystery Babylon is simply untenable, and his reasons for justifying such an interpretation are just as bad.

The Cup Full of Oil

The city of Mystery Babylon is pictured in several places as having a cup of wine in her hand (Revelation 17:4, 18:3). In Revelation 18:3 it is said that the nations become drunk on her wine:

> "For all the nations have drunk of the wine of the wrath of her fornication, the kings of the earth have committed fornication with her, and the merchants of the earth have become rich through the abundance of her luxury." (Revelation 18:3)

Walid Shoebat claims that the wine in the harlot's cup is oil, and since Saudi Arabia is a very large producer of the world's oil, this interpretation would obviously fit with his view that Saudi Arabia is Mystery Babylon. Shoebat argues that the nations will be intoxicated with their need for oil and this need for oil draws them into the Antichrist's system.

I will attempt to refute Shoebat's idea by taking a closer look at what Scripture says about this cup of wine Mystery Babylon is holding to see if his interpretation holds up to scrutiny.

Revelation 17:4 tells us the woman's cup is filled with "abominations and the filthiness of her fornication"

> "Having in her hand a golden cup full of abominations and the filthiness of her fornication." (Revelation 17:4b)

In Revelation 18:4 this is reiterated when it says the cup contains the "wine of the wrath (or fierceness) of her fornication."

Regardless of their ultimate viewpoint as to the identity of Mystery Babylon, scholars typically see this cup as a symbol of the harlot's fornication with the Antichrist. The picture being painted is that of a city having embraced the Antichrist and his doctrine with such passion that the rest of the world is made drunk by the intensity, or "wrath," of this city's religious fornication with the beast.

If we take Shoebat's view that this cup contains oil, then the descriptions given to the contents of the cup do not make sense. It would mean that oil in itself is an "abomination," "filthy," and considered to be "fornication." It's important to recognize that when it uses this strong language, it is clearly talking about the actual contents of the cup; therefore, one must be ready to conclude that oil, in itself, is an abomination to God.

It is highly unlikely that crude oil would be considered sinful by God. While it is no doubt true that many terrible things have come about because of the use of oil, many good things have come about as well, such as missionaries being able to travel all over the world. Other types of oil were used in biblical times for a variety of purposes, such as lamps and anointing kings. One might argue that this was olive oil or other types of vegetable oil and thus didn't need to be taken out of the ground. However, many other things, such as minerals, were taken out of the ground and made use of in biblical times. We never see a single hint in all of Scripture that using the natural resources of the earth is sinful in itself. However, believing that oil is inherently sinful is the logical outcome of Shoebat's interpretation because the text is so clear that the wine itself is an abomination, not the act of letting the kings drink it.

I would also argue that this interpretation strips Mystery Babylon of her harlot status because the wine of her fornication and abomination is the very reason she is pictured as a harlot in the first place. She is committing the worst kind of fornication and abomination by embracing the Antichrist and promoting him to the rest of the world. If you replace that wine with oil, all she is really doing is selling oil to people, which does not seem nearly a bad enough crime to warrant her being labeled as a whore.

This interpretation also seems to suggest that the world is made to worship the Antichrist primarily because of oil. While I agree that the threat of being cut off from Saudi Arabia's oil would be a major blow to the economy, it should be noted that, while they produce 13.80 percent of the world's oil (as of 2014), the United States produces 13.09 percent, almost exactly as much. I can hardly imagine that Saudi Arabia's refusal to sell oil to the world would lead the world to convert to Islam just to attain 13 percent more oil.

This idea of oil being the wine in the harlot's cup does not adhere to sound methods of interpreting the Bible. I would be surprised if there is a single scholar who would endorse such a view, and as far as I know, none do.

The Wilderness

In Revelation 17:3 John is taken by an angel to the wilderness to see a vision of Mystery Babylon. We are told this occurs "in the Spirit."

> "So he carried me away in the Spirit into the wilderness. And I saw a woman sitting on a scarlet beast which was full of names of blasphemy, having seven heads and ten horns." (Revelation 17:3)

This is similar to other visions that were given to Old Testament prophets like Ezekiel, who was also taken "in the spirit" to see part of God's plan in the form of a vision.

> "The hand of the Lord came upon me and brought me out in the Spirit of the Lord, and set me down in the midst of the valley; and it was full of bones." (Ezekiel 37:1)

Walid Shoebat makes the case in his book that the word *wilderness* here, which can just as easily be translated "desert," necessitates that the city in view here must be found in a desert. He believes this is an argument in support of his theory that Mystery Babylon is Saudi Arabia.

It does not seem at all clear that we are to understand the wilderness or desert to have a literal referent any more than the "waters" in which the beast sits. In 17:15 we are told by the angel that the water is a symbolic representations of many peoples and nations. Similarly we are told the woman in the vision is a symbolic representation of a city, and the beast's heads are really kings.

It could be said that the waters and the woman were only elements of the vision, but the desert was the location of the vision and so is to be taken more literally than the elements of the vision itself. While this could be true, we must also remember that John, in the book of Revelation, is carried by angels to several places, and not all of those places would fit if we applied Sheobat's methods. For example, in Revelation 13 John is taken to a seashore where he watches the Antichrist rise out of the sea. If we were to apply the same interpretation here, we must conclude that the Antichrist comes from somewhere in the Mediterranean Sea. Interestingly Shoebat, in the case of Revelation 13, sees the location of the vision as symbolic. Here in Revelation 13, he understands the sea to be symbolic of gentile nations, a point we will discuss in a later chapter. In essence, he is interpreting this in the exact opposite fashion that he does in Revelation 17. If this hermeneutic cannot be consistently applied in the same book, regarding the exact same seven-headed beast, it would seem to be a faulty method of interpretation.

To be fair there are many instances when the location that God took the prophets to have a vision has a clear correlation to the location of the events that he showed them. For example, Ezekiel is taken "in the Spirit" to Jerusalem to see the idolatry and Tammuz worship that was secretly going on in the temple (Ezekiel 8:1–13). However, in that case the vision was not at all symbolic; it was simply God showing Ezekiel the people and places He wanted Ezekiel to see. This correlation to the vision's location with the events shown may not be the case when the vision is highly symbolic in nature, like so many of the visions in the book of

Revelation. If we look at the vision of the valley of dry bones in Ezekiel 37, which is much more symbolic, we see that he has again been transported "in the Spirit" by God. In this case he is taken to an unnamed valley. Here he sees a symbolic vision of Israel coming back from desolation, pictured as bones coming back to life. He also sees symbolic pictures of the two houses of Israel being reunited, as well as the start of the messianic kingdom. In this case are we to understand that this valley is where all these events will take place? If the Bible commentaries are correct, this valley that Ezekiel was taken to is the same one mentioned in Ezekiel 3:22, namely a valley near Tel-Abib in Syria. Surely Shoebat wouldn't claim that the Messianic Kingdom will be centered in Syria because that is the location of this vision. If it is not a picture of that valley, then it could simply be a sort of "theater" in which to see symbolic visions. If this is the case, there is no reason to see the wilderness in Revelation 17 as the location for the symbolic events any more than the valley is the location for the symbolic events in Ezekiel 37.

For the sake of argument, let's assume that the wilderness/desert in Revelation 17:3 is not just a theater of sorts for John's vision, but rather that he was taken to some specific desert and this location plays a major role in the interpretation of the events in Revelation 17-18.

It should be noted that the most common usage for the Greek word translated as *wilderness* or *desert* in the New Testament refers to the wilderness of Judea. This desert is located less than five miles from the city of Jerusalem. It was in this desert that John the Baptist preached and Jesus spent forty days before he began His ministry. Jesus often went into this desert to pray. It is just as logical, if not more so, to understand the wilderness or desert in Revelation 17:3 as the Judean desert. I mention this to make the point that there are many possible places that could be in view in Revelation 17:3. To assume it is referring to Saudi Arabia above all the others, just because a wilderness is mentioned, would be very presumptuous.

It could also be the case that the Judean wilderness served as the theater for John to see the symbolic vision simply because of its significance to the events being described about the Antichrist. We know, for example, that the Antichrist will spend a great deal of time in Jerusalem, if not a majority of his time (Daniel 9:27, Matthew 24:15–16, 2 Thessalonians 2:4). Therefore watching a symbolic representation of the actions of the Antichrist from the Judean wilderness on the border of Jerusalem would be natural.

Wealth, Etc.

Most of the rest of Shoebat's arguments for Saudi Arabia being Mystery Babylon are very general and, as such, can and have been applied to just about every candidate for Mystery Babylon in history. For example Shoebat spends a great deal of time telling us that Saudi Arabia is very wealthy. This may be true, but if we put Saudi Arabia's wealth in context it is only the thirteenth richest nation in the world, just behind South Korea. It doesn't sound nearly as interesting when you put it that way.

I feel that many commentators miss the point with this type of argumentation. Mystery Babylon's wealth is related to the Antichrist and his massive conquests. We are told that he receives large amounts of gold from the nations he conquers during his rise to power (Daniel 11:43). In addition he seems to be able to control the buying and selling of all items sold in the world (Revelation 13:17), not to mention that he will be worshipped by the world. In other words, the Antichrist's wealth has not been made yet; his city won't become the political, military, and economic powerhouse it is said to be until he shows up. Therefore, all this talk about which nation is currently the strongest, the richest, or the most blasphemous is a waste of time. All we have are the words of Scripture to tell us what the Antichrist's kingdom will be once he arrives. To say this another way, the chapters about Mystery Babylon tell us of the capital city of a future empire. And though that city almost certainly exists today, it is almost a guarantee that it does not currently act as it will when it becomes the capital city of the Antichrist.

Additional Problems with the Saudi Arabia View

Before concluding this chapter about Mystery Babylon, I would like to make a few other points that were not specifically addressed by Walid Shoebat in his book.

The angel in Revelation 17:18, while interpreting John's vision, says the woman is a city.

> "And the woman which thou sawest is that great city, which reigneth over the kings of the earth." (Revelation 17:18)

Mystery Babylon is referred to as a city eight times in Revelation, and many of the things that happen to it in the narrative seem to be talking about a literal city. It is difficult to believe that the angel got this point wrong or that we are to understand the angel's interpretation as an allegory, considering the fact that the whole purpose of the angel's interpreting the vision was to explain the literal truth of John's allegorical vision.

Shoebat claims that Mystery Babylon is not a city but rather Saudi Arabia. It may be argued that Shoebat occasionally says Mystery Babylon is Mecca, a particular city in Saudi Arabia. For example, he wrote an article for World Net Daily called "Mystery Babylon Is Mecca Not Vatican."[20] Yet in that article he uses the same argument discussed in this chapter (that Arabian cities are mentioned in Isaiah 21), which can only be an argument for Saudi Arabia, not Mecca. If Shoebat does believe that Mystery Babylon is Mecca and not Saudi Arabia, then he should write a new book with new arguments because most of the arguments for Saudi Arabia used in his book are not interchangeable with Mecca at all.

Another point that argues against Mystery Babylon being Saudi Arabia is that Saudi Arabia cannot be said to contain the "blood of

---

[20] Shobat, Walid. "'Mystery Babylon' Is Mecca Not Vatican." *WND*. N.p., 31 May 2013. Web. 16 Jan. 2015. http://www.wnd.com/2013/05/mystery-babylon-is-mecca-not-vatican.

the prophets." It is true that Saudi Arabia is no friend to Jews or Christians, but if the term "prophets" in Revelation 18:24 refers to the biblical prophets, then we can say with certainty that Saudi Arabia is not in view, since no biblical prophets were killed there.

I believe that the best argument against Saudi Arabia, or any other candidate for Mystery Babylon, is the positive argument because if you truly have the correct view about Mystery Babylon or any other doctrine, then everything will fall into place. The difficult passage will no longer be difficult, and the mysteries will no longer be mysteries. I believe I know the correct view of Mystery Babylon (don't we all right?). I wrote a book about it a few years back. However because of my commitment not to use my own personal views to debunk the Islamic Antichrist view in this section, I will refrain from explaining my view here. If you would like to know more, I will include in Appendix 3 of this book a short summary of my views about Mystery Babylon.

Chapter 8
The Mark of the Beast

Walid Shoebat, in his book *God's War on Terror*, endorses a very unique approach to understanding the so-called "mark of the beast" in Revelation 13:18. Most Bible scholars and teachers have understood the mark of the beast in Revelation to be the number 666. Shoebat, however, proposes that John, the writer of the book of Revelation, did not intend for us to understand this mark as a number at all. Shoebat says that John was supernaturally shown the Arabic words for "in the name of Allah" and a picture of crossed swords when he was writing Revelation 13:18. John then supposedly wrote down these Arabic letters and symbols just as he saw them. Later generations of scribes, however, apparently misunderstood John's intentions due to the Arabic symbols resembling the Greek letters *Chi Xi Sigma*. These scribes wrote the Greek letters instead of the Arabic symbols when making subsequent copies, and since the Greek numbering system is based on letters, scholars mistakenly believe the mark of the beast to be the number 666.

Contextual Problems

I begin with the argument that the context of this passage does not support his thesis. The verse in question reads as follows:

> "Here is wisdom. Let him who has understanding **calculate** the **number** of the beast, for it is the **number** of a man: His **number** is 666." (Revelation 13:18)
> Notice the words "calculate" and "number" in the above verse. These words are quite blatantly telling us that we are to look for a number. Because we see phrases like "it is the number of a man," and "his number is," it would seem that John was well aware that he was intending the reader to understand the mark as a number.

Shoebat writes the following about this problem in his book:

> "Now consider the alternate translation that the Allah Theory could produce. The Greek word Psephizo, translated above as 'count,' can also quite naturally mean 'reckon' or 'to decide.' Likewise, the Greek word Arithmos, translated above as 'number' can also mean 'an indefinite number or multitude,' 'multitude,' in the case of more than one, such as a multitude of people. With this in mind, consider the following translation, as it makes very good sense:

> "Here is wisdom. Let him that hath understanding reckon (or decide, discern) the multitude of the beast, for it is the multitude of a man [that is, Mohammed and or the Mahdi-Antichrist] and his multitude [are identified through the following] 'In the Name of Allah and the two swords (or

Jihad).'"[21]

Count/Calculate

Let's start with the word *psephizo*, which is often translated as "count" or "calculate." Shoebat says the word can simply mean to discern or decide and doesn't necessarily have to do with counting anything. *Psephizo* is a very rare Greek word in the New Testament; in fact, the only other time it occurs in the Bible is in Luke 14:28:

> "For which of you, intending to build a tower, does not sit down first and **count** the cost, whether he has enough to finish it."

Here the word is obviously used in the sense of counting. Jesus is talking about a man counting his money to see if he has enough to finish a building project. The word is never used in a general sense, as in to discern or decide. The Greek language has a much better word for that (*dokimazō*), which is used quite often in the Bible, and if John had meant to simply say reckon/decide/discern in the sense Shoebat is using it, he almost certainly would have used *dokimazō*.

Shoebat says that the word *psephizo* (calculate/count), "can also quite naturally mean 'reckon' or 'to decide.'" In other words, it can be used without reference to numbers or counting. I can only imagine Shoebat looked at some Greek lexicons like Strong's or Thayer's and simply saw the word "reckon" and "decide" but failed to read the full lexicon entry carefully because these lexicons clearly define the word as related to counting something. I will show you an example of one such lexicon so you can see what I

---

[21] Shoebat, Walid; Richardson, Joel (2008-07-21). *God's War on Terror: Islam, Prophecy and the Bible* (p. 372). Top Executive Media. Kindle Edition.

mean.

STRONGS NT 5585: ψηφίζω

ψηφίζω; 1 aorist ἐψηφισα; (ψῆφος, which see); **to count with pebbles, to compute, calculate, reckon**: τήν δαπάνην, Luke 14:28; τόν ἀριθμόν, to explain by computing, Revelation 13:18. (Polybius, Plutarch, Palaeph., Anthol.; commonly and indeed chiefly in the middle in the Greek writings **to give one's vote by casting a pebble into the urn; to decide by voting**.) (Compare: συγψηφίζω, καταψηφίζω, συμψηφίζω.)[22]

The word "reckon" in the lexicon above is expected to be understood as synonymous with the other words in the definition, like "compute" and "calculate." Reckon, in this case, is limited to reckoning as it relates to counting. Similarly, notice that in the discussion of how the word was used in other Greek writings, psephizo meant "decide" in the sense of "deciding by voting," which is related to counting. After consulting every major Greek lexicon I have available, I have not found a single one that would allow psephizo to be used the way Shoebat uses it. If Shoebat would like people to believe his translation, I would suggest he needs to produce a Greek scholar or some very good argumentation sufficient to overturn the understanding of this Greek word in the scholarly world.

Number

The word number, which is used three times in Revelation 13:18, comes from the Greek word *arithmos*, which is where we get the English word arithmetic. Shoebat translates this word as "multitude." While it is true that the word *arithmos* can mean multitude, it cannot be used the way Shoebat is using it. Lexicons give two possible definitions for arithmos:

---

[22] "Thayer's Greek Lexicon". *STRONGS NT 5585*. N.p., n.d. Web. <http://biblehub.com/greek/5585.htm>.

1. A fixed and definite number.

2. An indefinite number, a multitude.

The second definition is only using "multitude" in the same way that English speakers use the word "number" to describe an indefinite number (e.g., There are a number of cats over there, or The number of homicides in the city has risen alarmingly.)

One way to show that Shoebat's translation is not possible is to first show you that the Bible already has a word for "multitude" when it is used the way that Shoebat is using it. The Bible uses the Greek word "*ochlos*" to refer to a crowd of people, and it does so 175 times in the Bible, including four times in the book of Revelation (7:9, 17:15, 19:1,6). When *ochlos* is used, it always describes a group of people.

> "Now when the multitudes saw it, they marveled and glorified God, who had given such power to men." (Matthew 9:8)

A good way to see the difference in these two words is to substitute "number/ *arithmos*" for "multitude/*ochlos*" in the sentence above:

> Now when the number saw it, they marveled and glorified God, who had given such power to men. (Matthew 9:8)

In this case we would wonder *the number of what?* It requires a subject because the second definition of *arithmos* simply means "an indefinite number," whereas *ochlos* means a group of people, that is, only people.

I again referenced every available lexicon I have available to me and did not find a single one that would allow for Shoebat's interpretation of this passage. When Shoebat says a Greek word "can also quite naturally mean" something else, he needs to give some significant reasons to believe him, especially considering that the reference material disagrees with him.

Restoration Scriptures True Name Edition

Shoebat, in an attempt to justify his translation of Revelation 13:18, says the *Restoration Scriptures True Name Edition* translates the passage in an almost identical way as he translates.

That leads us to a pretty interesting story. The *Restoration Scriptures True Name Edition* is a translation put together by one man, a messianic author and pastor from Florida named Moshe Koniuchowsky. Koniuchowsky has many sermons that preach, almost verbatim, the theories of Walid Shoebat, including this theory about the mark of the beast. I started to expect plagiarism on the part of Shoebat when reading over Koniuchowsky's material since it was written long before Shoebat published his books. Then I discovered the Simon Altaf connection.

Simon Altaf was a member of Koniuchowsky's ministry team at one time and heavily influenced Koniuchowsky's end times teachings. Walid Shoebat was a good friend of Altaf in the early days of his ministry; in fact, they wrote a book together called *This is Our Eden, This is Our End,* which is now out of print. Two years before Shoebat's book *God's War on Terror* came out, Altaf wrote a book called *Islam, Peace or Beast* about the Islamic Antichrist doctrine, which included the exact material on virtually every topic Shoebat covers, including the mark of the beast material that later appeared in Shoebat's book. Altaf accused Shoebat of plagiarizing his work in an article on his website and the two are no longer friends.[23]

Altaf's book was published originally by Your Arms to Israel, Moshe Koniuchowsky's ministry. Shoebat has since accused both Altaf and Koniuchowsky of being "cult leaders" who practice polygamy and bad doctrine.[24] It should be noted that both Altaf and Koniuchowsky do not

[23] Altaf, Simon. *Walid Shoebat Fraud Exposed.* African-israel.com, 26 Feb. 2009. Web. 16 Jan. 2015. http://www.african-israel.com/False%20Christians/Walid.html.

[24] Richardson, Joel. "A Public Rebuke and Warning from the Walid Shoebat Foundation." *Joel's Trumpet.* N.p., 21 July 2008. Web.

deny that they practice "plural marriages" and seem quite proud of that fact.

So to sum up this point, Walid Shoebat, in an attempt to justify his translation of Revelation 13:18, points us to a self-published Bible which he admits was written by a "cult leader" whom he personally knows. In addition, Shoebat clearly influenced the translation of Revelation 13:18 in Koniuchowsky's Bible, either directly or if you believe Simon Altaf, Altaf influenced Koniuchowsky with the exact same arguments that Shoebat would later steal from Altaf. Either way, this is an absolute mess, and Shoebat does not gain an ounce of credibility for his decidedly awful translation of Revelation 13:18 by citing Koniuchowsky's *Restoration Scriptures True Name Edition.*

The Greek Text

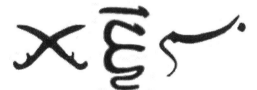

"In the Name of Allah"

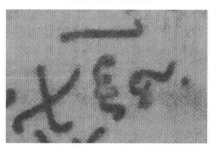

Mark of the Beast "666" in Codex Vaticanus

When making his case on the mark of the beast, Shoebat puts particular emphasis on the facsimile of *Codex Vaticanus* that is in the library of

Bob Jones University. Shoebat claims that when he visited the library, he was surprised to find that he could read the 666 section of Revelation 13:18 because "it was in Arabic."

The following is a picture of the two relevant images that are typically shown to demonstrate this theory. The top image is of the Arabic words "in the name of Allah," followed by a picture of crossed swords (Arabic is written from right to left). The bottom image is from the copy of *Codex Vaticanus* at Bob Jones University.

There are misrepresentations in virtually every aspect of these images, but the best place to start would be with regard to the history of this copy of *Codex Vaticanus* and its lack of relevance to Shoebat's thesis.

Throughout Shoebat's book he continually tells his readers that the codex he saw at Bob Jones University is dated to 350 AD. This is significant because Shoebat is trying to say that the earliest copies of Revelation 13:18 looked like the image he is presenting, so convincing his readers that the image he shows them is a very early copy is paramount to his theory.

The problem is that while much of the copy of *Codex Vaticanus* is dated to around 350 AD, the book of Revelation was not included in the original and was added by a scribe in the fifteenth century. The styles of writing between the early portions of the codex and the book of Revelation are vastly different. The style of the Greek text in the picture above is called "miniscule," and it wasn't even invented until around the ninth century.

All of the early Greek writings of the New Testament were written in a style known as Uncial, which looks nothing like Arabic.

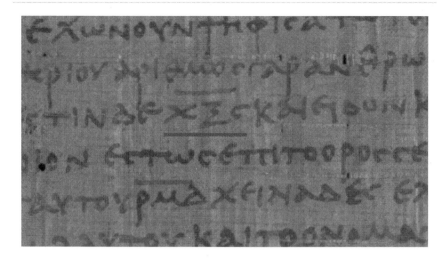

In the image above, from the p47 fragment of Revelation which is dated to around 250 AD, you will notice that the *Chi-Xi-Sigma* (666) looks very different from the way it is presented by Shoebat. The same is true with every single early copy of the book of Revelation, such as p115 (shown below) in which you can see that the sigma look very simple, like the English letter C.

In the p115 fragment (dated to around 300 AD), the number in p115 is actually 616, a variant reading of the text, which was recognized as wrong by church fathers such as Irenaus as early as 180 BC. In his book

Against Heresies, Irenaus explains that there were some copies of Revelation that read 616, but the majority of the texts read 666 which he explained was even the opinion of those who were taught by the Apostle John "face to face." The 666 vs 616 argument is irrelevant to our discussion at the moment. The important thing is that all early Greek writings were written in a completely different way than in the picture Shoebat shows. Remember, this is a picture which he dishonestly says was written in 350 AD, when in fact it was written over 1000 years later in a type of Greek writing that would have been completely foreign to John or any other Greek writer at the time.

Chi

As I said earlier, there are misrepresentations in every aspect of Shoebat's images, so I will need to take it section by section in order to debunk it. I will start with the Greek letter *Chi* which Shoebat says is really a picture of crossed swords.

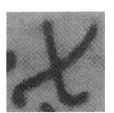

Crossed swords

Chi from
Codex Vaticanus

It should first be noted that there is no actual correlation with Chi, which looks like an X, to any Arabic letter or word. When Shoebat says he was surprised he could read this section of Revelation 13:18, he couldn't have been referring to the letter *Chi*, since there is no Arabic letter equivalent to it. Instead Shoebat claims that John was shown a picture of crossed swords, which Shoebat says, "is used universally throughout the Muslim world to signify Islam." So the first thing we must accept if we are to believe Shoebat's theory is that God showed John a mixture of Arabic words, as well as a picture. It seems more likely that Shoebat, when finding no way to incorporate the letter *Chi* into Arabic, had to resort to claiming it was a picture instead of an Arabic word.

It is obvious that Shoebat would need to really emphasize the "universality" of the crossed swords relationship to Islam in order to make this theory coherent, but the crossed swords symbol is far from a universal symbol of Islam. In fact, most Jihadist flags, banners, and badges don't contain any swords at all; some have only one sword, if any. There are a few that have two crossed swords, but only an extremely small minority of those contain the words "in the name of Allah." The most common Arabic phrase on Islamic insignia is the *"Shahada"* which says, *"There is no god but God, Muhammad is the messenger of God"* and looks nothing like the Greek symbols for *Chi-Xi-Sigma.*

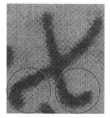 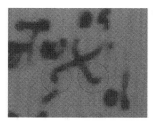

| Chi from the mark of the beast passage of Codex Vaticanus | Chi from another Revelation passage in Codex Vaticanus |

One of the many reasons Shoebat sticks to the version of Revelation 13:18 produced by this fifteenth century scribe is the way the scribe wrote the letter *Chi* which is different from other scribes. It should be noted that with Greek miniscule texts in the fifteenth century, it was common for scribes to have their own unique style. This particular scribe wrote the letter *Chi* with the flourishes on the bottom two legs of the X, which made it possible for Shoebat to claim they were sword handles.

There are two problems with this. The first is that this is how the scribe wrote the letter *Chi* in all the other instances of the letter in the book (see picture above). There is nothing unique about the scribe's letter *Chi* in Revelation 13:18 from any other instance of the letter *Chi*. He didn't add "sword handles" just to this verse, but apparently he added sword handles every time he wrote the letter. The second problem is that this scribe's particular style when writing the letter *Chi* (putting the flourishes on the bottom two legs) is different than other scribes of the era (see picture below), and indeed is not consistent with how the letter was written at any time, including all the earliest copies of the book of Revelation.

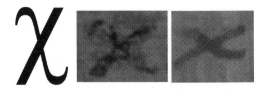

If flourishes were to be added to *Chi*, even in the much later miniscule texts, they were almost always on the same line. Shoebat's theory would not work with these images because that would mean one of the "swords" in the picture consists of just two handles, while the other is just two blades. We will keep running into reasons why Shoebat must stick to this particular fifteenth century scribe's version of Revelation.

Xi

Shoebat says that the Greek letter *Xi* in Revelation 13:18 corresponds to the Arabic word for "Allah."

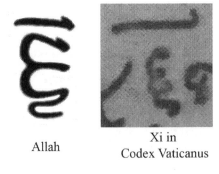

Allah

Xi in
Codex Vaticanus

The first thing to note is that this is not how *Xi* was written in John's day, nor is it the way it is written in the earliest copies of the book of Revelation.

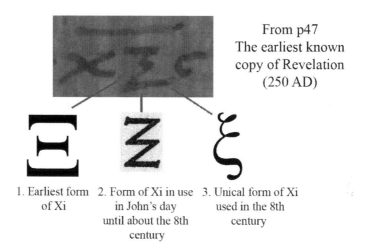

From p47
The earliest known
copy of Revelation
(250 AD)

1. Earliest form   2. Form of Xi in use   3. Unical form of Xi
of Xi   in John's day   used in the 8th
               until about the 8th   century
               century

Notice that the letter is not curvy at all in the oldest copies of Revelation. *Xi* was originally just three lines, but by John's day had developed into more of a jagged zig-zag form. It would be almost another 800 years before the letter *Xi* began to be written with the curvy fashion that Shoebat shows.

The Line Above Xi

Here again we will see an example of why Shoebat emphasizes the fifteenth century version of Revelation in *Codex Vaticanus* above all others. Notice that the line above the letter *Xi* is only above that letter; notice also the flourish that the scribe adds to the line.

"In the Name of Allah"

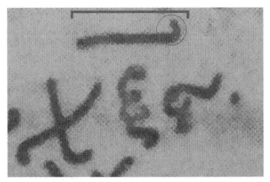

Mark of the Beast "666" in Codex Vaticanus

In other manuscripts the line extends over all the letters in this series (see image below) and does not contain the flourish that we see above. As mentioned previously the Greek alphabet doubled as the Greek numbering system. To avoid confusion, Greek writers would draw a line above letters that were intended to be read as numbers.

With the line clearly extending over all the letters and without the flourish, Shoebat's theory is wrong because in the oldest versions, this looks nothing like the word for Allah when the line designating numbers is shown in the correct way.

Upside Down Allah

Another thing Shoebat has to do to make his theory work is turn the word Allah on its side and then display its mirrored image. Here is how the word Allah is written in Arabic:

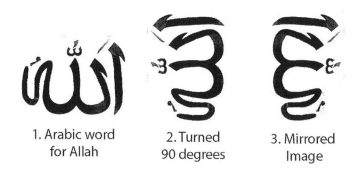

1. Arabic word   2. Turned   3. Mirrored
   for Allah   90 degrees   Image

It seems very odd to me that God would show John the word for Allah flipped on its side and reversed. It's even harder to believe that if John originally saw the word for Allah right side up that he would have decided to flip it around and reverse it himself.

Shoebat deals with this problem by saying that in some cases, like when the word for Allah is written on a circular object such as a coin, it can be written on its side. This may be true for circular objects, but it is not true in any other case, nor does this explain the reversal of the word. It's just as wrong for Arabic writers to write a word on its side and reversed as it is for an English writer to write an English word on its side and reversed. Just as in the case of the "crossed swords," Shoebat is doing everything he can to force Arabic words and symbols into the Greek alphabet.

Sigma

Shoebat says the Greek letter Sigma in Revelation 13:18 is really the

Arabic word *Bismi* which means "in the name of."

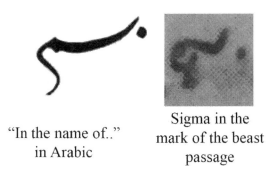

"In the name of.."
in Arabic

Sigma in the
mark of the beast
passage

Here again the Greek letter *Sigma* looks nothing like it would have in the era when the early copies of the New Testament were written.

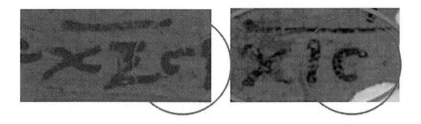

In the image above notice the absence of the dot that appears in the image below. In the case of *bismi*, the dot is a very important part of the Arabic word, but it is not and never has been a part of the Greek letter *Sigma*. The dot seen in the fifteenth century Greek text that Shoebat uses was actually a period, since the chapter ends with the number "666." Punctuation marks were not even added to this text until well after the fifteenth century.

Stigma (15th Century)
with a period
(punctuation marks were
added much later).

The Arabic word "bismi."
Here the dot is an actual
letter.

Conclusion

We have seen that Shoebat's theory fails in several ways. His attempt to rewrite Revelation 13:18 by explaining away the words for "count" and "number" and defining Greek words in a way that no Greek lexicon or Bible dictionary agrees with is not possible. His pointing to Koniuchowsky's *Restoration Scriptures True Name Edition* was almost funny, considering he influenced Koniuchowsky's translation and Shoebat himself considers Koniuchowsky to be a "cult leader."

We have also seen that Shoebat continually misrepresents his key text of the *Codex Vaticanus* in the Bob Jones University library (without which his theory cannot work) as being written in 350 AD when in fact the relevant section was written in the fifteenth century. We have seen that in order to make the Greek texts look like Arabic, he has to (1) insert an image (crossed swords) instead of letters; (2) turn the word "Allah" on its side and reverse it; (3) act as if the line used by the Greeks to designate numbers was connected only to *Xi*; (4) pretend that a period added very recently by a scribe was in the original and is actually an Arabic symbol; and above all, (5) act as if the Greek miniscule text was somehow known by scribes in the first century, despite the form of writing not being invented until the ninth century.

Chapter 9
Gog as the Antichrist

In his book *Mideast Beast,* Joel Richardson asserts that Gog of Ezekiel 38–39 is the Antichrist. He comes to this conclusion primarily by making a case that the Gog-Magog war is the same war as the Battle of Armageddon in Revelation 16:19. However, even if it were true that the Gog-Magog war was to be equated with Armageddon, this in itself would do nothing to prove that the Antichrist is a Muslim. Richardson therefore also concludes that Gog comes from Turkey, which has a sizable Muslim population.

Richardson has three chapters in his book that deal with his claim that Gog is the Antichrist. The first chapter argues that the correct timing of the Gog-Magog war is at the end of the 70th week of Daniel during the Battle of Armageddon. The second chapter goes through some of the similarities between Gog in Ezekiel and the Antichrist. The last chapter is an attempt to show that Gog comes from Turkey as opposed to Russia. I will attempt to refute Richardson's arguments in the order he presents them in his book beginning with his claim that the Gog-Magog war of Ezekiel 38-39 is the same war as the Battle of Armageddon.

The Timing of the Gog-Magog War

In this section I will present an overview of the views that Christians have about the timing of the Gog-Magog war and discuss some of their strengths and weaknesses. Though I have written this book with the intention not to present my personal views as arguments against the Islamic Antichrist theory, I need to make an exception in this chapter since I believe that understating the correct view of the timing of the Gog-Magog war is the best way to refute Richardson's claim that Gog is the Antichrist.

The Christian views about the timing of the Gog-Magog war are divided into four categories:

1. Pre-Seventieth Week of Daniel
2. Mid-Seventieth Week of Daniel
3. Armageddon (Richardson's view)
4. End of the Millennium

Though there are subsets for most of these categories—for example, at least two views of the timing of the war fall under the umbrella of "pre-seventieth week of Daniel"—I'm limiting this discussion to these four broad categories, as the problems with the main category applies to all of its subsets as well.

Pre-Seventieth Week of Daniel

The problems with viewing the Gog-Magog war as occurring before the seventieth week of Daniel begins are as follows:

1) Ezekiel 39:7 says Yahweh's name is never to be profaned again after the end of the Gog-Magog war:

> "So I will make My holy name known in the midst of My
> people Israel, and I will not let them profane My holy name

anymore. Then the nations shall know that I am the LORD, the Holy One in Israel." (Ezekiel 39:7)

The seventieth week of Daniel, the time of the Antichrist, is characterized by blasphemy and rebellion against God, both on the part of the Antichrist, who is particularly blasphemous, and those who follow him. For example, Scripture says that people will "blaspheme the God of heaven because of their pains and their sores" (also see Revelation 17:3, 13:6, and 16:9–11).

The people in Israel rejoice at the deaths of the two witnesses (Revelation 11:10), which doesn't sound like people who are finished with rebellion against God. If the Gog-Magog war occurs before the seventieth week of Daniel, then we need to explain how the blasphemy and rebellion by the Antichrist and the people of the earth in the end times do not constitute a defiling of God's name. This problem is insurmountable, in my opinion.

2) The nations recognize the sovereignty of God as a result of the Gog-Magog war:

> "I will bring you against my land so that the nations may acknowledge me, when before their eyes I magnify myself." (Ezekiel 38:16b)
> "I will exalt and magnify myself; I will reveal myself before many nations. Then they will know that I am the LORD." (Ezekiel 38:23)
> "Then the nations will know that I am the LORD, the Holy One of Israel." (Ezekiel 39:7b)

The nations are explicitly in rebellion against God throughout the seventieth week of Daniel (Revelation 11:2, 18:3, 16:14). In fact, it seems that the "kings of the earth" who are gathered to battle against Christ at Armageddon include all or most of the nations of the earth. So we would need to explain how this contradiction is reconciled.

3) Israel also recognizes the Lord's sovereignty in totality (Northern and Southern Kingdoms) after Gog-Magog:

> "So the house of Israel shall know that I am the LORD their God from that day forward." (Ezekiel 39:22)

The salvation of Israel en masse cannot happen before the conclusion of the seventieth week of Daniel. The whole point of the seventieth-week prophecy is that the entirety of the seventy weeks (including the last seven years) needs to be completed before the salvation of Israel will occur:

> "Seventy weeks are determined
> For your people and for your holy city,
> To finish the transgression,
> To make an end of sins,
> To make reconciliation for iniquity,
> To bring in everlasting righteousness,
> To seal up vision and prophecy,
> And to anoint the Most Holy." (Daniel 9:24)

This also violates the purpose of the "time of Jacob's trouble," which is a purifying event for the Jews during the last half of the final seven-year period, culminating in their repentance and recognition of God. They will not be completely saved until after this purification event is completed.

4) Phrases like "dwelling securely," "dwelling in a land that has undergone a restoration from the sword," "a land of unwalled villages," "peaceful people, who dwell safely, all of them dwelling without walls, and having neither bars nor gates" are all inconsistent with Israel's geopolitical situation currently or for the foreseeable future. Nor could one argue that this is some kind of false security brokered by the Antichrist, since that event isn't supposed to occur until the first day of the seventieth week.

Mid-Seventieth Week of Daniel

Those who hold to the view that the Gog-Magog war occurs sometime in the midst of the seventieth week of Daniel usually see the abomination of desolation, which occurs at the midpoint, as the time when Israel comes to know God. They see references to "dwelling peacefully" and "without walls" explained by the false peace of the Antichrist during the first three-and-a-half years of Daniel's seventieth week. A number of different proposed scenarios place the Gog-Magog war within the seventieth week, all of which suffer from similar problems:

1) There is no indication that after the Gog-Magog war, Israel will once again be subjected to conquest. This would necessarily be the case if it occurred at the midpoint, since a great deal of destruction and conquest begins at that time (Matthew 24:15–21). Ezekiel says there will be no one to "make them afraid" and God will leave "none of them captive any longer" after the war. The mid-seventieth week view essentially has Israel being miraculously delivered by God, only to be handed over to the Antichrist again for the final part of the seventieth week. Zechariah 13:8–9 says that two-thirds of Israel will be killed during this time, and Revelation 11:2 says the Gentiles will trample Jerusalem for three-and-a-half years after this point. This is hardly consistent with the language of a final victory and establishment of universal peace that seem to come after the Gog-Magog war.

2) Israel is said to bury bodies for seven months and use the weapons of the dead soldiers for fuel for seven years after the Gog-Magog war. This is inconceivable during the Great Tribulation, when the saints are hunted and killed and the trumpet and bowl judgments take place.

3) Related to the previous point, the burying of bodies is described in Ezekiel 39 as a triumphant event that cleanses the land:

> "For seven months the house of Israel will be burying them, in order to cleanse the land. Indeed all the people of the land will be burying, and they will gain renown for it on

the day that I am glorified," says the Lord GOD." (Ezekiel
39:12–13)

How can the land be considered cleansed or even begging to be cleansed
during a time before the final judgments found in Revelation, such as,
turning the sea into blood and killing all life in the sea? A plain reading
of Ezekiel 38–39 is a picture of a final destruction, followed by
restoration; but this view anticipates that the Gog-Magog war is followed
by the worst persecutions and devastation the world has ever seen.

4) This view presumes that phrases like "dwelling securely" or "a
peaceful people, who dwell safely, all of them dwelling without walls,
and having neither bars nor gates" refer to a false peace given by the
Antichrist at the beginning of the seven-year period. This is a classic
example of reading one's preconceived notions into the text. I don't think
anyone who holds to this view would disagree that there is absolutely no
suggestion in Ezekiel 38–39 that this is a false peace. The idea must be
read into the text. Not one word in Ezekiel would give the reader the
notion that this peace is from anyone else but God and that it will be
anything but everlasting. Indeed, the destruction of Gog-Magog seems to
only prove that the original peace is genuine, since the armies are
destroyed by God before they even have a chance to attack.

There has been a good deal of scholarly work showing that the specific
phrases used by Ezekiel to describe the peace are used elsewhere to
describe the millennial peace. Ralph H. Alexander has said the following
in his paper, "A Fresh Look at Ezekiel 38 and 39":

> "The expression 'in the last days'(be'aharit hayyamim),
> found in Ezekiel 38:16, places these events at the end time,
> for this phrase is most frequently employed to designate the
> time of Israel's final restoration to the land and the period
> of Messiah's rule (cf. Isa. 2:2; Jer. 23:20; 30:24; Hosea
> 3:5; Mic. 4:1; Dan. 10:14).... Another significant factor in
> these chapters is the employment of the expression 'living
> securely' (a form of yasab followed by labetah) in Ezekiel

38:8, 11, 14 and Ezekiel 39:26. This phrase is often employed in reference to millennial security, especially in Jeremiah and Ezekiel (cf. Jer. 23:6; 32:27; Ezek. 28:26; Zech. 14:11). This expression is used previously by Ezekiel in this series of messages to describe a definitely millennial picture (Ezek. 34:25-28; cf. Mic. 4:4).… These chronological notices in Ezekiel 38 and 39, in conjunction with the temporal *emphasis of the entire context of* these six night messages, argues strongly that the events of Ezekiel 38 and 39 transpire at the end time when Israel has already been restored to the land, the Messiah is present, and she has entered into the Peace covenant with Yahweh her Lord."[25]

The mid-seventieth-week view also suffers from the problems of the pre-seventieth week view, namely, that Yahweh's name will be profaned again and the subjection of the nations and Israel cannot occur until the end of the seventieth week.

End of the Millennium

I will skip for now Richardson's view that the war of Gog is the same as the Battle of Armageddon. I will come back to that view after I have presented the final view, since I believe that understanding the view that the war of Gog occurs after the Millennium will help us see Richardson's view in a different light.

The view that the Gog-Magog war occurs after the end of the millennial reign, when Satan is let out to gather nations to battle Jerusalem but is defeated by God, is the only view on the timing of this war that enjoys explicit biblical support. It is the only view that has no inherent contradictions and makes sense of the entire prophecy of Ezekiel, beginning in chapter 33 and continuing through chapter 39. The

---

[25] R. H. Alexander, "A Fresh Look at Ezekiel 38 and 39," in JETS 17 (1974).

arguments leveled against it are often superficial and will be dealt with at length at the end of this chapter.

Let me start by explaining what I mean when I say that this view enjoys explicit biblical support. In Revelation 20, the apostle John states when the battle of Gog and Magog will occur:

> **"Now when the thousand years have expired**, Satan will be released from his prison and will go out to deceive the nations which are in the four corners of the earth, **Gog and Magog**, to gather them together to battle, whose number is as the sand of the sea. They went up on the breadth of the earth and surrounded the camp of the saints and the beloved city. And fire came down from God out of heaven and devoured them. The devil, who deceived them, was cast into the lake of fire and brimstone where the beast and the false prophet are. And they will be tormented day and night forever and ever." (Revelation 20:7–10, emphasis added)

John says this event will occur when the "thousand years have expired" after the Millennium and after Jesus has been ruling on earth during an unprecedented time of peace. John uses the exact phrase "Gog and Magog," a phrase used only one other time in Ezekiel 38–39, and the details of the battle John describes are consistent with what is described by Ezekiel, though obviously in an abbreviated version. Ralph Alexander says of this reference to Gog-Magog:

> "The strong basis for this position is the explicit reference to Gog and Magog in Revelation 20:8. Such an explicit reference cannot be dismissed lightly, as is often the case. The terms employed in Revelation 20:8 are the same as those in Ezekiel 38 and 39. Normal hermeneutics would require the identification of the two passages (since the terms Gog and Magog are used nowhere else in the Scriptures) unless strong reasons can be brought forth to

deny such an equation."[26]

It is so frustrating to hear commentators and preachers speak about this passage and dismiss it with a wave of their hands. The excuses they give for its dismissal are not at all convincing, and sometimes even misleading. For example, they almost always say something similar to this: "The armies in Ezekiel come from the north; but in Revelation 20 the armies come from the 'four corners of the earth.'" This objection is easily dealt with by noting that in Ezekiel 38:5, 6,13 and 39:6, nations from all the compass points are specifically mentioned: Persia from the east, Cush (Ethiopia) from the south, Put (Libya) and the people who dwell 'carelessly in the isles' from the west, and Gomer and Togarmah from the north. Why they insist that the armies in Ezekiel only come from the north is beyond me.

Some argue that the term "four corners of the earth" suggests a worldwide invasion, whereas Ezekiel is describing a coalition that is based primarily in the Middle East. This can be easily refuted by noting that the term "four corners of the earth" or "four winds," which are often used interchangeably,[27] are terms which often refer only to the four compass points within a Middle Eastern context (Daniel 11:4; Jeremiah 49:36).

Another reason given for dismissing Revelation 20 is that in Ezekiel, Gog is the main aggressor, a man, whereas in Revelation 20, Satan is said to be the aggressor. To this I would say that there is no reason to expect that after the Millennium Satan will be incarnate and will physically lead these nations to battle. In fact, there is explicit evidence that he operates in the same way he always has after he is released: He tempts these nations to go to war.

"Now when the thousand years have expired, Satan will be released from his prison and will go out **to deceive the**

---

[26] [26] R. H. Alexander, "A Fresh Look at Ezekiel 38 and 39, " in JETS 17 (1974).
[27] See Jeremiah 49:36 and Revelation7:1.

> **nations** which are in the four corners of the earth, **Gog and Magog, to gather them together to battle,** whose number is as the sand of the sea." (Revelation 20:7–8, emphasis added)

What could be clearer than that? Satan deceives Gog and Magog to go to battle. He is not leading these armies himself. Even the simplest reading of both Ezekiel 38 and 39 and Revelation 20:7–9 proves this argument impotent, as both passages clearly say that Gog is leading human armies in each case.

Another reason given for dismissing Revelation 20:7–9 is that in the passage in Ezekiel, bones are left to be buried, but in Revelation, the fire God sends on the armies completely consumes them, bones and all. Like the others, this argument is reading way too much into the text. Let's take a look at what is said: "And fire came down from God out of heaven and devoured them" (Revelation 20:9b).

People who argue this point say the word translated "devoured" must mean the armies are completely consumed, bones and all. But I would suggest that far too little information is given here to state dogmatically that the bones must be consumed as a part of this devouring. If we look at Zechariah 14:12, which some say is a picture of the destruction of Gog and his armies, we see what looks like a fire that certainly could be described as "devouring," but apparently leaves the bones intact, as it seems to only target the soldier's flesh.

> "And this shall be the plague with which the LORD will strike all the people who fought against Jerusalem: Their flesh shall dissolve while they stand on their feet, Their eyes shall dissolve in their sockets, And their tongues shall dissolve in their mouths." (Zechariah 14:12)

It's just as likely the word John used that is translated as "devouring" can refer to an event like we find in Zechariah 14, which is limited to devouring flesh.

I hope you will see that the reasons given for dismissing Revelation 20:7–9 are easily dismissed themselves. The importance of this passage cannot be understated. If this interpretation is correct, we do, in fact, have a clear biblical basis for saying that the Gog-Magog war occurs after the Millennium when Satan is released.

Similarities

Despite the fact that John only spends a few verses summarizing Ezekiel's prophecy, the similarities between the two passages are striking:

1) Both armies march against Israel.
2) Both armies are destroyed by God Himself.
3) Both armies are defeated before they attack.
4) Both armies are destroyed by fire.
5) Both armies are coalitions of many countries.
6) Both armies are led by Gog.
7) The armies come upon people who have been living during an unprecedented time of peace.
8) The war will be followed by true and everlasting knowledge of God.

Problems Solved

If the Gog-Magog war occurs at the end of the Millennium, as Revelation 20 says, then the following problems concerning the other views are solved:

1) Yahweh's name will never be defiled again after the war is over.
2) All the passages about dwelling securely can be seen in their normal context, as Israel would have been dwelling in peace for one thousand years before this rebellion breaks

out.

3) There is no need to divorce Ezekiel 38–39 from the previous chapter (chapter 37), which is part of the same prophecy and ends with a clear reference to the millennial kingdom, where Jesus is ruling over a restored Israel.

4) The millennial phrases throughout Ezekiel can mean what they mean in other places (i.e., they are references to the Millennium).

5) References to weapons made of wood and horses can be seen literally, as opposed to being allusions to high-tech missiles. It can be reasonably assumed that during the Millennium, people will go back to a simpler way of life in which horses and wooden weapons would be used, especially if there had been no need for weapons for a thousand years.

6) The various promises of final restoration after the war, such as the cleansing of the land and a true peace with no more threats of any kind, can be seen as totally true, since there will be no more wars or evil after Satan is thrown into the lake of fire.

Arguments against a Post-Millennial Gog-Magog War

1. Argument about the chronology of Ezekiel: The main reason people reject this notion is because chapters 38 and 39 in Ezekiel are followed by an obvious description of the Millennium in chapters 40–48. They assume that since chapters 40–48 talk about the Millennium, the Gog-Magog war, which is found in the two preceding chapters, must occur before the Millennium. There are indeed many occasions in Scripture where this kind of chronological connection would be valid, but, as we will see, this is definitely not one of them.

Ezekiel begins each prophecy with a description of the date when he received it; he does this thirteen times throughout the book. The section that includes the prophecy against Gog begins in chapter 33, verse 21: "And it came to pass **in the twelfth year** of our captivity, in the tenth month, on the fifth day of the month, that one who had escaped from Jerusalem came to me and said, 'The city has been captured!'" (emphasis added).

Everything Ezekiel was given to write about Gog and Magog is included in this prophecy, which continues for six chapters and ends after the section about the Gog-Magog war in chapter 39. The nine chapters that follow this prophecy about the Millennium are part of a completely different prophecy given to Ezekiel thirteen years later. Chapter 40 begins this way: **"In the twenty-fifth year** of our captivity, at the beginning of the year, on the tenth day of the month, in the fourteenth year after the city was captured, on the very same day the hand of the LORD was upon me; and He took me there" (Ezekiel 40:1).

In his paper, "Rethinking Ezekiel's Invasion by Gog[28]," Dr. J. Paul Tanner says:

> "We need not expect [chapters] 40–48 to chronologically follow [chapters] 38–39 since these chapters are part of a separate vision."

If we place the dates of Ezekiel's thirteen visions in chronological order, the list would look like this: Ezekiel 1:1; 8:1; 20:1; 24:1; 29:1; 26:1; 30:20; 31:1; 33:21; 32:17; 40:1; and 29:17. Notice that three of the visions are not in chronological order; more importantly, Ezekiel 29:17, which is about Egypt being conquered by Nebuchadnezzar, was written later than the prophecy of the Millennium that begins in Ezekiel 40. A simple understanding of the nature of the book of Ezekiel would prevent anyone from building doctrine based on the order of the visions in Ezekiel.

---

[28] J. Paul Tanner, Rethinking Ezekiel's Invasion By Gog, Journal of the Evangelical Theological Society, March 1996, vol. 39

Ironically, if we apply the idea correctly and see a chronological connection within a particular vision of Ezekiel—in this case, the one that begins in chapter 33 and goes through 39—we would conclude that the Gog-Magog war must come after the Messiah is ruling on earth, since chapter 37 is so clear that the Millennium has begun and the throne of David is occupied at that time. To say it another way: if we limited chronological connections to the same vision, then it is absolutely necessary to conclude that the Gog-Magog war comes after the Millennium.

Some people even suggest that the last nine chapters of Ezekiel are a part of a separate book altogether. Josephus states that Ezekiel "left behind two books" (*The Antiquities of the Jews,* 10:5.1). And while we don't have enough information to say conclusively what Josephus meant, it would make sense if the last nine chapters of Ezekiel were distributed separately. It would mean that the book of Ezekiel originally ended with the Gog-Magog war, which would be fitting since the book of Revelation essentially ends with the Gog-Magog war also. Admittedly, this point is too speculative to be dogmatic about.

2. Israel would have no reason to burn the invaders' weapons or bury bodies in the eternal kingdom: There are many variations of the argument, but the main idea is based on an assumption that in the eternal state that follows the Millennium, there is no reason to bury bodies or burn weapons for fuel. The people who are making this argument assume a great deal about life after the Millennium, but the fact is that we have very little information about what life will be like in the eternal kingdom. However, the information we do have in Revelation 21–22 seems to suggest there will indeed be life on earth, much like there was during the Millennium; therefore, there will be a reason to bury bodies and make fires.

> "Then I, John, saw the holy city, New Jerusalem, coming down out of heaven from God, prepared as a bride adorned for her husband. And I heard a loud voice from heaven saying, 'Behold, **the tabernacle of God is with men, and**

He will dwell with them, and they shall be His people. **God Himself will be with them** and be their God.'" (Revelation 21:2–3, emphasis added)

The New Jerusalem is a massive structure 1,400 miles in length, width, and height. The notable point here is that this city comes from heaven to earth and "the tabernacle of God is with men, and He will dwell with them." God is going to dwell on earth in the eternal kingdom. Therefore, we would expect some semblance of the laws of nature that govern earth to be in effect during this time, even if radically modified. It should also be noted that it is prohibited for anyone to enter the New Jerusalem who might defile it.

> "And they shall bring the glory and the honor of the nations into it. But there shall by no means enter it anything that defiles, or causes an abomination or a lie, but only those who are written in the Lamb's Book of Life." (Revelation 21:26–27)

I only suggest that the little information we do have about the eternal state seems to indicate there will be life on earth outside the New Jerusalem as well. It may be that only those who are dead in Christ dwell in this 1,400-mile-square city. But the existence of earthly life outside the city seems to be implied, and one would assume there would be need to cook food with fires, etc.

The argument that there will be no need for people to bury bodies or burn weapons in the eternal state could be a moot point anyway. After all, we are not told how much time elapses between the Gog-Magog war and the eternal state. Dr. Tanner makes the following observations regarding this:

> "A closer look at Revelation 20 reveals that there are a thousand years from the beginning of Christ's millennial rule until the release of Satan. It does not tell how much

time transpires between Satan's release and the eternal state. Following the thousand years, several things must take place before the eternal state: (1) Satan will be released for 'a short time' (v. 3), (2) Satan will have time to deceive the nations and move them to attack Israel, (3) Satan, the beast, and the false prophet will be thrown into the lake of fire (v.10), and (4) all the unrighteous dead will be brought before the great white throne, judged by God and thrown into the lake of fire.

"In all honesty, we don't know how much time there may be, but nothing in the text precludes a period of seven years in which the weapons of war could be burned.

So the argument concerning burning weapons and burying bodies is based on various speculations and presuppositions about things we are not yet privy to know completely, such as the timing between the thousand years and the eternal state and the exact nature of life on earth in the eternal state. I suggest the information we do know about the eternal state certainly allows for a post-millennial Gog-Magog war.

3. Ezekiel 38–39 says that after the war "the nations shall know that I am the LORD" and He will "make his name known" in the midst of Israel. But this would have already occurred during the Millennium.

It is true that the nations and Israel will be subservient to Christ in the Millennium, but several passages in Scripture make it known that it is far from a sin-free state (see Isaiah 65:20, 11:3–5; Zechariah 14:16–21). Those passages say that "wicked" people and "sinners" are still there. In fact, that is the probably the reason Jesus rules during this era with a "rod of iron" to quickly and decisively give out judgment to those who are sinning. It is generally accepted that during the Millennium, people will still need to accept Christ as their Savior in addition to their King, and not everyone on earth is automatically saved.

Writer Arthur Pink said this of the millennial kingdom:

> "In spite of the fact that Satan will have been removed from the earth, and that Christ reigns in person over it, yet conditions here will not be perfect even in the Millennium. Unregenerate human nature will remain unchanged. Sin will still be present, though much of its outward manifestation will be restrained. Discontent and wickedness will not be eradicated from the hearts of men, but will be kept beneath the surface by means of the Iron Rod. Multitudes will yield to Christ nothing but a 'feigned obedience'" (Ps. 18:44, margin). This 'feigned obedience' will be the product of power not grace; it will be the fruit of fear not love."[29]

The fact that not everyone is saved is quite obvious considering that when Satan is released at the end of this thousand years, he is able to tempt so many people to go to war against Jesus that their numbers are like the "sands of the sea." The Millennium is obviously a blessed time, but it is not perfect, and it is not doctrinally correct to say that every person on earth is saved or "knows God" in the salvific sense at this time. Therefore, only after the attack described by John in Revelation 20 and the beginning of the eternal kingdom does true universal salvation appear to occur.

Armageddon

Most of Richardson's arguments for equating the war of Gog with Armageddon are similar to the arguments that I just made for placing the war at the end of the Millennium. For example, he uses the same arguments concerning the verses that tell us that after the war of Gog and Magog the nations will "know God," and there will be no more blasphemy, etc. In this I think he is more correct than those who hold to

---

[29] Arthur Pink, *The Redeemer's Return*, p. 379.

the various views that place the war of Gog at some point before the return of Christ. The problem, however is, that he, at no point, discusses the view that the war of Gog takes place at the end of the Millennium, where John specifically says it takes place. He either doesn't realize or simply doesn't address the fact that a majority of his arguments for equating the war of Gog with Armageddon are better suited to the timing of the war that John gives us, such as "when the thousand years have expired" (Revelation 20:7). If Richardson wants us to believe that the same arguments used for putting the war of Gog at the end of the thousand years are best suited to Armageddon (which occurs before the thousand years even begin), then he should at least attempt to interact with the post-Millennium view of the war of Gog to show why the arguments he uses are not better applied there.

There are in fact a number of reasons that the war of Gog in Ezekiel 38-39 cannot be the same as the Battle of Armageddon. For example, the idea that Israel would be "dwelling securely" in the way described by Ezekiel just before the battle of Armageddon is absurd. As mentioned previously, if there were ever a time that Israel is *not* dwelling in peace, it would be the time just before Armageddon when there is no more grass, clean water, or fish in the sea. This is a time when the Antichrist's persecution is at its height, when all those who do not worship the beast are killed, and when Jerusalem has been trampled by the Gentiles for the last three-and-a-half years.

Richardson attempts to deal with the multiple references to what seems to be a true and everlasting peace in Ezekiel 38-39 by making somewhat vague allusions to the "peace agreement" the Antichrist will supposedly make with Israel (Daniel 9:27). This falls far short of helping his case because, according to the same passage in Daniel 9:27, this supposed peace agreement will be broken at the mid-point of the seven-year period, resulting in the worst persecution of all time. This persecution is so bad that Jesus warned anyone in the city of Jerusalem at that time to flee to save their lives (Matthew 24:15-22).

Since the Battle of Armageddon does not occur until the end of this seven-year period, are we to believe the Antichrist will relent from this persecution at some point during the last three-and-a-half years? Will he perhaps strike a second peace agreement with Israel that he never breaks, which would then allow them to "dwell securely" in Israel in the time before Armageddon? The idea is preposterous and completely without biblical basis. Any attempt at trying to describe the people who live just before the Battle of Armageddon as "dwelling securely" or "a peaceful people, who dwell safely, all of them dwelling without walls, and having neither bars nor gates" has insurmountable problems.

Another set of problems for Richardson relates to the reference to the Gog-Magog war in Revelation 20:7-9. There is an unbroken chronology of events from John's description of the Battle of Armageddon at the end Revelation 19 all the way to John's description of the war of Gog and Magog in Revelation 20:7 which shows us without any doubt that John understood the two wars to be distinct, not to mention separated by over a thousand years.

It is true that portions of the book of Revelation can be seen as out of chronological order, but it is just as true that certain sections of the book are clearly meant to be taken in chronological order. One of the ways we can tell that one event occurs before the next event listed is by such chronological phrases as "and then,." as well as contextual clues that the passage is following a consistent forward progression of events. John concludes his discussion of the war of Armageddon in the last verse of Revelation 19. He then begins the next chapter (note that chapter breaks were not in the original) with the words:

> "**Then** I saw an angel coming down from heaven, having the key to the bottomless pit and a great chain in his hand. He laid hold of the dragon, that serpent of old, who is the Devil and Satan, and bound him for a thousand years."(Revelation 20:1-2)

Here I don't think I would find any opposition with my claiming that Revelation 20:1-2 is to be understood as John explaining a chronological progression of events. There are few, if any, premillennial scholars who would disagree with the idea that the Battle of Armageddon in Revelation 19 is followed by an angel binding Satan for a thousand years

(Revelation 20:1-2). Both the word "then" in verse 1 as well as the context of this passage make this point clear.

Revelation 20:3–6 continues with this description of events in chronological order, making several references to the "thousand years" mentioned in verse 2.

Then in Revelation 20:7–10 John says:

> **"Now when the thousand years have expired**, Satan will be released from his prison and will go out to deceive the nations which are in the four corners of the earth, Gog and Magog, to gather them together to battle, whose number is as the sand of the sea."

Because of this clearly unbroken chronology of events from the Battle of Armageddon in Revelation 19 to the war of Gog and Magog in 20:7, those who try to say that John, in Revelation 20:7–10 was just re-telling the events of the war of Armageddon, have a great deal of explaining to do. Why would John use several phrases like "and then" leading up to this verse if he was not explaining a progression of events, and why use the very strong phrase "now when the thousand years have expired" when they believe he is referring to an event that happens before the thousand years even begin?

In my opinion the only hope for someone still wanting to hold to the idea that Armageddon is the same war described by Ezekiel in chapters 38-39 is to see the war that John describes in Revelation 20:7-10 as another war altogether. In this view they would at least not have to deny that such a war will occur at the end of the Millennium, though they would still have to come up with a reason why John says this war will be led by Gog and Magog, not to mention why all the events of this post-millennial war look so much like the war that Ezekiel describes.

If Richardson takes this view that there is, in fact, a war led by Gog that will occur "when the thousand years have expired" but that is not to be understood as the same war as the one Ezekiel describes, then there are still a host of problems for his theory. The main problem is that the majority of arguments he makes in his book concerning the timing of the Gog-Magog war are not best suited for the battle of Armageddon because he rightly sees the verses he cites as demanding there be no more sin, rebellion, or lack of salvation after the war of Gog-Magog. As we have seen in the arguments above, all of those things will in fact be present in the Millennium to some degree, and especially in the time after Satan is released at the end of the thousand years. In other words, Richardson consistently claims that the descriptions of the world after the war of Gog in Ezekiel 38-39 are only possible after Armageddon, but in reality, such descriptions are truly only possible after the Gog-Magog war John describes in Revelation 20:7-10.

What the True Timing of the Gog-Magog War Means for the Gog / Antichrist Theory

The logical outcome of seeing the Gog-Magog war as occurring "after the thousand years have expired" is the theological impossibility of the Antichrist playing a role in the Gog-Magog war in any way.

We are told in Revelation that the Antichrist and False Prophet are thrown alive into the "lake of fire" at the end of the battle of Armageddon.

> "Then the beast was captured, and with him the false prophet who worked signs in his presence, by which he deceived those who received the mark of the beast and those who worshiped his image. These two were cast alive into the lake of fire burning with brimstone." (Revelation 19:20–23)

Later on, after the thousand years have expired and the battle of Gog and Magog has occurred, Satan is also thrown into the lake of fire with the Antichrist. When this event is described, we are told this is where the Antichrist and False Prophet have been the whole time.

> "The devil, who deceived them, was cast into the lake of fire and

brimstone where the beast and the false prophet are. And they will be tormented day and night forever and ever." (Revelation 20:10)

Since the Antichrist was thrown alive into the lake of fire just after Armageddon (Revelation 19:20-23) and clearly spends the entire 1000 year period there, (confirmed in Revelation 20:10), then he cannot be Gog, since John tells us Gog's entire rebellion occurs while the Antichrist is in the lake of fire.

A Concession

Though I firmly believe, for the reasons I have stated above, that the war Ezekiel describes in chapters 38–39 must have its ultimate and most literal fulfillment in the war described by John in Revelation 20:7-10, I am not opposed to the idea that the war of Armageddon is a kind of type fulfillment of the Gog-Magog war. I do believe there are certain aspects of Armageddon that parallel the Gog-Magog war. For example, the description of the birds feasting on the bodies is very similar in Ezekiel 39 and Revelation 19. But like other prophecies in Scripture that have a near and far fulfillment the earlier event has some aspects that could be said to have been fulfilled, while the final event will fulfill all aspects of the prophecy perfectly and literally. Take, for example, the prophecies of Antiochus Epiphanies given to us by Daniel. Quite a few people, mostly preterists, would say that those prophecies were completely fulfilled by Antiochus, but most premillennial scholars recognize it would be impossible for Antiochus to have fulfilled all of those prophecies himself and the future fulfillment with the Antichrist is required to fulfill the prophecy completely and literally. Jesus endorses this understanding of the prophecies about Antiochus awaiting their most accurate fulfillment in the future with the Antichrist when he tells his followers to look for the "Abomination of Desolation," which was spoken of by Daniel." Similar near/far fulfillments follow this same pattern.

All this to say that it is possible we are to see Armageddon as a limited or near fulfillment of Ezekiel 38-39, but because of the various problems with equating Armageddon with the war of Gog listed above, it simply cannot be the fullest or most literal fulfillment. That distinction must go to the Gog-Magog war mentioned by John in Revelation 20.

More From Richardson On Equating Gog with the Antichrist

In Richardson's second chapter about the war of Gog he gives a few additional reasons why Gog should be seen as the Antichrist. At the end of this chapter he summarizes his arguments with twenty items that he considers comparisons with Gog and the Antichrist. Some of these comparisons are superficial and would be expected in any battle that takes place in Israel, as both of these wars undoubtedly will. For example number four on his list is "Both armies attack each other."

Other comparisons on his list of similarities we have already dealt with to some degree, such as the "bird feast" which occurs in both passages. I maintain that because of the near/far nature of Ezekiel's prophecy, we should expect some of these types of similarities. In the same way we would say that Antiochus Epiphanies was surely in view in Daniel 11, but that he was only a shadow of the ultimate fulfillment that will occur in its fullness with the Antichrist.

Other comparisons on his list are based on various presuppositions that he has argued for in earlier parts of his book. For example, number eight says that "both come from the same region." This is true only if you buy his earlier argument about the "Assyrian" in Isaiah and Micah. If you have read and agree with the chapter in this book which argues against Richardson's view that "the Assyrian" is the Antichrist, then there is no reason to believe that number eight on his list is true at all.

Similarly about seven of the items on Richardson's list have been refuted in the previous section of this book on the timing of the war of Gog. For example, number fifteen says: "After both of their deaths, the surviving nations will come to a saving knowledge of God." As discussed earlier, this isn't true, at least with regard to Armageddon. Though the people in the Millennium are certainly in better place than we are today, "wickedness," "sin," and unsaved people still exist in the Millennium (see Isaiah 65:20, 11:3–5; Zechariah 14:16–21). What Richardson refers to will not be fully true until after the war described by John in Revelation 20:7–10; after this the Great White Throne Judgment occurs, the New Jerusalem descends, and the "eternal state" begins.

Additional Problems

Richardson also provides what he sees as answers to various criticisms about his view that Gog is the same person as the Antichrist. For example, he addresses the problem that Gog is described as being buried in Ezekiel 39:11 whereas the Antichrist is said to be "thrown alive" into the lake of fire.

Ezekiel 39:11 says of Gog:

> "It will come to pass in that day that I will give Gog a burial place there in Israel, the valley of those who pass by east of the sea; and it will obstruct travelers, because there they will bury Gog and all his multitude. Therefore they will call it the Valley of Hamon Gog." (Ezekiel 39:11)

Of the Antichrist it is said:

> "Then the beast was captured, and with him the false prophet who worked signs in his presence, by which he deceived those who received the mark of the beast and those who worshiped his image. These two were **cast alive** into the lake of fire burning with brimstone." (Revelation 19:20, emphasis added)

Of this seeming contradiction Richardson says Revelation 19:20 is only speaking of the soul of the Antichrist being "cast alive" into the lake of fire, not his body. I find it very hard to believe that the Greek word for "alive" would be used here if it were really only trying to convey that his soul would go to hell when he died.

Richardson's reasoning for this is based on two passages that seem to suggest that the Antichrist is killed at Christ's *parousia* (second coming). The first passage is found in Daniel 7:11-12.

> "I watched then because of the sound of the pompous words which the horn was speaking; I watched till the beast was slain, and its body destroyed and given to the burning flame. As for the rest of the beasts, they had their dominion taken away, yet their lives were prolonged for a season and a time." (Daniel 7:11-12)

It should be noted that in Daniel 7 the "beast," which verse 11 says will be destroyed, is almost certainly a reference to the kingdom and not the person of the Antichrist. I can say this with some confidence because the beasts in this chapter are consistently described as "kingdoms" (Daniel 7:23), while the horns on the beast are described as "kings" (Daniel 7:24). The Antichrist himself is pictured as a particular horn on the beast's head, but the beast in which the horns are found is his kingdom. I would not deny that the Antichrist must be included in this destruction of the beast in some way, as he is obviously a part of the beast; but I would say that using this verse to prove the Antichrist physically dies is sketchy because what is being described as "destroyed" is what has been earlier defined as a kingdom. It is especially good to be cautious in light of the verse in Revelation 19:20 where the Antichrist is clearly in view and is described as being thrown "alive" into the lake of fire.

The second verse that Richardson uses to try to prove the physical death of the Antichrist is 2 Thessalonians 2:8:

> "And then the lawless one will be revealed, whom the Lord will consume with the breath of His mouth and destroy with the brightness of His coming." (2 Thessalonians 2:8)

This verse presents a much stronger case since clearly the Antichrist himself is being referred to here. I would simply make the case that the Greek word used here for "destroyed" *katargeō* is sometimes translated "do away with" or "made to cease." It could be consistent with the

Antichrist being "thrown alive" into the lake of fire and certainly that would be a type of *katargeō* or destruction. This is in contrast to the much clearer words the Bible uses when bodily death is meant. For example, *apokteinō*, which is used seventy-five times in the Bible, always means to kill the body, slay, to be put to death. Similarly another Greek word *anaireō*, used twenty-three times in Scripture and is often translated "kill or killed," would have been better than *katargeō* if Paul wanted to let us know that physical death was in view. In conclusion on this point, *katargeō* is in fact a good description of the Antichrist being "thrown alive" into the lake of fire, and if physical death was intended, *apokteinō* or even *anaireō* could have been used over *katargeō*.

Is Gog From Turkey

Islamic Antichrist theorists such as Joel Richardson place the locations of many of the northern nations mentioned in Ezekiel 38 and 39 (Magog, Meshech, and Tubal) in Turkey, which is primarily a Muslim nation. They use this premise to conclude that the Antichrist must be a Muslim because, as we have seen, they see the Antichrist as Gog, and Gog is said to come from the region where Magog, Mesech and Tubal are located.

As detailed in the preceding chapter, the evidence strongly supports the idea that this war will not occur until the end of the thousand-year reign of Christ on earth. This means that identifying the exact locations of the nations mentioned by Ezekiel has only limited value for the believer since this war will be at least a thousand-plus years in the future. Attempting to force the circumstances of this war onto the modern, premillennial world can only lead to confusion and error. That being said, I do think Scripture gives us the tools we need to discover the location of many of the nations involved in this war. I believe there is value in such a study if for no other reason than to show the errors of the theorists who try to force Ezekiel's prophecy into our modern context. I will try to remain as neutral as I can in this study, something uniquely possible for those who hold to the view that the Gog-Magog war won't occur until after the Millennium. Christians from every era of the church have attempted to identify these countries in light of their current political circumstances; they identified the countries involved as the primary "boogey men" of their day. Because I don't need to try to fit these countries into a modern context, it is easier to follow the evidence wherever it leads. Even if you disagree with me about the timing of the war, I hope this study on the players involved will be useful for that reason alone.

Nations Mentioned In Ezekiel 38–39

At least eleven nations are mentioned in Ezekiel 38 and 39, including Magog, Meshech, Tubal, Persia, Cush, Put, Gomer, Togarmah, Sheba, Dedan, and Tarshish. For many of these nations, there are virtually no disagreements about their location, but others have been the focus of longstanding debates. For example, few would argue that Persia refers to modern Iran, but there are many different opinions about the location of Magog, Meshech, and Tubal. These three nations are of particular importance for our purposes as it is said that Gog is the chief prince of Magog, Meshech and Tubal. Therefore, it is believed by those who see Gog as the Antichrist that simply determining the location of Magog, Meshech, and Tubal, one can discover the nation of origin of the Antichrist. For this reason I will focus primarily on the locations of these particular nations in this study.

Millennial Occurrences

Before identifying the countries involved, I would like to make a point often overlooked by commentators, one I believe reinforces the idea that the war Ezekiel describes occurs after the Messiah has been ruling over Israel during the Millennium. Four of the countries mentioned by Ezekiel are also said to exist during the Millennium: Cush (Psalms 68:31; Isaiah 11:11; Zephaniah 3:10), Tubal (Isaiah 66:19), Sheba (Psalms 72:10; Isaiah 60:6), and Tarshish (Psalms 72:10; Isaiah 2:16, 60:9, 66:19). I could add more to this list, but will limit the references I cite to passages that unquestionably speak of the Millennium. I mention this to invoke a little humility among those attempting to identify these nations, as we simply cannot guess the exact way Christ will divide the nations during

His rule. It may be that during His earthly reign these nations will actually be called by the ancient names Ezekiel uses or have different borders. All we know for sure is that the Bible tells us many of the nations in Ezekiel 38 and 39 are also present during the Millennium. That being said, these nations have also existed in the past, and it is possible to discover a great deal about their locations. It is reasonable to assume that the locations and borders of these countries in the past will have a great deal of correlation with their millennial counterparts.

Another interesting point that reinforces the idea that we are to understand the nations mentioned in Ezekiel 38-39 as nations existing during the Millennium can be seen by looking at all of the areas that will be involved in the Gog-Magog war (see map). If you do this, an interesting question comes up: Why aren't the nations closest to Israel involved? It seems there is a kind of buffer zone of nations that separate Israel from its enemies.

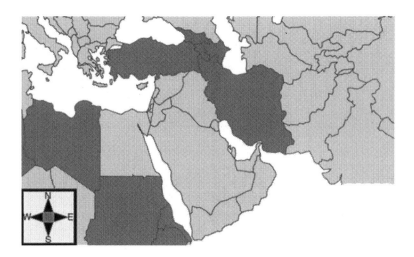

Why, for example, isn't Egypt involved? Historically it has been a major enemy of Israel, not to mention Jordan, Saudi Arabia, Iraq, and Syria, which constitute the biblical Assyria. The answer lies in Isaiah 19:23–25, which says that during the Millennium, Egypt and Assyria will be in a special relationship with the Lord and Israel.

"In that day there will be a highway from Egypt to Assyria,

and the Assyrian will come into Egypt and the Egyptian
into Assyria, and the Egyptians will serve with the
Assyrians. In that day Israel will be one of three with Egypt
and Assyria—a blessing in the midst of the land, whom the
LORD of hosts shall bless, saying, 'Blessed is Egypt My
people, and Assyria the work of My hands, and Israel My
inheritance.' (Isaiah 19:23–25)

So it would seem that those nations closest to Israel, namely Egypt and
Assyria (modern-day Jordan, Saudi Arabia, Iraq, and Syria) will be allied
with Israel in a special way during the Millennium, and when the time
comes for Satan to be released at the end of the thousand-year period,
they remain true to the Lord. I believe this is the best way to explain the
conspicuous absence of these historical enemies of Israel in the Gog-
Magog war.

Gog, of the Land of Magog, the Prince of Rosh, Meshech, and Tubal

Let's begin our study of the geographical locations of the nations
mentioned in Ezekiel 38-39.

Gog, the primary instigator of the war, is described as being from the
land of Magog and prince over Rosh, Meshech, and Tubal: "Son of man,
set your face against Gog, of the land of Magog, the prince of Rosh,
Meshech, and Tubal, and prophesy against him" (Ezekiel 38:2).

Since all of the areas mentioned in this passage are a part of Gog's
kingdom (Magog, Rosh, Meshech, and Tubal), determining the location
of even one of these areas with a measure of certainty will help to narrow
the scope of our search. I like to start any research on the location of a
biblical nation within the pages of Scripture itself, because while the
views of ancient writers and historians are useful, we should not rely
upon them dogmatically as they often have different opinions. While
Gog, Magog, and Rosh are mentioned in other places in Scripture, those

passages don't offer additional clues to their locations. Magog is only mentioned in the genealogies of Japath (Genesis 10:2; 1 Chronicles 1:5), the prophecy in Ezekiel 38–39, and in Revelation 20:8. Other than the fact that Ezekiel 38:15 says Gog will come from the "far north," we are left with no specific details that might help determine which nation or nations from the far north are being referred to. The identification of Rosh is difficult as well for reasons we will come to later. Of these four nations associated with Gog, only Meshech and Tubal are found in another place in Scripture that might give us a clue as to their whereabouts.

Meshech and Tubal

In Ezekiel 27, we find a prophecy against the city of Tyre in modern-day Lebanon. Tyre has been a commercial shipping port for thousands of years, going back to the ancient Phoenician merchants. Ezekiel 27 describes many of the nations, including Meshech and Tubal, that traded with Tyre, as well as the specific goods they traded: "Javan, Tubal, and Meshech were your traders. They bartered human lives and vessels of bronze for your merchandise" (Ezekiel 27:13).

We can gather two important clues about Meshech and Tubal from this passage:

1. They traded with Tyre in Ezekiel's day (593–565 BC).
2. They traded bronze and slaves with Tyre.

Normally, we could gather very little about the location of a biblical nation based on the goods that it traded, but the mention of bronze narrows the field considerably. Bronze wasn't something that just anyone could make during this time; the process was very specialized and limited to a handful of nations. The field narrows even further when we consider that this nation also must be from the north and must have been able to trade with Tyre in Ezekiel's day.

This brings us to the end of the biblical clues that can help us determine the location of Meshech and Tubal. Even though it seems like only a little information, I think you will agree it is more than enough to confirm or deny the extrabiblical and historical data that we will now look at.

The *Jewish Encyclopedia* identifies Meshech and Tubal with Moschia (which the Assyrians called "Mushki" or "Muski") and Tubal (which the Assyrians called "Tabal").

> "Meshech...are probably the Moschi (Assyrian: Mushku and Musku), the inhabitants of the Moschian mountains, between the Black and the Caspian seas, which contained rich copper mines. 'Tubal' (Assyrian, Tabal), which is always mentioned in connection with Meshech, is the name of the Tibareni, who lived to the south-east of the Black Sea."[30]

There are many reasons to take this view seriously. I mentioned before that the production of bronze was important. Well, Mushku and Tabal were two of the few places in the world where bronze was produced at this time; in fact, they were famous for it—they were even two of the inventors of Iron Age metallurgy. The legend of King Midas, who was said to be able to turn everything he touched into gold, is actually based on Mita, a historic king of Moschia. Assyrian records refer to the Assyrians receiving huge amounts of bronze vessels as tribute from Moschia and Tabal—the very goods that Ezekiel said these nations traded with. In addition, it is known that trade between these countries and Tyre was well established at the time of Ezekiel's writing.

It is interesting that these two places, Moschia and Tabal, are so often mentioned together in ancient writings, because Meshech and Tubal are almost always mentioned together in the Bible as well (Ezekiel 27:13,

---

[30] "Armenia." *Jewish Encyclopedia*, 1906. http://www.jewishencyclopedia.com/articles/1787-armenia.

32:26, 38:2, 3, 39:1; Genesis 10:2). One scholar believes that even Rosh is mentioned along with Meshech and Tubal in one Assyrian text.

> "There is even one cuneiform document from the reign of the Assyrian King Sargon II (ruled 722–705 B.C.) which actually names all three peoples [Rosh, Meshech, Tubal] mentioned by Ezekiel 38–39. Sargon II writes in this badly broken inscription:
> "I deported (the people) of the lands of Kashu, **Tabalu**, and Hilakku. I drove out Mite (Midas), king of the land of **Muski**...the lands of **Rashi** and Ellipi which are on the Elamite frontier."[31] (emphasis added)

This view is also consistent with what we know from ancient writers like Josephus, who identified the people from Meshech and Tubal as the Mosocheni (from Moschia) and Thobelites (from Tabal). The identification of Meshech and Tubal as Moschia and Tabal has a massive amount of support in the modern scholarly community as well.[32] It's probably safe to call it the majority view among scholars.

A few people have claimed that Meshech and Tubal refer to the modern Russian cities of Moscow and Tobolsk. There is no historical support for this claim whatsoever. It is based solely on the similar sounds of both words. Even people like Thomas Ice who support the idea that Russia is

---

[31] Clyde Billington. "The Rosh People in History and Prophecy," vol. 3: *Michigan Theological Journal* Volume 3. 1992 (2) (170–171). Plymouth, Michigan: Michigan Theological Seminary.

[32] R. H. Alexander, "A Fresh Look at Ezekiel 38 and 39, " in JETS 17 (1974), pp. 161 f.; E. M. Blaiklock, *Pictorial Bible Atlas* (Grand Rapids: Zondervan, 1969), p. 45; John J. Davis, *Paradise to Prison* (Grand Rapids: Baker, 1975), pp. 138 f.; J. D. Douglas, ed., *The New Bible Dictionary* (Grand Rapids: Eerdmans, 1962), p. 811; C. F. Pfeiffer, H. F. Vos, and J. Rea, eds., *Wycliffe Bible Encyclopedia* (Chicago: Moody, 1975), II, pp. 1105 f., 1751;J. B. Taylor, Ezekiel (London: Tyndale, 1969), p. 244.

in view with the northern coalition of Gog reject the idea that Meshech and Tubal indicate Moscow and Tobolsk.[33]

The modern location of Meshech and Tubal is on the southeast side of the Black Sea, south of the Caucuses Mountains, primarily in modern-day Georgia, as well as parts of Armenia and eastern Turkey. There is some debate as to whether Tubal should also be associated with the Tibareni on the Black Sea coast, which would push the location a bit more into central Turkey, but that connection is not as certain.

Gog and Magog

The location of Gog and Magog are much more difficult to determine, either with Scripture or historical accounts. Gog, of course, is a proper name designating the leader of this future coalition. Some people attempt to find a reference to a king named Gog in ancient texts, namely Gugu of Lydia (western Turkey), but the general consensus seems to be that this connection is inconclusive.

The location of Magog is also less clear than Tubal or Meshech. There is not very much to go on in Scripture or history, though we can reasonably assume that Magog would be close to Meshech and Tubal, based on the biblical account that seems to link the three nations geographically   and the fact that the migrations of Japheth's sons would likely be close together. Jewish sources have traditionally put Magog very close to Meshech and Tubal (see map).

---

[33] Thomas D. Ice, "Ezekiel 38 & 39" (2009). Article Archives. Paper 1,

http://digitalcommons.liberty.edu/pretrib_arch/1 .

Josephus said: "Magog founded those that from him were named Magogites, but who are by the Greeks called Scythians."[34] The Scythians were a band of ethnically diverse nomadic tribes that spanned great distances in the Eurasian Steppe. There are several problems with understanding the term "Scythians" used by Josephus the same way we do today. The term was applied very generally by the Greeks as any nomadic tribe north of the Black Sea. Other scholars have pointed out that the terms "Scythians" and "Cimmerians" were used interchangeably.[35] The Cimmerians started out dwelling north of the Caucuses Mountains, but by Ezekiel's day had migrated south due to wars with Sargon II, settling in the general area of Meshech and Tubal, specifically around modern-day Armenia, Georgia, and parts of Turkey. The *Encyclopedia Biblica* places Magog in the same area using a totally different method to come to its conclusion.[36] I believe that the evidence is conclusive that Magog should be placed in roughly the same area as Meshech and Tubal, in modern-day Georgia, Armenia, and parts of eastern Turkey.

---

[34] Flavius Josephus, *Antiquities of the Jews*, Book 6, chapter 1.

[35] Maurits Nanning Van Loon. *Urartian Art. Its Distinctive Traits in the Light of New Excavations,* Istanbul, 1966, p. 16.

[36] *Encyclopedia Biblica*, 1899. Entry on "Gog and Magog."

The Rosh Problem

There is considerable debate among scholars to this day as to whether the Hebrew word "*Rosh*" in Ezekiel 38:3 is a proper noun designating another nation or an adjective related to "prince" (i.e., "chief prince"). A review of different Bible translations will demonstrate the differences in opinion among scholars:

> "and say, 'Thus says the Lord GOD: "Behold, I am against you, O Gog, **the prince of Rosh**, Meshech, and Tubal."'"
> (Ezekiel 38:3 NKJV, emphasis added)

> "and say, 'Thus says the Lord GOD: "Behold, I am against you, O Gog, **chief prince of Meshech** and Tubal."'"
> (Ezekiel 38:3 ESV, emphasis added)

The basic idea is that if "*Rosh*" is a proper noun, then Gog is also the prince of a place named Rosh. If it's not a proper noun, then it should be translated as the word "chief," meaning Gog is the chief prince of only Meshech and Tubal and there is no place called Rosh. This argument seems to be primarily motivated by those trying to either prove a connection to Rosh and modern-day Russia and those who are trying to deny such a connection. In my opinion, both sides are letting their determination to prove their points affect their ability to honestly deal with the issue.

The early Greek texts of the Old Testament, such as the *Septuagint* and the *Theodosian*, translate "Rosh" as a proper noun. But Jerome, when writing his Latin translation of the Bible known as the *Vulgate*, decided to translate "Rosh" as "chief." He did this not because of any grammatical clue, but rather, in his own words, because "we could not find the name of this race [i.e., the Rosh people] mentioned either in Genesis or any other place in the Scriptures, or in Josephus."[37]

---

[37] Jerome, *Commentariorum in Ezechielem*, col. 357.

Though Jerome couldn't find any references to the Rosh people, there do indeed seem to be such references in ancient history. Clyde E. Billington, in his three-part paper "The Rosh People in History and Prophecy," does a good job of tracking down the references to the Rosh people. I disagree with part 3 of Billington's paper, in which he claims the references to "Rosh" in Ezekiel should be understood as modern-day Russia, but I do agree with him that the Rosh were an ancient people in Ezekiel's day.

The Rosh people, according to Billington, migrated often during their history, but he believes they primarily occupied a particular area south of the Caucasus Mountains in modern Armenia, Azerbaijan, Georgia, and northeastern Turkey.[38] In other words, he agrees that the Rosh were located in the same areas as Meshech, Tubal, and Magog. It is especially notable that this was the primary location of the Rosh people when, as mentioned earlier, the Rosh were mentioned in the same Assyrian inscription with Meshech and Tubal, linking them all to the same basic geographic region.

Billington and others who attempt to equate the Rosh mentioned by Ezekiel to modern Russia do so by arguing that the Rosh people, long after the time of Ezekiel, migrated north of the Caucasus to modern-day Ukraine. They also argue that the Varangian Rus, Vikings of Scandinavian origin who conquered Russia from the north in the ninth century AD and are why we call the land Russia today, got the second part of their name (Rus) from intermarriage with the Rosh people in the south in an attempt to integrate with their conquered population. While this argument is feasible, from what I can tell, this has little bearing on the identification of the Rosh in Ezekiel 38 and 39 for the following reasons:

1. It is clear that Ezekiel believed Magog, Rosh, Meshech, and Tubal were closely related. Even Billington admits that in Ezekiel's day, all of these places were geographically centered in the areas around Georgia, Armenia, and eastern

---

[38] Billington, 168.

Turkey. It is far more reasonable to assume that this is the area the northern coalition will come from.

2. Ezekiel 27 not only mentions Meshech and Tubal as trading with Tyre, but also almost every other nation that is a part of this future war, namely Put, Togarmah, Dedan, Sheba, Tarshish, and Persia. It is inconceivable to think that Russia was trading with Tyre in Ezekiel's day.

3. The method of interpretation that Billington and others use is called the ancestral migration method, which attempts to identify nations in Scripture not by the geographic location of the nation during the relevant times, but rather by tracing the bloodlines of the people throughout history.

The bottom line is that all the nations mentioned in Ezekiel 38:3—Magog, Rosh, Meshech, and Tubal—can be shown to have been located in modern-day Georgia, Armenia, and parts of eastern Turkey. This area was a relatively small area to the far north of Israel, that traded with Tyre with the same goods mentioned in Ezekiel 27. There is every reason to believe that this will be the area the northern coalition will come from in the Gog-Magog war as well.

Joel Richardson never mentions Georgia or Armenia when discussing the locations of Magog, Meschech, or Tubal, probably because they are not Muslim nations. For example, Georgia is 90 percent Christian and Armenia is 95 percent Christian, so mentioning that Meshech and Tubal were primarily located in these countries would be counterproductive to his agenda. I believe this is somewhat deceptive on his part because of the nine atlas entries he cites[39] to show that these areas are in the "regions of Turkey." Most of them actually make clear that Georgia and Armenia are just as much if not more in view than Turkey. This omission seems unlikely to be chalked up to ignorance on his part since the

---

[39] Richardson, Joel (2012-06-08). *Mideast Beast: The Scriptural Case for an Islamic Antichrist* (p. 215). Joel Richardson. Kindle Edition.

information is in the sources he cites. It is more likely to be a result of his desire to divert attention from information that would cast his theory in a negative light.

Chapter 10
Beheadings in Revelation

On page 162 of *God's War on Terror,* Walid Shoebat makes the claim that the beheading of Christians mentioned in Revelation 20:4 must mean that the Antichrist system will be Islamic since beheadings are "the very heritage of Islam." I would not deny that beheadings are an important part of Islamic doctrine or that this practice is terrible and frightening, but I would dispute the claim that Revelation 20:4 is necessarily a clue to the Islamic nature of the Antichrist's system. Let's begin by looking at the verse in question.

> "And I saw thrones, and they sat on them, and judgment was committed to them. Then I saw the souls of those who had been beheaded for their witness to Jesus and for the word of God, who had not worshiped the beast or his image, and had not received his mark on their foreheads or on their hands. And they lived and reigned with Christ for a thousand years." (Revelation 20:4)

I believe the reason the Antichrist beheads people at this point is related to when these beheadings take place. The context of this passage in Revelation 20 makes clear that the people being beheaded are those who are on the earth after the rapture. These are the people that were not saved prior to the first resurrection and thus were alive during the Day of the Lord judgments that follow the rapture. This is significant because after the Day of the Lord judgments begin, which are intended to torment the wicked people on Earth, it seems to be difficult for people to die in the normal way.

> "In those days men will seek death and will not find it; they will desire to die, and death will flee from them." (Revelation 9:6)

I will admit the following is speculation, but it seems reasonable to understand Revelation 9:6 as God supernaturally preventing men from dying as a way to escape the judgments He has prepared for them during the Day of the Lord. If this is true, then we could easily assume that this moratorium on death will be equally distributed to all those alive at the time the Day of the Lord begins, including those people who would later become Christians after the rapture. If this premise is correct, then it would seem that beheadings were chosen as a way of execution during this time for a very practical reason, that is, it would be one of the only sure ways to kill a person during the Day of the Lord.

It is notable that the word translated "beheaded" in Revelation 20:4 is the only occurrence of that word. In other places where the Antichrist's wrath on Christians is mentioned, a much more general word for killing is used. It is, therefore, quite possible that the Antichrist only resorts to beheadings after the Day of the Lord begins and beheading becomes the most efficient way to ensure the death of Christians. Therefore, it is not at all necessary to see the beheadings taking place in Revelation 20:4 and equate it with Islam.

Part 2

Chapter 11
Islamic Eschatology

The "end times" or eschatological beliefs in Islam play a major role in the promotion of the Islamic Antichrist theory. In fact Joel Richardson's first book, *Antichrist: Islam's Awaited Messiah*, later republished as *Islamic Antichrist*, was entirely about Islamic eschatology. That book attempts to prove that the Antichrist will be Islamic by comparing Islamic beliefs about the last days to Christian beliefs. The thesis of Richardson's *Islamic Antichrist* book is, in short, that Islamic eschatological beliefs are preparing the Muslim world to accept the Antichrist and False Prophet. We will discuss this thesis in much more detail later, but for now I only want to point out that Islamic Antichrist theorists such as Joel Richardson put a particular emphasis on Islamic eschatological beliefs when trying to convince people of their theory.

General Overview of Islamic Eschatology

Before we discuss what Joel Richardson and others claim about the end times beliefs of Islam, I will first offer a brief overview of the subject of eschatology in Islam to provide some context for the rest of this chapter.

There are some significant differences of opinions about the end times among Sunni and Shiite Muslims; however, both sects do share many common beliefs as well. I will attempt to limit this overview to only those ideas that are common to both groups.

In Islam, the "day of judgment" or the "day of resurrection" is preceded by several signs. These signs are categorized into two groups by Islamic scholars, the minor signs and the major signs. Many of the minor signs are very general; for example, a few minor signs include "an increase in killing" and "much wine is drunk." It is generally believed by Muslims that some of the minor signs have already happened while others have either not yet occurred or have begun but have not yet concluded. Not many of the minor signs are used to support the Islamic Antichrist theory and thus will be largely ignored in this book.

The major signs are much more important for this study as they basically give an outline of the major events the average Muslim expects to happen as the day of resurrection approaches. Most Islamic scholars agree that none of the major signs have happened yet.[40] I will list a few of the most relevant major signs in chronological order.[41]

1.) The emergence of the Mahdi
The Mahdi is said to be unite the Muslim world to fight several battles, including the conquest of Constantinople. He shares the wealth that he acquires through conquest with the people. He rules the world for five, seven, eight, nine, or nineteen years (Islamic sources differ) before Isa returns.

---

[40] Darussalam; Al Areefi, Dr Muhammad (2014-01-07). *The End of the World* (Kindle Location 669). Darussalam Publishers. Kindle Edition.
[41] There is some debate about the chronological order of the major signs, but relevant Hadiths Islamic scholars generally agree on the basic order. This order is the one I will attempt to present.

2.) The appearance of the Dajjal

The Masih ad-Dajjal (literally the false messiah) will appear after the battle of Constantinople. He will be blind in one eye and his other eye will be deformed. He will travel the entire world deceiving people. He will gather many followers (mostly Jews and women) and his powers of persuasion are said to be almost irresistible. He will draw the Mahdi's armies to fight him in battle, though it will actually be Isa (the Muslim Jesus) who kills him.

3.) The return of Isa (Jesus)

Isa, who Muslims believe to be a prophet but not God, will return just as the Mahdi's armies are preparing to battle the Dajjal's armies. Isa will kill the Dajjal and all the Dajjal's followers and help to convert many people to Islam. After this, Isa will rule over a supernaturally restored Earth until he dies forty years later.

4.) Ya'jooj and Ma'jooj (Gog and Magog war)

Two tribes of vicious beings which had been imprisoned by Dhul-Qarnayn will break out. They will ravage the earth, drink all the water of Lake Tiberias, and kill all believers in their way. They will kill so many people that even Isa has to flee, though later Isa prays to Allah who sends destruction on Gog-Magog.

There are many more major signs, but these four are relevant to the Islamic Antichrist theory and, thus, will be my primary focus.

Islamic Antichrist Theorist Claims About Islamic Eschatology

The basic idea proposed by those holding to the Islamic Antichrist theory is that the events described above will actually come to pass more or less like Islamic people expect them to. They would, however. say the Mahdi, in Islamic tradition, will actually be the Antichrist; that Isa, the Muslim Jesus, will be the False Prophet; and that the Dajjal, the Islamic version of the Antichrist, is actually the real Jesus.

This line of thinking relies on listing a number of similarities between the prominent eschatological figures in Islamic and Christian traditions. For example, in the case of the Mahdi, Richardson suggests that both the Mahdi and the Antichrist are to be world political and religious leaders who kill Christians and Jews. In the case of the Isa and the False Prophet, Richardson points out that Isa and the Mahdi are kind of a team in the end times, in the same way the Antichrist and False Prophet are said to be. He suggests that Isa is said to have many of the same roles as the False Prophet, and thus, are the same people. In the case of the Dajjal, Richardson points out that the Dajjal will most likely claim to be the Jewish Messiah and should, therefore, be seen as the return of the real Jesus who is, of course, the Messiah to the Jews. This is a very incomplete overview of the similarities of these figures suggested by Richardson. I will offer a much more in depth look at his claims later in this chapter as I critique his theory.

I will attempt to refute Richardson's arguments about Islamic eschatology in several ways. I will begin with a discussion of the history and origins of the Islamic beliefs about the end times. I will then look very closely at the supposed similarities of each of these figures and attempt to offer a detailed refutation of the idea that these similarities are profound, or in some cases, exist at all.

The Origins of Islamic Eschatology and Why It Matters

To fully understand the problems with the Islamic Antichrist proponents' views about Islamic eschatology, it is necessary to understand how Islamic traditions about the end times came about in the first place. This is partly because there seems to be some acceptance on the part of Islamic Antichrist theorists that the end times events in Islamic tradition are going to occur more or less like Muslims say they will, with only minor changes. I feel that they give these Islamic prophecies far too much credibility.

The idea that the False Prophet of Revelation 13 will claim to be the Islamic version of Jesus and force everyone to be a Muslim is certainly not an explicit teaching about the False Prophet in the Bible. The theorists look at the prophecies about Isa in Islamic tradition and assume they are demonically inspired prophecies that have something to tell us about how the end times will play out. They then force the idea that the False Prophet will be a Muslim Jesus into Revelation 13.

Understanding the history of Islamic eschatology demystifies it completely. Hopefully, once you see how Muslims have come to believe what they do about the end times, you will understand that these Islamic prophecies have absolutely nothing to teach us about how the last days will actually play out and, assuming they do provide some kind of guideline can only lead to error.

An Overview

Most of the ideas about Islamic end-times beliefs do not come from the *Quran*, the central text in Islam, but from the *hadiths*, a word that means "tradition." The *hadiths* are a collection of sayings attributed to Mohammed, compiled by his followers over the hundreds of years after his death in AD 632. Even within Islam, many of these hadiths are considered spurious. By the ninth century, the number of these sayings had grown exponentially to about 60,000. Some of them clearly contradict each other. Islamic scholars had to decide which ones were authentic and which had been invented for political or theological purposes.[42]

It is important to note that ideas about the end times in Islam arose at least 600 years after the book of Revelation was written; most of them came about much later than that. The people who constructed Islamic eschatology, therefore, were very aware of Christian and Jewish views about the end times and, as we will see, liberally borrowed from them.

---

[42] John L. Esposito. *Islam: The Straight Path*. 81. 4th ed. Oxford University Press, 2010.

How Islamic Eschatology Developed

There are two main ways that Islamic end times beliefs came to be. The first way, which is the most common, is by borrowing from the Bible itself. Since Islam claims to accept both the Old and New Testaments of the Bible as true, they also accept the end times views expressed in the Bible as true. For example, Muslims believe in the resurrection of the dead, the return of Jesus to reign on Earth, the Antichrist, the Gog-Magog war, and many other Christian doctrines about the end times. However, since Muslims also believe that Christians and Jews have corrupted the Bible, they feel this gives them a license to rewrite certain aspects of the Bible to make Islam out to be the victorious religion in the end times. This results in *hadiths* that, on their face, are obviously taken from the Bible but include substantive changes that are necessary to make Islam out to be the true religion.

For example, the following *hadith* describes what the world will look like when Isa, the Muslim Jesus, returns and rules the world.

> "Eesa ibn Maryam [Jesus son of Mary] will be a just judge and ruler among my Ummah…Grudges and mutual hatred will disappear and the venom of every venomous creature will be removed, so that **a baby boy will put his hand in the mouth of a snake and it will not harm him;** a baby girl will make a lion run away and it will not harm her; and **the wolf will be among the sheep like their sheepdog.** The earth will be filled with peace just as a vessel is filled with water. The people will be united and none will be worshipped except Allah. War will cease and Quraysh will no longer be in power. The earth will be like a silver platter, with its vegetation growing as it did at the time of Adam, until a group of people will gather around one bunch of grapes and it will suffice them, and a group will gather around a single pomegranate and it will suffice them. An ox will be sold for such and such an amount of money, and a horse will be sold

for a few dirhams."[43]

An astute student of the Bible will notice several commonalities with this description of the Earth when Isa returns and the descriptions of the messianic age in the book of Isaiah.

Children playing with snakes:

> "The nursing child shall play by the cobra's hole,
> And the weaned child shall put his hand in the viper's den.
> They shall not hurt nor destroy in all My holy mountain,
> For the earth shall be full of the knowledge of the LORD
> As the waters cover the sea." (Isaiah 11:8–9)

Wolves and lambs coexisting:

> "The wolf also shall dwell with the lamb,
> The leopard shall lie down with the young goat,
> The calf and the young lion and the fatling together;
> And a little child shall lead them." (Isaiah 11:6)

In the *hadith* quoted above, we see many other commonalities with descriptions of the messianic age in the Bible, such as the depictions of peace and abundance of materials. It is clear, at least in part, this *hadith* is based on the descriptions of the messianic age in the Bible.

Highlighting the differences in these two versions is also important for our study. For example, we see in the *hadith* above that "Allah" is the God the world worships during this time. This is an example of the aforementioned insertion of Islamic doctrine into biblical concepts to make Islam look like the ultimate victor. This particular *hadith* also inserts the idea that "the *Quraysh* will no longer be in power." The *Quraysh* were a powerful merchant tribe that controlled Mecca and its

---

[43] Publishers, Darussalam; Al Areefi, Dr Muhammad (2014-01-07). *The End of the World* (Kindle Locations 4587-4596). Darussalam Publishers. Kindle Edition.

Ka'aba during the time this *hadith* was written. They caused various problems for Mohammed and his followers, resulting in many conflicts and wars. Here we see that the *hadith* writers were also prone to adding ideas from their current political circumstances to their eschatological doctrines.

One way to show how much Islamic eschatology is based on the New Testament is by listing a few Islamic doctrines concerning Isa and comparing them to Christian eschatological beliefs concerning Jesus. For example, Muslims believe the following things about Isa:

1.) He was born of the Virgin Mary.
2.) He was a prophet.
3.) He performed many miracles.
4.) He ascended into heaven.
5.) He is coming back in the last days.
6.) He will destroy the Antichrist.
7.) He will destroy the wicked people on earth.
8.) He will rule the world with justice and peace in a restored Earth.

The aspects of Isa that differ from the Christian understanding of Jesus are all related to maintaining Islam doctrine concerning Isa. For example, instead of having Jesus return as a champion of Christianity, they made him return as a champion of Islam and antagonistic toward Christians. This doesn't mean that we should actually expect a false Jesus to come back as a champion of Islam; it simply is the typical way Muslims use the Bible for their own ends. They read the Bible and switch the religions in view to make Islam look good.

This tactic can be seen in the Islamic version of the story of Abraham almost sacrificing his son Isaac in Genesis 22. In the Islamic version of this story, they switch Isaac with Ishmael, since Ishmael is supposedly the progenitor of the Muslim people. This is a typical example of how Islamic doctrine is based on the Bible, yet liberally altered in order to glorify Islam over Judaism and Christianity.

So the first way that Islamic eschatology developed is by *hadith* writers looking at what the Bible said about the end times and changing certain details to make Islam appear to be victorious in the end times. This, of course, required them to make the heroes all Muslim and the bad guys Jews and Christians. There is nothing about this process that should make us think their version of the end times, where they differ from the Bible, is going to come to pass any more than we should expect the Mormon or Jehovah's Witness's versions of the end times to come to pass.

Extra-Biblical Texts

One of the more fascinating research projects I have undertaken while writing this book is the second way Islamic eschatology developed, which is by borrowing early Christian beliefs about the end times found in extra-biblical sources. There are many aspects about Islamic eschatology that are completely foreign to the Bible, and I have often wondered if the writers of the *hadiths* were simply coming up with these new ideas about the end times out of thin air. However, after examining in detail the early apocalyptic writings of Christians, especially those written in Syria, I was astounded to see that the Islamic writers of the hadiths seemed to be borrowing huge amounts of information from these spurious Christian sources. Then, much like in the case of their borrowing from the Bible, they changed small details to make these extra-biblical writings compatible with Islamic doctrine.

Apocalyptic Pseudepigrapha

The primary texts used to fill in the gaps of Islamic eschatology are the apocalyptic pseudepigraphical writings of the early Christian church. The word *pseudepigrapha* means "false name" and refers to texts that are falsely attributed to other people, usually biblical apostles or prophets. For example, many people have heard of the gnostic gospels such as the Gospel of Thomas or the Gospel of Judas. These are examples of pseudepigraphical writings.

In addition to being falsely attributed to ancient writers, apocalyptic pseudepigraphical writings were written in an apocalyptic style like the book of Revelation. Some examples of apocalyptic pseudepigraphical writings are the *Apocalypse of Pseudo-Methodias*, the *Apocalypse of Pseudo-Ephraim*, the *Apocalypse of Pseudo-Baruch*, as well as many others.

Apocalyptic pseudepigraphical writings were partially based on the events described in the book of Revelation, but they often added new details, events and characters which are not found in the Bible. Usually these additions pertained to the current political circumstances at the time they were written. These writings became extremely popular in early Christianity and often the new details about the end times that they offered were considered as authoritative as the biblical writings. The acceptance of these forgeries was due, in part, to a lack of biblical literacy, as well as the inability to accurately date documents at the time. It wasn't until the late Middle Ages that these spurious writings were widely understood to be fakes. As a result the Islamic writers of the *hadiths*, who were writing at a time when these spurious Christian documents were widely accepted as true, incorporated many elements from these apocalyptic pseudepigraphical writings into their *hadiths*, while making various changes to suit Islamic doctrine.

Examples of Islamic Borrowing from the Pseudepigrapha

One of the more obvious examples of Islamic writers borrowing from Christian pseudopigraphical writings is the Islamic version of the Gog-Magog war. The following is a summary of the *hadiths* concerning the Gog-Magog war from an influential Islamic scholar named Imam Ibn Kathir, who wrote in the 1300's in Syria. This is also the standard understanding of the Gog-Magog war among Muslims today.

> "At the time of Abraham (p.b.u.h.), there was a king called Dhool-Qarnayn. He performed Tawaaf around the Kabah with Abraham (p.b.u.h.) when he first built it; he believed and followed him. Dhool-Qarnayn was a good man and a great king;

Allah gave him great power and he ruled the east and west. He held sway over all kings and countries, and traveled far and wide in both east and west. He traveled eastwards until he reached a pass between two mountains, through which people were coming out. They did not understand anything because they were so isolated; they were Gog and Magog. They were spreading corruption through the earth, and harming the people, so the people sought help from Dhool-Qarnayn. They asked him to build a barrier between them and Gog and Magog. He asked them to help him to build it; so together they built a barrier by mixing iron, copper and tar.

"Thus Dhool-Qarnayn restrained Gog and Magog behind the barrier. They tried to penetrate the barrier, or to climb over it, but to no avail. They could not succeed because the barrier is so huge and smooth. They began to dig, and they have been digging for centuries; they will continue to do so until the time when Allah decrees that they come out. At that time the barrier will collapse, and Gog and Magog will rush out in all directions, spreading corruption, uprooting plants, killing people. When Jesus (p.b.u.h.) prays against them, Allah will send a kind of worm in the napes of their necks, and they will be killed by it."

Many elements in this story have no correspondence with the biblical account of the Gog-Magog war. However, when you look at the Christian pseudepigraphical writings which were popular when these *hadiths* were written, you find in them the same basic elements. The following is an example of the teaching on Gog Magog found in the *Apocalypse of Pseudo-Methodias*:

"Hear now then in true fashion how these four empires were joined, the Ethiopian with the Macedonian and the Greek with the Roman. They are the four winds that move the great sea (Dan. 7:2). Philip the Macedonian was the father of Alexander and took to wife Chuseth, the daughter of King Phol of Ethiopia. From her was born Alexander, who was made ruler of the Greeks. He founded Alexandria the Great and reigned nineteen

years. He went to the East and killed Darius, king of the Medes.
He was the ruler of many regions and cities and he destroyed the
earth. He even went as far as the sea which is called the region of
the sun where he beheld unclean races of horrible appearance. . .
. He gave orders and gathered them all together with their
women and children and all their villages. Leading them away
from the East, he restrained them with threats until they entered
the northern lands where there is no way in or out from East to
West to visit them. Alexander prayed to God without
interruption and He heard his prayer. The Lord God gave a
command to the **two mountains** which are called the "Breasts of
the North," and they came together to within twelve cubits.
Alexander built **bronze gates and covered them with unmixed
bitumen**, so that if anyone wished to force them open by steel or
to melt them with fire, he would be able to do neither, but
immediately every fire would be extinguished...Who are the
nations and the kings that Alexander concealed in the North?
Gog and Magog…"

"Then [in the last days] the 'Gates of the North' will be opened
and the strength of those nations which Alexander shut up there
will go forth. The whole earth will be terrified at the sight of
them; men will be afraid and flee in terror to hide themselves in
mountains and caves and graves. They will die of fright and very
many will be wasted with fear. There will be no one to bury the
bodies. The tribes which will go forth from the North will eat the
flesh of men and will drink the blood of beasts like water. They
will eat unclean serpents, scorpions, and every kind of filthy and
abominable beast and reptile which crawls the earth. They will
consume the dead bodies of beasts of burden and even women*s
abortions. They will slay the young and take them away from
their mothers and eat them. They will corrupt the earth and
contaminate it. No one will be able to stand against them.

"After a week of years, when they have already captured the city
of Joppa, the **Lord will send one of the princes of his host and
strike them down in a moment.**"

Beside the fact that the king who built the gates to imprison Gog-Magog is given a different name in each account, "Dhool-Qarnayn" in the Islamic version and Alexander the Great in the Christian version, all the other elements are virtually identical. In fact even many Islamic scholars recognize that Dhool-Qarnayn is probably a reference to Alexander.[44] The name Dhool or Dhul Qarnayn literally means "having two horns" and is probably a reference to the fact that Alexander is sometimes pictured as having two horns in ancient Greek inscriptions and coins.

Here are some other areas of correspondence between the Islamic sources and Christian pseudopigrapha regarding Gog and Magog.

- Both kings were godly men who traveled to the Far East.
- Both kings found an unruly race of people there named Gog and Magog who needed to be imprisoned.
- Both kings imprisoned Gog and Magog by herding them between two mountains.
- Both kings built a gate between the two mountains using bronze and tar.
- Gog and Magog were unable to get out of the gates until God/Allah decreed.
- At the end of time both texts say that Gog and Magog will get past the barrier and cause destruction.
- Both texts say that God/Allah will cause their destruction suddenly.

The similarities shared by the Islamic *hadiths* and Christian forgeries should be quite obvious. Here again the differences are telling as well. It is likely that Islamic writers didn't like the idea of having a pagan king (Alexander the Great) as the hero of this story, so they simply obscured his identity by giving him a fictitious name and claiming that he was a good Muslim, saying that he "performed *Tawaaf* (an important Islamic ritual) around the *Kabah* with Abraham."

---

[44] "Alexander the Great." Oxford Islamic Studies Online. http://www.oxfordislamicstudies.com/article/opr/t125/e113?_hi=0&_pos=5.

It is interesting to note that the Christian sources actually stole this story from the much earlier *Alexandrian Romance* stories and adapted it for their purposes by adding the parts about biblical prophecy. The Alexandrian Romances were fictional stories about Alexander the Great that often depicted him in fanciful situations, like fighting mythical monsters. These stories were extremely popular shortly after Alexander's death and remained so for hundreds of years, undergoing numerous adaptions by various groups. So the Islamic writers of the *hadith* basically stole their version of the Gog-Magog story from Christian forgers who had originally stolen it from the *Alexander Romance* stories and adapted it to fit with their end times beliefs.

The Origin of the Dajjal in Apocalyptic Literature

The Islamic version of the Antichrist, the Dajjal, is, on the one hand, clearly an adaption of the biblical version of the Antichrist. However, many descriptions of the Dajjal's characteristics and actions in Islamic tradition are not found in the Bible. I will attempt to show in this section that when the descriptions of the Dajjal differ from the biblical account, it is clear that the information is being adapted from the Christian psuedopigraphical material.

I will begin by showing that the physical descriptions of the Dajjal were borrowed from the Christian pseudopigripha. In the Bible there is very little if any discussion about what the Antichrist looks like; however, in the extra-biblical Christian psuedopigrapha, physical descriptions of the Antichrist became a very common theme. He is often described as having an odd complexion, thick hair, one blind eye, one deformed eye, and elongated physical features, as well as having three letters that mean "deny" or "reject" written on his forehead. Given what we have seen so far, it is not surprising that every one of these physical descriptions were later incorporated into the physical descriptions of the Dajjal found in the *hadiths*.

Deformed Eyes

From the Christian pseudopigrapha:

> "His right eye like the star that rises in the morning, and the other without motion." (*The Apocalypse of Pseudo-Ezra*)

> "He shall be bald-headed, with a small and a large eye." (*Pseudo-Daniel*)[45]

> "His right eye like the star which rises in the morning, and the other like a lion's." (*Apocalypse of Pseudo-John*)

From Islamic Hadiths:

> "His right eye will be punctured, and his left eye would be raised to his forehead and will be sparkling like a star."[46]

> "Ad-Dajjal is blind in the right eye and his eye looks like a bulging out grape."[47]

In both the Islamic and Christian traditions we see the theme of the Antichrist/Dajjal having two deformed eyes one of them is blind and the other is said to be like a star. These traditions vary slightly from source to source, but the basic characteristics are enough to suggest that the Islamic writers were borrowing from the Christian writers who preceded

---

[45] Bousset, Wilhelm (2014-09-08). *The Antichrist Legend* (Kindle Location 1926). Evergreen Books. Kindle Edition.

[46] Bilgrami, Sayed Tahir (2005). "6.". *Essence of Life, A translation of Ain al-Hayat* by Allama Mohammad Baqir.

[47] Sahih al-Bukhari, 3:30:105.

them. This will become more of a certainty as we see more instances of this type of borrowing.

Three Letters on His Forehead

In the Bible the Antichrist is said to cause his followers to receive a mark on their right hand or forehead. This mark is said to be the number 666. However, in the apocalyptic Christian literature as well as the Islamic *hadiths*, we see a significant variation of this teaching. They both claim it will be the Antichrist/Dajjal himself that has this mark, not necessarily his followers; and the mark is actually three letters, not numbers, that mean "reject" or "deny." As in the previous case, the fact that this tradition cannot be found in the Bible and that both Islamic and Christian traditions share almost identical views of this non-biblical teaching show that Islamic borrowing from the earlier Christian pseudopigraphical material is very likely.

From the Christian pseudopigrapha:

> "And he [the Antichrist] also has upon his forehead three letters; A, K, T. And the A signifies: 'I deny,' the K: 'And I completely reject,' the T: 'The befouled dragon.'" (*The Apocalypse of Pseudo-Daniel*)

From Islamic Hadiths:

> "Anas b. Malik reported that Allah's Messenger (SAW) said: Dajjal is blind of one eye and there is written between his eyes the word 'Kafir.' He then spelled the word as k. f. r., which every Muslim would be able to read." [48]

At first glance the only similarities between the Christian and Islamic traditions about the mark of the beast is that it would be on the Antichrist/Dajjal's forehead, as opposed to his followers', and that it would be three letters as opposed to numbers. However the fact that

---

[48] Sahi Muslim Hadith # 7009, Chapter 41.

these three letters are different (A.K.T. in the Christian tradition and K.F.R in the Islamic tradition) should not be seen as a true difference because both writers made the letters on the Antichrist's forehead mean the same thing (i.e., to "deny" and "reject,") despite the letters being different.

The writer of *Pseudo-Daniel* does not tell his readers why A.K.T should mean to "deny" and "reject." He seems to suggest that there is a kind of secret meaning to the letters that is not able to be discovered by normal means. The writer of the *hadith*, however, changes the letters to K.F.R,. a reference to the Arabic word *Kafir*, which literally means "to deny or reject." In other words, the three letters on the Antichrist/Dajjal's forehead mean the same thing in both traditions, though the letters were changed in the Islamic version, possibly to avoid the need to interpret the letters in an esoteric way, as is the case in *Pseudo-Daniel*.

Skin and Hair

The last of the physical descriptions of the Antichrist and the Dajjal found in the extra-biblical traditions that I will discuss are those regarding his skin and hair.

From the *Christian Pseudopigrapha*:

> "The appearance of his face is dusky; the hairs of his head are sharp, like darts" (*Apocalypse of Pseudo-John*)

From Islamic *hadiths*:

> Ubada ibn Saamit narrates that the Prophet... "The hair on his head will be Aja'd "(coarse and curly).[49]

> "Dajjal is blind of left eye with thick hair."[50]

---

[49] "The Dajjal (Anti-Christ)" *Discovering Islam*. N.p., n.d. Web. 17 Jan. 2015. http://www.discoveringislam.org/anti-christ.htm
[50] Sahih Muslim Book 041, Number 7010, reported by Hudhalfa

"Red complexioned, fat, with coarse hair"[51]

The emphasis that the Christian pseudopigrahical material puts on the coarseness of the Antichrist's hair seems to be reflected in the *hadith* writers using the Arabic word *Aja'd* (coarse) to describe the Dajjal's hair. The complexion of the Dajjal is variously described in the *hadiths* as reddish or sometimes fair. This variation on the skin color in the *hadith* may be related to the original Christian sources being somewhat vague, using the word "dusky" to describe the Antichrist's skin.

Description of the Antichrist's Actions

A number of descriptions about the actions of the Antichrist are found in extra-biblical Christian traditions but cannot be found in the Bible. Here again we will see these non-biblical teachings showing up in Islamic traditions.

Three Years of Drought

From the *Christian Pseudopigrapha*:

> "Antichrist; he shall be exalted even to heaven, and shall be cast down even to Hades, making false displays. And then will I make the heaven brazen, so that it shall not give moisture upon the earth; and I will hide the clouds in secret places, so that they shall not bring moisture upon the earth… And again I said: Lord, and how many years will he do this upon the earth? And I heard a voice saying to me: Hear, righteous John. Three years shall those times be." (*Apocalypse of Psuedo-John*)

From Islamic *hadiths*:

> "There will be three hard years before the Dajjal. During them,

---

[51] Sahih Bukhari Volume 4, Book 55, Number 650:

people will be stricken by a great famine. In the first year, Allah will command the sky to withhold a third of its rain, and the earth to withhold a third of its produce. In the second year, Allah will command the sky to withhold two thirds of its rain, and the earth to withhold two thirds of its produce. In the third year, Allah will command the sky to withhold all of its rain, and it will not rain a single drop of rain."[52]

In both the Christian and Islamic traditions God will withhold rain for three years because of the Antichrist. Though the Christian version is not specific on the matter, it seems to suggest that the three years of drought come during the reign of Antichrist, whereas the Islamic tradition says the drought precedes the appearance of the Dajjal. In addition the Islamic tradition suggests an incremental drought as opposed to the Christian version where the drought is total for the duration of the three years. Despite these slight differences the similarities are telling.

A Test with Enoch and Elijah

From *Christian Pseudopigrapha*:

> "And then I shall send forth Enoch and Elias to convict him; and they shall show him to be a liar and a deceiver" (*The Apocalypse of Pseudo-John*)

From Islamic *hadiths*:

> "Two angels resembling two Prophets, one on either side will accompany him [the Dajjal]. This will be to test mankind. Hence Dajjal will ask, 'Am I not your lord? Do I not give life and death?' One of the angels will reply, 'You are a liar.' However nobody will be able to hear this reply besides the other angel. The second angel addressing the first angel will say, 'You are speaking the truth.' Every body will hear what this second angel said and will think that an angel is testifying that the Dajjal is

---

[52] Sahih Al-Jami` as-Saghir, no. 7875.

Allah though in reality this second angel was addressing the first and agreeing with his reply that you are speaking the truth that the Dajjal is certainly a liar."

The Christian source here refers to "Enoch and Elijah," the Old Testament prophets who many Christians, both then and now, believe will be the two witnesses of Revelation 11. Islamic tradition mentions "Two angels resembling two Prophets." The description in the *hadith* is also slightly different in intent from the Christian text, but it is notable that both the Islamic and Christian traditions describe the two witnesses performing a test to prove the Antichrist/Dajjal is a "liar."

There are many other similarities between the Antichrist in pseudopigraphical texts and Islamic *hadiths* and much more work needs to be done in comparing the two traditions. I will, however, assume that the reader has enough information to see the similarities for themselves by this point, and I will move on the commonalities between the Mahdi and the Last Roman Emperor.

The Origin of the Mahdi in Apocalyptic Literature

Now that you have seen the significant dependence that the writers of the Islamic *hadiths* had on early extra-biblical Christian writings, it should be much easier to convince you that the concept of the Mahdi was derived entirely from the same apocalyptic Christian writings.

In the case of the Islamic Isa and the Dajjal, there is a clear one-to-one comparison with the Christian Jesus and the Antichrist. As we have seen, Isa is based primarily on the Christian Jesus with adjustments for Islamic doctrine. The same is true for the Dajjal where we have seen that the basic concept of the biblical Antichrist was used.

The Islamic Mahdi, on the other hand, is much more interesting in this respect since there is no obvious figure in the Bible that corresponds directly to him. The Bible never mentions a human king who fights religious wars and restores a temporary orthodoxy before the appearance of the Antichrist and the return of Jesus. It would seem at first glance that the writers of the *hadith* have come up with an entirely new end times character. However, I will attempt to show that it was, in fact, the early Christian writers of the pseudopigrapha that came up with this brand new eschatological character, which was then copied and adapted by the writers of the *hadiths* to form their concept of the Mahdi.

The new end times character that the Christian extra-biblical apocalyptic writers introduced was a divinely guided monarch who would overcome the present tribulations and usher in a time of temporary peace before the return of Jesus. Though he was not given a name at the time, he would come to be known as the Last Roman Emperor. The primary text that popularized the idea was *Pseudo-Methodius,* written in the early seventh century, but the *Syrian Apocalypse of Daniel* played a role as well. The Last Roman Emperor was said to arise at a time when Roman Christianity was in great distress. He would fight a number of wars with the enemies of Christianity and restore Roman Christianity to its previous place of prominence. He would rule for seven to ten years which are described as being particularly plentiful. Then, just before the Antichrist and the Gog-Magog war broke out, Jesus would return, defeat the rebellion, judge the enemies of God, and The Last Roman Emperor would give Jesus his crown.

It is difficult to explain how prominent this idea was at the time. In his paper "The Last Roman Emperor and the Mahdi, " Andras Kraft says that the Last Roman Emperor was given "near-canonical status" at that time and in the centuries that followed. The figure eventually developed into the so-called "Great Monarch," a concept still believed in certain Catholic circles today. The Last Roman Emperor was also mentioned by Christopher Columbus in his *Book of Prophecies* written in the early 1500s.

Considering that the concept of the Last Roman Emperor was believed to be true biblical teaching by so many Christians at the time, it is not surprising that Islamic writers incorporated the idea into their eschatology as well. Many of the same early Christian texts from which the *hadith* writers were borrowing were the same texts that speak of the Last Roman Emperor. In other words, if the Islamic writers were already constructing their doctrines about the Gog-Magog war, the Dajjal, and Isa from *Pseudo-Methodius* and other similar texts, it is no surprise that they also incorporated the Last Roman Emperor from those same documents into their theology.

The Islamic Antichrist proponents try very hard to find similarities between the Mahdi and the Christian Antichrist. I will argue later that this can only be done in a very general way. But if you choose to compare the Islamic Mahdi with the Last Roman Emperor figure instead of the Antichrist, you can produce a much more impressive list of similarities.

The Mahdi and the Last Roman Emperor share the following characteristics.

They both are human kings.

> Both the Mahdi and the Last Roman Emperor are described as purely human, not angelic or divine. Any supernatural things that happen during each of their careers are attributed to God/Allah. The idea in both cases is that God/Allah supports each of these kings and therefore guides and protects them.

They both come at a time of great trouble for their respective religions.

> Last Roman Emperor in *Pseudo-Methodius*:

> "Then suddenly tribulation and distress will arise against them. The king of the Greeks, i.e., the Romans, will come out against them in great anger."

> The Last Roman Emperor is preceded by signs very similar to

the Islamic "minor signs" which describe a moral decline:

"Men will get themselves up as false women wearing prostitutes' clothes. Standing in the streets and squares of the cities openly before all they will be adorned like women; they will exchange natural sex for that which is against nature."

The *Mahdi* in Islamic tradition:

The Mahdi is frequently mentioned to come on the scene as a result of *fitan* (trials and tribulations). He is preceded by many of the "minor signs" which describe a time of moral decline. More specifically he is said to come to power to combat the *Sufyani*, a Muslim tyrant who causes great trouble. The Mahdi is said to defeat the *Sufyani* once he gains power.

They both are reluctant to rule.

Last Roman Emperor in *Pseudo-Methodius*:

"[The Last Roman Emperor will be] roused [in order to rule] as from a drunken stupor like one whom men had thought dead and worthless."

The Mahdi in Islamic tradition:

"And he [The Mahdi] will accept it [the rule] reluctantly. He will not know, and they will not know, that he is the expected Mahdi, and previously there will be no calls for him to be Mahdi, and he will not even know himself, but God will choose him, and the people will choose him suddenly."[53]

---

[53] *Tawila, `Abd al-Wahhab `Abd al-Salam. 1999. Al-Masih al-muntazar wa-nihayat al-`clam. Cairo: Dar al-Salam.* p. 65

They both fight wars to destroy other human kings opposed to their religious system.

Last Roman Emperor in *Pseudo-Methodius*:

"He will go forth against them from the Ethiopian sea and will send the sword and desolation into Ethribus (Southern Arabia) their homeland...Egypt will be desolated, Arabia burned with fire, the land of Ausania burned, and the sea provinces pacified. The whole indignation and fury of the king of the Romans will blaze forth against those who deny the Lord Jesus Christ."

The Mahdi in Islamic tradition:

"Although the uprising of Hadrat al-Mahdi ('atfs) will commence in Mecca, he will conquer the land of Hijaz" (a large section of Arabia).[54]

"He will have a sword with him, which he will unsheathe, and through him God will conquer the lands of Rome, China, Turkistan, Daylam, Sind, Hind, Kabul, Sham, and Khazar."[55]

"God will send al-Mahdi ('atfs) and through him the religion will regain its grandeur and through him and for Him, glorious victories will be attained."[56]

The primary enemy that he destroys will be a Muslim king who rules over Syria and kills women and children.

In *Pseudo-Methodius*, the Last Roman Emperor put particular emphasis on destroying Syria:

---

[54] *Ibn Hummad, Fitan*, p. 95; *Muttaqi Hindi, Burhan*, p. 141; *Ibn Tawus, Malahim*, p. 64; *Al-Mukhtasar*, p. 23
[55] *Nu'mani, Ghaybah*, p. 108; *Bihar al-Anwar*, vol. 52, p. 348.
[56] *'Uyun Akhbar ar-Rida*, p. 65; *Ihqaq al-Haqq*, vol. 13, p. 346; *Ash-Shi'ah wa'r-Raj'ah*, vol. 1, p. 218.

"The land of Syria will be empty and reduced; those dwelling in her will perish by the sword. . . . Egypt and the East and Syria will be under the yoke and hemmed in by great tribulations. They will be constrained without mercy...The inhabitants of Egypt and Syria will be in trouble and affliction, seven times the greater for those in captivity."

The reason that the world is in tribulation when he arises is due to the Muslim threat from those regions. The people he destroys are described as "casting lots for children."

The Mahdi in Islamic tradition:

The Mahdi also places a particular emphasis on destroying Syria when he comes to power. This is because of a threat from "the *Sufyani*" an Arabic king who rules of Syria. The *Sufyani* also is said to treat women and children badly.

"A man will emerge from the depths of Damascus [Syria]. He will be called *Sufyani*. Most of those who follow him will be from the tribe of Kalb. He will kill by ripping the stomachs of women and even kill the children. A man from my family will appear in the Haram, the news of his advent will reach the *Sufyani* and he will send to him one of his armies. He [referring to the Mahdi] will defeat them. They will then travel with whoever remains until they come to a desert and they will be swallowed. None will be saved except the one who had informed the others about them. (Mustadrak Al-Hakim)"

They both rule only briefly
Last Roman Emperor in *Pseudo-Methodius*:

"After this the king of the Romans will go down and live in Jerusalem for seven and half-seven times, i.e., years. When the ten and a half years are completed the Son of Perdition will appear."

The Mahdi in Islamic tradition:

The hadiths give different times for the Mahdi's rule (five, seven, eight, nine or nineteen years), but in any case it is a brief rule. Perhaps one reason for the contradictions in the *hadiths* is because of the odd way that the length of the rule of the Last Roman Emperor is described in *Pseudo-Methodius* (i.e. "seven and half-seven times").

They both succeeded in restoring orthodoxy to their religion, but only briefly.

Last Roman Emperor in *Pseudo-Methodius*:

The Last Roman Emperor destroys the enemies of Christianity and sets up his religious rule, but this time is followed by terrible destruction, such as the Gog-Magog war and the appearance of the Antichrist.

The Mahdi in Islamic tradition:

Similarly the Mahdi succeeds in destroying the enemies of Islam and setting up a religious peace, but that peaceful time is followed by the Gog-Magog war and the appearance of the Dajjal, both of those events cause immeasurable destruction to the earth and to Islam.

They both rule over a temporary time of peace and prosperity.

Last Roman Emperor in *Pseudo-Methodius*:

"The whole indignation and fury of the king of the Romans will blaze forth against those who deny the Lord Jesus Christ. Then the earth will sit in peace and there will be great peace and tranquility upon the earth..."

The Mahdi in Islamic tradition:

> "The Mahdi will appear. Allah will grant him rain, the earth will bring forth its fruits, he will give a lot of money, cattle will increase and the *ummah* will become great."[57]

"He will fill out the earth with peace and justice"[58]

Both of their reigns will be followed by the Gog-Magog war.

Last Roman Emperor in *Pseudo-Methodius*:

The description of the peace the Last Roman Emperor will win for himself is followed by the description of the Gog-Magog war.

> "Then the 'Gates of the North' will be opened and the strength of those nations which Alexander shut up there will go forth."

It is clear from the context that follows that the initial peace of the Last Roman Emperor is followed by the Gog-Magog war.

The Mahdi in Islamic tradition:

In Islamic tradition it is clear that the Gog-Magog war takes place after the initial peace of the Mahdi. In addition Isa, not the Mahdi, is ruling at the time of the Gog-Magog war, which conclusively puts the war after the Mahdi's initial time of peace.

---

[57] *Mustadrak al-Hakim*, 4: 557-558
[58] *Sahih al-Tirmidhi*, v2, p86, v9, pp 74-75

The Antichrist figure comes on the scene at the end of his career.

Last Roman Emperor in *Pseudo-Methodius*:

> "After this the king of the Romans will go down and live in Jerusalem for seven and half-seven times, i.e., years. When the ten and a half years are completed **the Son of Perdition will appear**."

The Mahdi in Islamic tradition:

> In the *hadiths* it is quite clear that the Dajjal does not appear until after the Mahdi has defeated Constantinople, an event that occurs toward the end of his career. Isa is said to appear as the Mahdi's armies, recently returned from Constantinople, are preparing to fight the Dajjal. Isa's appearance marks the beginning of the end of the Mahdi's rule.

In both cases Jesus returns at the end of his time after the Antichrist has been revealed.

Last Roman Emperor in *Pseudo-Methodius*:

> Though the actual return of Jesus is not mentioned in *Pseudo-Methodius*, it does describe the Last Roman Emperor going to Golgotha (the cross of Christ) and laying his crown on the cross (symbolically giving his throne to Jesus). He does this because of the appearance of the Antichrist.

The Mahdi in Islamic tradition:

> As mentioned earlier Isa appears after the conquest of Constantinople, when the Mahdi hears of the appearance of the Dajjal. Isa seems to appear for the expressed purpose of

defeating the Dajjal, something the Mahdi apparently cannot do.

In both cases he does not defeat the Antichrist.

Last Roman Emperor in *Pseudo-Methodius*:

As mentioned in the previous point, the Last Roman Emperor, upon hearing of the Antichrist's appearance, goes to give his throne symbolically to Jesus. He dies at this point. The last words of *Pseudo-Methodius* make clear that the Antichrist is still on earth after the Last Roman Emperor's death.

> "When the Cross has been lifted up on high to heaven, the king of the Romans will directly give up his spirit. Then every principality and power will be destroyed **that the Son of Perdition may be manifest**."

The Mahdi in Islamic tradition:

Here again the Islamic traditions are quite clear that Isa, not the Mahdi, defeats the Dajjal.[59]

> "And Allah would then send Jesus son of Mary who would resemble 'Urwa b Mas'ud.' He (Jesus Christ) would chase him [the Dajjal] and kill him."[60]

In both cases Jesus will rule after him.

---

[59] It should be noted that a small group of Shia Muslims do believe it is the Mahdi who kills the Dajjal, though they are in the minority.

[60] *Sahih Muslim*, 41:7023

Last Roman Emperor in *Pseudo-Methodius*:

This is seen by the Last Roman Emperor abdicating his throne to Jesus and then dying. The text presumes that Jesus will then return to Earth and rule after this. Other material from the time, such as the *Apocalypse of Daniel,* make this point much more clear.

The Mahdi in Islamic tradition:

It is difficult to know exactly how long the Mahdi lives after Isa arrives. Some Muslims believe he will immediately be killed by a bearded woman or give up the rule of the world to Isa and be killed later. Others believe there will be a short time in which they rule together before Isa takes over. In any case, since Isa is said to rule for forty years after his return and the Mahdi's rule is said to be much shorter, it is clear that Isa rules after the Mahdi dies.

When you add to this the supplemental information we have already discussed, such as the Gog-Magog war similarities in both versions or the descriptions of the Antichrist/Dajjal having one blind eye and one that shines like a star, it becomes nearly impossible to see these similarities as coincidences. The Mahdi idea, just like so many of the other non-biblical concepts in Islamic eschatology, is based on the peculiar ideas found in the extra-biblical traditions of the early Christian church. It should be noted that, in the case of the Mahdi and the Last Roman Emperor, the writers of the *hadiths* continued with their method of reversing the religions involved in the original story to make Islam out to be the victor. So in this case, instead of this eschatological hero being a Roman king who fights for Christianity, he is an Islamic king (Caliph) who fights to restore Islam. This is all that is needed to explain the development of the Mahdi idea. That being said, I would recommend the paper I mentioned earlier "The Last Roman Emperor and the Mahdi" by Andras Kraft for more of the background on this subject.

Chapter 12
A Closer Look at the Comparisons Provided by the Islamic Antichrist Proponents

Isa and the False Prophet

In his book *Islamic Antichrist,* Joel Richardson compares the Islamic version of Jesus (Isa) to the biblical False Prophet. As previously noted, his theory is that a fake Muslim Jesus who calls himself Isa will appear in the future and his real identity will be the False Prophet of Revelation 13. Richardson provides a list of four main similarities between Isa and the False Prophet. I will discuss each in the order they appear in his book.

An Unholy Partnership

The first similarity Richardson proposes is that Isa has a partnership with the Mahdi in the same way that the False Prophet has a partnership with the Antichrist. Since Richardson believes the Mahdi is the Antichrist, he also believes that Isa must be the False Prophet, based on the belief that Isa and the Mahdi are said to have a partnership of some kind.

Is Isa Subordinate to the Mahdi?
In order to make the partnership of Isa and the Mahdi look anything like the Antichrist and False Prophet, Richardson and others need to convince their readers that Isa will actually be subordinate to the Mahdi in the same way the False Prophet is subordinate to the Antichrist. The problem with this idea is that, despite Islamic Antichrist theorists constantly saying Isa is subordinate to the Mahdi, many Islamic sources vehemently disagree and maintain it is actually Isa who outranks the Mahdi, not the other way around.

They have very good reasons for saying this. The first is an important doctrine in the Quran that says prophets outrank all other created beings.

> "The statement of Allah Most High after naming numerous prophets, 'each one We preferred above all beings.'" (6:86)

In his commentary, Imam Baydawi said of this verse: "There is proof in this for their superiority over those other than them from among created things."

This idea is confirmed several times in the *hadiths*:

> "The Prophet (Allah bless him and grant him peace) said, 'Allah selected my companions over all created things apart from the messengers and prophets.'"

Since Isa is a prophet in Islam, and the Mahdi is only an Imam and a Caliph, Isa outranks the Mahdi. This is not my opinion; it is the common understanding of the relationship between the Mahdi and Isa by the majority of Muslims.[61]

---

[61] A quote from Ustadh Salman Younas on this issue: "All of the above goes to show that the rank of a prophet is superior to the rank of a non-prophetic figure.

This should also be quite obvious from the *hadiths* previously discussed in this book. For example, we have seen that it is Isa who destroys the Dajjal, executes judgment on the world, defeats Gog and Magog (through prayer), and rules the world after the Mahdi serves his role. This is clearly a more exalted set of tasks when compared to the Mahdi, who fights regular wars with human enemies and achieves temporary peace and prosperity.

So what kind of arguments do Islamic Antichrist theorists like Joel Richardson make to support the Mahdi outranking Isa? They point to the *hadiths* that describe Isa allowing the Mahdi to pray a ritualistic prayer before the battle with the Dajjal. They claim that when Isa allows the Mahdi to pray this prayer, it is essentially the same as saying the Mahdi is of a higher rank than Isa.

Here is the *hadith* in question:

> "This hadith has been narrated on the authority of Jabir Ibn Abdillah al-Ansari that I heard the Messenger of Allah saying: 'A group of my Ummah will fight for the truth until near the day of judgment when Jesus, the son of Mary, will descend, and the leader of them will ask him to lead the prayer, but Jesus declines, saying: "No, Verily, among you Allah has made leaders for others and He has bestowed his bounty upon them.""'

A prominent Islamic theology website[62] makes the following points when discussing this *hadith*:

> "The fact that our liege-lord `Isa (Allah bless him) was offered to lead [the prayer] indicates that people understood his superiority

---

As Imam Mahdi is a non-prophetic figure, it is contrary to our creed to consider him superior to our liege-lord `Isa (Allah bless him)."

[62] Younas, Ustadh Salman. "Does the Mahdi Have a Higher Rank Than Prophet `Isa." *Seekers Hub Global*. N.p., 31 May 2012. Web. http://seekershub.org/ans-blog/2012/05/31/does-the-mahdi-have-a-higher-rank-than-prophet-isa-peace-be-upon-him/.

over all others."

"These very narrations indicate the reason for our liege-lord
`Isa's (Allah bless him) refusal to lead prayer when offered to do
so, namely to show how Allah has honored the community of
Muhammad (Allah bless him and grant him peace). Thus, when
requested to lead he will reply, 'No, for some of you are leaders
upon others out of Allah's honoring this community.'" [Muslim]

Basically what is being pictured here is the Mahdi asking Isa to lead the
prayer since he understood Isa's general superiority over him, but Isa
refuses on the grounds that the Mahdi is the leader of the men who are
present.

It should be noted that certain sections of Shite Muslims, which
constitute about 10 to 20 percent of Muslims,[63] do in fact take this
passage to mean the Mahdi is superior to Isa. Because of this, I will not
state too strongly what Muslims believe about the relationship between
Isa and the Mahdi. However, I will say that Richardson and others who
tell Christians that Muslims believe Isa is subordinate to the Mahdi are at
best only talking about 20 percent of the Muslim population. As we have
seen, there are good arguments to support the Sunni position, such as Isa
ruling the world after the Mahdi; Isa, not the Mahdi, destroying the
Dajjal and Gog-Magog; the contextual evidence that shows the Mahdi
offered the prayer to Isa first; and the Quran passages which state that
prophets are always superior to non-prophets.

The most important similarity that Richardson makes when talking about
the "unholy partnership" is that Isa is subordinate to the Mahdi in the
same way the False Prophet is subordinate to the Antichrist. If that
premise is called into question—which I very much think it should be—
then the rest of this theory about the supposed similarities between Isa
and the False Prophet or the Mahdi and the Antichrist is on thin ice.

---

[63] "Religions.". CIA. *The World Factbook*. 2010. Retrieved 2010-08-25.

The Enforcer

The next similarity between Isa and the False Prophet, suggested by Richardson, is that both are enforcers of the orders from their leader. In the case of the False Prophet, this is more or less true. The False Prophet institutes the mark of the beast system and carries out its implementation (Revelation 13:16–17). He is also the one who sets up the "image of the beast" which the world is forced to worship (Revelation 13:14–15). Finally, he is clearly doing all these things so the Antichrist, not himself, will be glorified (Revelation 13:12).

It is only when Richardson tries to show that Isa is "the Mahdi's chief enforcer" that I must disagree. Despite the relevant section in his book being titled "The Muslim Jesus as the Mahdi's Chief Enforcer," he doesn't offer a single argument to prove this. Instead he shows that Isa is an enforcer of Islam in general when he becomes the ruler of the world. For example, he cites that Isa is said to convert Christians to Islam, abolish the *Jizya*h tax, and judge the world with Islamic law. None of these *hadiths* suggest that Isa is doing this on behalf of the Mahdi. The Mahdi is said to rule for seven to nineteen years and most, if not all, of these years take place before Isa even shows up. Isa is said to rule for forty years, so it is clear that Isa does not need the Mahdi to help him rule since he is said to be doing so long after the Mahdi is dead.

The Executioner

Richardson's third point is that both Isa and the False Prophet set up systems that will ultimately lead to the death of those who hold to any other religion. The False Prophet, for example, sets up the mark of the beast system. If people do not receive this mark, they will be executed. Isa, on the other hand, abolishes the *Jizya* tax that allows non-Muslims to live peacefully with Muslims. Although not expressly stated in the *hadiths*, it is presumed that this would lead to the death of non-Muslims. I submit that the similarity here is minimal and, in any case, this kind of general similarity is to be expected since the *hadith* writers, as we have seen, based their Isa on biblical and extra-biblical accounts of the

Christian Jesus in the kingdom age. Jesus rules the earth with an "iron rod," demands religious obedience,[64] pilgrimage,[65] and gifts.[66] He is also said to "slay the wicked"[67] during His earthly reign. If Muslims were simply basing their Isa on the biblical prophecies about Jesus in the kingdom age, such general similarities as the one Richardson proposes here are to be expected.

Two Horns Like a Lamb

Richardson's final attempt to equate Isa with the False Prophet is related to the following verse about the False Prophet in Revelation 13:11:

> "And I beheld another beast coming up out of the earth; and he had two horns like a lamb, and he spake as a dragon."

Richardson argues that because the False Prophet is said to have "two horns like a lamb," the False Prophet is attempting to imitate Jesus, who is often referred to as "the Lamb."

I believe the correct way to interpret this passage is in light of Jesus' warnings about false prophets in Matthew 7:15, which says:

> "Beware of false prophets, who come to you in sheep's clothing, but, inwardly, they are ravenous wolves." (Matthew 7:15)

Jesus said that in the last days false prophets would come in sheep's clothing, but would inwardly be like wolves. In this passage, it seems clear that Jesus is not using the sheep imagery to refer to Himself but to suggest that false prophets would act as though they are meek and harmless like lambs. He is essentially using the sheep imagery the same way He does in many other places in Scripture,[68] in a generic sense, to

---

[64] Romans 14:11
[65] Zechariah 14:16
[66] Isaiah 56:7, Ezekiel 45:13–46:15, Zechariah 14:16–18
[67] Isaiah 11:4
[68] John 21:15–16 is notable because it shows that lambs and sheep are

speak of people who are meek and harmless, like his church.

In Revelation 13:11 it seems that lambs are to be understood in this way (e.g. a meek person), and not a reference to Jesus because the verse goes on to contrast the False Prophet's looking like a harmless lamb with his dragon-like speech:

> "Then I saw another beast coming up from the earth. He had two horns like a lamb, **but** was speaking like a dragon." (NET)

This is virtually the same illustration Jesus gave in Matthew 7:15 about false prophets who dress up like sheep but are really wolves. However, in this case, a dragon is used instead of a wolf, which is probably to link the speech of the False Prophet to the satanic (dragon[69]) doctrine he will be teaching.

The idea that the False Prophet has two horns like a lamb is, therefore, to be understood as him trying to seem like a genuine lamb (a meek and harmless person) because this is the normal number of horns a lamb will grow just after they are weaned. In other words, the concept of having two horns like a lamb is to be connected with the idea of having "sheep's clothing." This has been noted in many Bible commentaries, such as theologian Johann Peter Lange's *Commentary on the Holy Scriptures: Critical, Doctrinal, and Homiletical, Volume 10*:

> "We do not translate, like **the** lamb...The two horns, therefore, are not to be placed in the category of a defect...has but two horns, and is thus distinguished, as a natural sheep."

In addition, I draw the reader's attention to how Jesus used the term "false prophets" in the Olivet Discourse, which almost certainly has the False Prophet of Revelation 13 in mind:

---

interchangeable.

[69] Satan is referred to as a dragon several times in the book of Revelation.

"Then, if anyone says to you, 'Look, here is the Christ!' or 'There!,' do not believe it. For false christs and false prophets will rise and show great signs and wonders to deceive, if possible, even the elect." (Matthew 24:23–24)

In this verse Jesus is contrasting the false prophets who show "great signs" (the same Greek phrase John uses to describe the False Prophet's signs in Revelation 13) with false christs. The fact that Jesus makes a clear distinction between these last-days false christs and false prophets makes it very unlikely that the False Prophet will also be a false christ as Richardson is suggesting. It seems clear Jesus is warning of two distinct types of last-days deceivers and not one deceiver who will be both a false christ and a false prophet.

A More Plausible Explanation

I will once again suggest that the best way to refute an argument is to offer a more plausible explanation than the one you are attempting to refute. In the case of the False Prophet, I think I have a much better theory than the one proposed by Richardson, one that takes into account all the information the Bible offers about the False Prophet. However, since I am determined to keep my personal views out of the main body of this text, I will include my thoughts on the False Prophet in Appendix 4.

The Mahdi and the Antichrist

Islamic Antichrist theorists compare the Islamic Mahdi to the biblical Antichrist. They basically believe when the Antichrist shows up, he will claim to be the Mahdi of Islamic traditions. Joel Richardson offers a list of similarities between the Mahdi and the Antichrist in his book, and just like in the case of the Isa/False Prophet comparisons, I will take each supposed similarity one by one.

A Powerful Political and Military World Leader

Richardson points out that both the Mahdi and the Antichrist are said to be powerful political and military world leaders. This is true, but it should be noted that this is a very general statement that can be applied to just about everyone we have discussed in this section of the book. For example, the Islamic Isa certainly could be described as a powerful political and military world leader, even more powerful than the Mahdi. In addition, the Last Roman Emperor from the Christian pseudopigraphical material could also be described as a powerful political and military world leader.

As we have already discussed, the concept of the Mahdi is almost certainly based on the Last Roman Emperor idea in Christian tradition. The pattern that will develop as we go over this list of similarities is Richardson will describe commonalities that are much more applicable to the Mahdi and the Last Roman Emperor than to the Mahdi and the Antichrist. We will also see that differences between the Mahdi and the Antichrist are the same as the differences between the Last Roman Emperor and the Antichrist. This is why the majority of Richardson's similarities must by necessity be extremely general.

For example, in this case, though the Mahdi and the Last Roman Emperor are powerful political and military leaders, they differ from the Antichrist in that they both die, allowing Jesus/Isa to rule the world after their very short reign. This is certainly not the case with the Antichrist and the False Prophet. The fact that Isa, not the Mahdi, is the one who restores the world to a state in which the lambs and wolves graze together and the vipers no longer bite people is a testament to the primacy of Isa over the Mahdi in the Islamic system. My point is that the general comparisons made by Richardson could be very specific comparisons if he were equating the Mahdi to the correct counterpart (i.e. the last Roman Emperor), who is a political and military world leader who rules the world before Jesus takes his throne. However, since Richardson is determined to equate the Mahdi with the Antichrist, he must minimize the importance of Isa as the final ruler in Islamic tradition.

The Mahdi as a Spiritual World Leader

Richardson's next point is that the Mahdi and the Antichrist are both said to be spiritual world leaders. Again this is true in a general sense, but this has the same problem with the previous point that this general statement is actually truer of Isa and the Last Roman Emperor. In the case of Isa, he is the one who actually converts the world to Islam and judges the world in accordance with Islamic law. It is only after the Mahdi dies and Isa begins his rule that the universal peace and justice based on Islamic law begins. The Mahdi should be considered more of a forerunner, preparing the way for Isa's new world.

The actual type of "spiritual world leader" the Mahdi is said to be is much more like the spiritual world leader the Last Roman Emperor is said to be. That is, they both come at a time when the world has lost faith, they both fight limited wars with the nations that oppose their religion to restore orthodox religion, they both set up a limited peace based on their religion, and this peace lasts until the Antichrist/Dajjal arrives, in which case they both look to Isa/Jesus for help.

The Mahdi Kills Jews and Christians

Next Richardson says that both the Mahdi and the Antichrist kill Jews and Christians and, therefore, should be equated with one another. There are several problems with this comparison. The first is that, while it is true that the Mahdi does kill Jews and Christians during his wars, he begins his military campaign against the *Sufyani*, a Muslim leader from Syria. The Mahdi also conquers many other Islamic countries, including parts of Iraq and Saudi Arabia. The Mahdi is even said to team up with the Christians at one point to fight their common Arab enemies; the Christians and Muslims even conquer Constantinople together. However this Christian/Islamic coalition ends when the Christians claim the victory was due to Christ and the Muslim armies claim it was due to

Allah.

There is no systematic killing of Christians whatsoever by the Mahdi, certainly not in the way the Antichrist is said to do. The systematic killing on religious grounds will only happen after Isa arrives to judge the world by Islamic law. So here again we have the same problem. Richardson's supposed similarities with the Mahdi and the Antichrist are truer of Isa than the Mahdi.

The actual type of killing of Jews and Christians done by the Mahdi is the same type of killing the Last Roman Emperor is said to do. The Last Roman Emperor is said to fight wars with those who oppose him and his religion. His killing of people is all military in nature. There is no hint of executing civilians because of their religion, but rather he is pictured as subduing the nations that oppose him. Those who die, die in battle with the Mahdi's armies, just like the Last Roman Emperor.

The Mahdi Conquers and Rules From Jerusalem

Richardson says that both the Antichrist and the Mahdi conquer and rule from Jerusalem. This initial statement is only half true. In the *hadiths,* Jerusalem seems to be conquered before the Mahdi arrives, and the people who fight there are Arabs.

> "Then, another black banner (army battalion) will come from Khorasan. Their turbans are black and their clothes are white. At their front end will be a man named Shuayb bin Salih, from Tamim (tribe). They will defeat supporters of the Sufyani [a Muslim leader] (and proceed further) until he (Shuayb bin Salih) arrives to Jerusalem (where) he will lay the foundation for the Mahdi's (future) dominion. He will be supplied with three hundred (men) from AshSham (Syria). From the time, he comes out (from Khorasan) until he hands over the matter (rule) to the Mahdi, there will be seventy two months (six years).'" (Nuaim Ibn Hammad's Kitab Al-Fitan)

I cannot find many *hadiths* that state specifically the Mahdi will actually rule his Caliphate from Jerusalem; but, as in the case of the *hadith* above, there is enough to at least suggest that he does. Unlike the Antichrist, however, there is certainly nothing in the *hadiths* that describe the Mahdi setting up the temple or allowing Jewish people to start the daily sacrifices again (Daniel 9:27), let alone sitting in the Jewish temple and declaring himself to be God. So I would again submit that the part of the similarity that is true is a general statement that better applies to Islamic Isa, who, without question, is said in the *hadiths* to rule from Jerusalem.

There are two probable reasons why the *hadith* writers felt compelled to incorporate Jerusalem into their eschatology. First, the Bible is clear that Jerusalem is where the kingdom age will take place. Even though Islamic writers obviously had no problem with making certain editorial changes of biblical stories, the centrality of Jerusalem in the last days was too significant to tamper with. The last battle with the Dajjal is, therefore, said to be in Jerusalem and Isa is said to rule the world from Jerusalem, just like in the Bible. The *hadith* writers' dependence on the Bible for the basic framework of their eschatology forced them to make Jerusalem the center of the last days despite their probable preference for making it Mecca or Medina. This is the first reason that Jerusalem was included, though I would argue the majority of Islamic texts that mention the city apply to Isa, not the Mahdi.

The only reason the Mahdi has any relationship to Jerusalem at all is probably related to the Last Roman Emperor. It should not be overlooked that both the Mahdi and the Last Roman Emperor are said to travel from Constantinople to Jerusalem after hearing of the Antichrist's appearance. This very specific similarity should be enough to show that the Mahdi is being patterned after the apocalyptic writings regarding the Last Roman Emperor, which explains the mention of Jerusalem in relationship to the Mahdi, since Jerusalem is where both men give up their rule to Jesus/Isa.

The Seven-Year Peace Agreement

This is the first of the similarities Richardson suggests that does not have the problem of being too general; in fact, it's quite specific. He quotes a *hadith* that says the Mahdi will make a seven-year treaty with the Romans. And since he also believes that Daniel 9:27 is speaking of the Antichrist making a seven-year treaty with the Jews, he says they must be a reference to the same thing. I will quote the *hadith* in question below:

> "The Prophet said: There will be four peace agreements between you and the Romans. The fourth will be mediated through a person who will be from the progeny of Hadrat Aaron [Honorable Aaron—the brother of Moses] and will be upheld for seven years. The people asked, 'O Prophet Muhammad, who will be the imam [leader] of the people at that time?' The Prophet said: 'He will be from my progeny and will be exactly forty years of age. His face will shine like a star.'"[70]

The first problem is this *hadith* is almost certainly referring to an event other *hadiths* talk about at great length, namely the treaty that unites the Roman armies and the armies of the Mahdi to fight against their common enemies. As previously noted, this treaty ends because of a disagreement between the soldiers about which God has been responsible for their victories. Note that in the following *hadith* the treaty is said to be for ten years, not seven.

> "You will enter into a reconciliation treaty with them [the Romans] for 10 years. You and the Romans will invade an enemy behind Constantinople. When you return for that invasion, you will see Constantinople... Then, together, you will invade Al-Kufa (a Shia city in Iraq) ... Then, you and the Romans together will invade some of the people of the East. You will capture women, children and money (possessions and wealth) The Romans will tell you: Give us our share of the children and women. The Muslims will say: No, we cannot based on our religion, but take from the rest of things (meaning from the possessions, etc). The Romans say: We will not take

---

[70] Tabarani as quoted by Mufti A.H. Elias and Muhammad Ali ibn Zubair Ali.

except from every thing. The Romans say: You won (the battle against the common enemies) because of us and our Cross. The Muslims will say: No, Allah granted victory and support to its religion. So, they will raise the Cross. Muslims become angry. A (Muslim) man will jump on to the Cross and break it. The Romans will leave angry and when you reach their king, they will tell him: The Arabs deceived us and withheld from us what we are entitled to and they broke our Cross and killed some of us. Their king becomes very angry and amasses a large army and reconcile with other nations. They will marsh against the Muslims."[71]

Though the timing of the Roman treaties is very hard to pin down due to multiple contradictory accounts, it seems likely that some *hadith* writers wrote seven years as opposed to ten years because of the time between the Constantinople battle and the Dajjal, which is occasionally said to be seven years.

> "Abdullah bin Busr reports that the Prophet said: 'Between the Malhama (the final War or Battle) and the conquest of the City (i.e. Constantinople), there will be six years, and the Dajjal (Antichrist) shall appear in the seventh year'"

To further illustrate the unreliability of these *hadiths*, especially concerning the amount of years involved, the "seven years" in the above *hadith* about the length of time between the conquest of Constantinople and the Dajjal is sometimes referred to as being "seven months."

> "Al-Malhama Al-Kubra conquest of Constantinople, and the coming of Dajjal (Antichrist) will be (occur) within (a period of) seven months." (Abu Dawud and Ibn Maja)

Richardson wants to equate this seven-year treaty with the Romans to the Antichrist "making a covenant" in Daniel 9:27. He suggests that the treaty the Mahdi makes with the Romans would allow the Jews to rebuild

---

[71] Nuaim bin Hammad's *Kitab al-Fitan.*

the temple, but it seems clear what Muslims believe this treaty is about and it has nothing to do with the Jewish temple. It is a military alliance with Romans to help the Muslims destroy various enemies. The treaty is broken when the soldiers get in a fight about religion.

As alluded to earlier, there is also a problem with the number of years mentioned in the *hadith* quoted by Richardson. The treaty with the Romans is almost always referred to in other *hadiths* as being ten years long, not seven. As far as I know, the only *hadith* that says it will be seven years is the one Richardson quotes. *Hadiths* are notorious for having contradictory statements, especially when it comes to numbers, but to choose the *hadith* with the number that best suits your theory, in light of it being the only *hadith* on the subject containing that number, is not good.

The Treaty is Not With the Jews

Another problem with this theory is that this treaty in the *hadith* that Richardson quotes does not include the Jews at all! It is true that a Jew from the tribe of Aaron mediates the treaty, but the treaty itself is actually between the Romans and the Muslims. So when Richardson says this treaty will have something to do with the temple being rebuilt in Jerusalem, I have to ask why? The Jews are not entering into any kind of agreement, with the Muslims, Romans, or anyone else in this *hadith*; they are simply acting as a middleman between the Muslims and the Christians.

Rethinking the "Peace Treaty"

Finally I submit that this entire issue may be moot since it may not even be a "peace treaty" that the Antichrist makes. The actual words used in Daniel 9:27 are "make firm a covenant"; and while a covenant can mean a contract or perhaps treaty, it certainly can be a reference to an actual covenant in the biblical sense of the word, as well. Again my self-imposed limitations prevent me from detailing my personal thoughts about this here, but I will include a discussion about the covenant made by the Antichrist in <u>Appendix 5</u>.

Richardson's White Horse Misquotation

The last comparison Richardson makes is actually very deceptive, that is, if he knew beforehand what he was doing. However, I will give him the benefit of the doubt and chalk this up to an honest mistake on his part.

Richardson says an influential Islamic scholar in the Middle Ages believed the Mahdi is in view in Revelation 6:1–2 in which a rider on a white horse, typically understood to be the Antichrist, is seen. I will quote Richardson directly on this point:

> "For in seeing the Antichrist on the white horse with a crown and conquering, Muslim scholars see a clear picture of the Mahdi. As mentioned in the earlier chapter on the Mahdi, the early Muslim transmitter of hadiths, Ka'b al Ahbar is quoted as saying:
> "I find the Mahdi recorded in the books of the Prophets... For instance, the Book of Revelation says: 'And I saw and behold a white horse. He that sat on him...went forth conquering and to conquer.'"[72]

When I first read this I was skeptical for several reasons. The first reason was because there is absolutely nothing that says the Mahdi rides on a white horse in any *hadith* or Quran verse that I have found. The second reason is that the person he is supposedly quoting, "Ka'b al Ahbar," wrote at a time when the concept of the Mahdi was not very well developed, certainly nothing like it is today. I found it very unlikely that he would say such a thing, so I went about trying to track down this quote.

What I found is a quote from a book by two Egyptian writers, Muhammad ibn Izzat and Muhammad Arif, in their book *Al-Mahdi*,

---

[72] Richardson, Joel (2009-07-28). *The Islamic Antichrist: The Shocking Truth about the Real Nature of the Beast* (p. 50). Midpoint Trade Books. Kindle Edition.

published in 1997. The actual quote reads like this:

> **"Kaʻb al-Ahbar said: "I find the Mahdi recorded in the books of the Prophets. There will be no injustice or oppression in his rule."** [This is when the actual quote from Kaʻb al-Ahbar stops (Note the quotation marks). The rest of this paragraph is commentary from the authors of this book] **For instance the Book of Revelation says: 'And I saw and behold a white horse. He that sat on him ... went forth conquering and to conquer.' It is clear that this man is the Mahdi who will ride a white horse and judge by the Qur'an (with justice) and with whom will be men with the marks of prostration on their foreheads."**[73]

Richardson took out the last part of the actual quote from al-Ahbar which said "There will be no injustice or oppression in his rule" and added in its place a quote from the authors of this book: "For instance, the Book of Revelation says: 'And I saw and behold a white horse. He that sat on him…went forth conquering and to conquer.'" Therefore, he is telling his readers a prominent Islamic scholar believes this when, in fact, this is the belief of two Egyptian men in 1997 who, in other places in their book, show that they have rather unorthodox views about the end times.

If you look up the idea of the Mahdi riding a white horse, you will not find the idea in the *hadiths* or the Quran. Instead, you will find Christians citing Joel Richardson who attributes the words of a recent book to the Middle Ages Islamic scholar Kaʻb al-Ahbar.

Dajjal as the Real Jesus

In his book *Islamic Antichrist*, Joel Richardson claims the Dajjal, the Islamic Antichrist, will in reality be the real return of Jesus. The primary

---

[73] Arif, Muhammad Ibn Izzat Muhammad (2012-08-07). *Al Mahdi* (Kindle Locations 166-171). Dar Al Taqwa. Kindle Edition.

reason he makes this claim is because many Muslims believe the Dajjal will claim to be the Jewish Messiah, just as Jesus will. Richardson doesn't spend very much time trying to point out similarities with the Dajjal and the real Jesus since there are virtually no similarities. The two characters are very different in their attributes and actions, and the reason they are so different is, as we have seen, the Dajjal is based on the biblical and extra-biblical Christian views of the Antichrist.

When attempting a comparison of these two figures, Richardson highlights only two items. The first is that the Dajjal is believed to be the Jewish Messiah, like Jesus; and second is that the Dajjal "defends Israel" from the Mahdi in the same way Jesus defends Israel from the Antichrist. I think this second point should be called into question since it takes a bit of imagination to understand the *hadiths* about the Dajjal's actions as "defending Israel." With that being said, even if we accepted these two premises as true, all this really proves is that the Dajjal is modeled after the early Christian views of the Antichrist and it is not a prophecy of the return of Jesus hidden in Islamic traditions.

Even if someone doesn't believe the Antichrist will claim to be the Jewish Messiah, no one would disagree that this was the earliest view of the church and it was certainly the prominent view at the time the *hadiths* were written. In other words, the Islamic *hadith* writers believed the Christian Antichrist would claim to be the Jewish Messiah and that is the reason the Dajjal also claims to be the Jewish Messiah. Similarly the Bible says the Antichrist will gather the nations to Armageddon in Israel to fight the last battle, a battle in which Jesus defeats the Antichrist. Given all we have discovered in this chapter, it is no surprise then that the Islamic *hadiths* also place their last battle in Israel where Isa, their version of Jesus, destroys the Dajjal. That is an exact match! This is very simple—the *hadith* writers were basing the Dajjal on the Antichrist, not Jesus.

I would invite you to consider how irresponsible Joel Richardson's theory about the Dajjal is. He is taking a character, who is unambiguously molded after the Antichrist, and telling Christians not just that the Islamic version of events will more or less come to pass, but that when they do, they should embrace the Dajjal as their savior! Even if there is the slightest chance that the Antichrist will actually claim to be the Jewish Messiah or Jesus Himself, then Richardson's theory is setting up the Christians who take his theory seriously for disaster. I will spend a considerable amount of time in the last chapter of this book explaining how much damage this theory could cause.

Conclusion

In this section we have looked at Islamic eschatology in detail. We saw that the writers of the *hadiths* based their end times doctrine partly on the Bible and partly on the extra-biblical beliefs of Christians at the time. We have seen that the Islamic Isa is based on Jesus, the Dajjal is based on the Antichrist, and the Mahdi is based on the so-called Last Roman Emperor. We have looked at the theories of Islamic Antichrist proponents like Joel Richardson who believe the Islamic version of the end times will actually come to pass more or less like the *hadiths* say, but that Isa is really the False Prophet, the Mahdi is the Antichrist, and the Dajjal is the real Jesus. I hope I have presented enough to show the flawed reasoning behind this theory and that the simplest explanation, which is that the *hadith* writers were simply plagiarizing Christian sources, is the correct one. There is absolutely no reason to expect the Islamic version of the end times to come to pass or to be true in any way.

Part 3

Chapter 13
Logical Problems with the Islamic Antichrist Theory

We know a great deal about the Antichrist and his actions from the Bible. In this section I will examine those characteristics and actions of the Antichrist that we can be relatively sure will occur. I will show how the Islamic Antichrist theory fails to explain these actions in a way that is logically consistent.

The Antichrist Claims to Be God

There are several places in Scripture that make it clear the Antichrist will claim to be God (i.e., 2 Thessalonians 2:4, Daniel 11:36). This seems very unlikely to occur with the Mahdi since in Islam the belief that a man can be God is considered blasphemy and is the primary reason Islam is opposed to Christianity.

No matter how many signs and wonders the Antichrist does, he would have a very difficult time convincing the Muslim world that a man, any man, is in fact Allah. At the very least, one could say there is no hint in Islamic tradition that the Mahdi is anything other than a man, not even a prophet. Therefore, if anything like this does occur, it would be inconsistent with the writings of the Quran and the *hadiths*.

The Antichrist Sits in the Jewish Temple

In the Bible it seems clear that the Antichrist will sit in the Jewish temple in Jerusalem, (2 Thessalonians 2:4). It is not just that the Antichrist "allows" the Jewish temple to be rebuilt; he actually plans on using it for the declaration of his deity. This is so contrary to Islamic doctrine I am surprised the point is not raised more often. Nothing could be more offensive to a Muslim than a man sitting in the Jewish temple, claiming to be God. One of the main reasons the Jews don't consider rebuilding the temple today is because such a move would spark a war with Islam. This action would be a tacit acceptance of the Jewish version of history and religion. Many Muslims, especially those in Israel, deny that the Jewish temple ever sat on the temple mount.

The Daily Sacrifice

Daniel 9:27 says that the Antichrist will allow the daily sacrifice, a Jewish ritual performed twice a day, to begin again. And even though he stops this sacrifice after three-and a-half years, the Islamic Antichrist proponents still need to explain why a man who is supposed to be intolerant of other religions, especially Judaism, allows Jewish people to sacrifice animals on the temple mount in Jerusalem. Islam denies the need for daily blood sacrifices to atone for sin, yet Jews believe that the daily sacrifice must start again if they are to truly obey the Mosaic covenant. The Muslims who currently control the temple mount won't even allow Jewish people to pray on the temple mount, so can you imagine a man, who is supposed to be such a champion if Islam, allowing animal sacrifices to the Jewish God to start again?

Will the Jews Accept an Islamic Messiah?

The idea that the Jews will accept the Antichrist as their Messiah seems to be clear from several passages in the Bible:

> "I have come in My Father's name, and you do not receive Me; if another comes in his own name, him you will receive." (John 5:43)

In this passage Jesus is talking to the Jewish leadership and saying that though they rejected Him, they will accept "another." This one "who comes in his own name" is widely considered to be a reference to the Antichrist.

> For many will come in My name, saying, 'I am the Christ,' and will deceive many." (Matthew 24:5)

> "Then if anyone says to you, 'Look, here is the Christ!' or 'There!' do not believe it. For false christs and false prophets will rise and show great signs and wonders to deceive, if possible, even the elect. See, I have told you beforehand." (Matthew 24:23-25)

Here Jesus says that a person claiming to be the "Christ" (the Jewish Messiah) will "deceive many."

The idea that a Muslim man who promotes Islam will be considered to be the Messiah by the Jews is preposterous. Jewish expectations are that the Messiah will be from the line of David (who was of the tribe of Judah). The *Encyclopedia Judaica* says: "The rabbis agree he is of Davidic lineage (based on Hos. 3: 5 and Jer. 30: 9)."[74] The *Jewish Encyclopedia* adds that being from the Davidic line is "essential to the

---

[74]   *Jewish   Virtual   Library.*   "Messiah,"   2008.   http:// www.jewishvirtuallibrary.org/ jsource/ judaica/ ejud_0002_0014_0_13744. Html.

198 | L o g i c a l   P r o b l e m s …

Messianic mission." [75]

Even if the Jews would be able to bend on the idea that the Messiah would be an ethnic Jew, they would certainly never bend on the concept that he must be a religious Jew. There is no imaginable scenario in which the Jews would accept as their Messiah a man who promoted Islam as the true religion.

While reading reviews of Walid Shoebat's book *God's War on Terror*, I came across an interesting story from someone who asked Walid Shoebat about this issue when he visited their church.

> "He [Shoebat] also taught in our Sunday school class and I asked the question, 'Why would the Jews accept a Muslim as their Messiah?' His response, 'That's a stupid question!'"

The point is that despite the Islamic Antichrist proponents telling us that the Antichrist will be a champion of Islam, most of what we know about the Antichrist from the Bible suggests that he is uniquely focused on Jewish rituals and customs. He makes Jerusalem his capital city and chooses the Jewish temple of all places to reveal himself. All of this seems logically inconsistent with the Islamic Antichrist idea.

What About Christians?

Sometimes it is overlooked that the deception of the Antichrist is primarily intended to deceive those who claim to be Christians, not the unsaved world. Considering that Islam is so feared and hated by the Western world, it seems unlikely that the Antichrist would choose a religion that has become such a "boogeyman" to win the hearts and minds of these people. I will not say that such a scenario is impossible, as I do in the case of the Jews, but I will say that of all the religious systems the Antichrist could choose to win over Christians, Islam is probably the worst.

---

[75] "Bar Kokba and Bar Kokba War" *Jewish Encyclopedia*, 1906. http:// www.jewishencyclopedia.com/ articles/ 2471-bar-kokba-and-bar-kokba-war.

The Wars of the Antichrist

One of the logical problems with the idea that the Antichrist will be Islamic is that Daniel 11:40-45 describes the Antichrist systematically destroying the Muslim world. In this chapter, I will discuss these wars and attempt to show that the military actions the Bible attributes to the Antichrist are not consistent with a man who is supposed to be a champion of the Islamic world.

One of the clearest doctrines of the Antichrist is that he is a man of war. He seems to come on the scene by conquering a number of countries that surround Israel (Daniel 11: 40-45). One of the things that most impresses the people who worship the Antichrist in Revelation 13 is his ability to defeat his enemies in war:

> "They worshiped the beast, saying, 'Who is like the beast? Who is able to make war with him?'" (Revelation 13:4b)

In Daniel 11:38–39 we're told that the Antichrist's war-making capability is empowered by his worship of a "god of fortresses," which I believe is a reference to Satan. Revelation 13:2 and 4 state directly that it is the "dragon" (a clear reference to Satan) who gives the Antichrist his power to subdue the nations with war. Regardless of who, exactly, this is, it is evident the Antichrist uses the "god of fortresses" to help with his supernatural military victories.

The Lord also tells us in Matthew 24 that, just preceding the abomination of desolation event, which occurs at the midpoint of the seventieth week, there will be "wars and rumors of wars." In addition, the first seal (Revelation 6:1–2) describes the Antichrist going out "conquering and to conquer."

The last few verses of Daniel 11 names the very kings the Antichrist will defeat:

> "At the time of the end the king of the South shall attack him;
> and the king of the North shall come against him like a
> whirlwind, with chariots, horsemen, and with many ships; and he
> shall enter the countries, overwhelm them, and pass through."
> (Daniel 11:40)

The "king of the South" is a reference to Israel's historic enemy Egypt
and has been used to refer to Egypt throughout the first part of this
chapter. This point is not contested by many; in fact, the word "Egypt"
even appears explicitly twice, a few verses later, in a passage that speaks
of the subjection of Egypt to the Antichrist:

> "He shall stretch out his hand against the countries, and the land
> of Egypt shall not escape. He shall have power over the treasures
> of gold and silver, and over all the precious things of Egypt; also
> the Libyans and Ethiopians shall follow at his heels." (Daniel
> 11:42–43)

It is interesting to see that Egypt attacks the Antichrist first (verse 40).
The Islamic Antichrist theorist must come up with a plausible reason
why Egypt, a thoroughly Islamic nation, attacks the Antichrist if the
Antichrist is supposed to be a Muslim.

Conservative expositors and scholars debate the identity of the "king of
the North," who is the second conquest of the Antichrist (verse 40).
During the Cold War, it was proposed that the king of the North was
Russia. However, that view seems to have been based more on the
geopolitics of the day rather than any clue from the text itself. These
days, it is generally accepted that the king of the North represents the
same thing it has throughout the earlier portion of the chapter, which
includes parts of modern-day Iran, Iraq, Turkey, Syria, Afghanistan, and
a few others. For more on this, I recommend the excellent paper by Dr. J.
Paul Tanner, *"Daniel's 'King of the North': Do We Owe Russia an
Apology?"* Dr. Tanner concludes his paper this way:

"To be hermeneutically consistent, the "'king of the North' ought to be interpreted in light of the meaning the phrase has had throughout the chapter…I would like to submit that the 'King of the North' is a confederation of northern Arab nations that will attack the Antichrist and his forces in this military conflict centered in the Middle East."[76]

So, to sum up the first part of this passage, the Antichrist is attacked by Egypt and a northern coalition of Arab states. But, even though he is attacked first, the Antichrist completely crushes these historic enemies of Israel, subdues them, and takes their resources.

Why isn't the fact that the Antichrist will destroy and subdue the enemies of Israel talked about more in modern prophecy teaching? The answer is that it doesn't fit with most of the modern views of the Antichrist. Why would the Antichrist, who they think is either a man of peace or a Muslim, destroy the Muslim world? It doesn't fit with many of the mainstream views, so almost no one dwells on this passage.

In my book *False Christ* I continue following the Antichrist's wars in Daniel 11:40-45 to show that literally every nation he attacks is Muslim.[77] However, I will limit the discussion in this book to just the wars he fights against the king of the North and the king of the South so that I can spend adequate time answering the objections that Richardson would raise to the points I have already discussed.

The King of the North Debate

It should be noted that even though Joel Richardson agrees that the king of the North in verse 40 is not Russia, but is in fact a coalition of Arab forces, he claims that the correct way to interpret this passage is not that

---

[76] J. Paul Tanner, "Daniel's 'King of the North': Do We Owe Russia an Apology?" JETS 35 (1992): 315–28.
[77] Even this invasion of the "Glorious Land" in Daniel 11:41 is an attack on the Muslim groups that surround Israel, "Edom, Moab, and Ammon," not on Israel itself.

202 | Logical Problems…

the Antichrist defeats this coalition but rather that the Antichrist *is* the king of the North.

Since we will be spending quite a lot of time discussing this passage, I will quote it again for your reference:

> "At the time of the end the king of the South shall attack him; and the king of the North shall come against him like a whirlwind, with chariots, horsemen, and with many ships; and he shall enter the countries, overwhelm them, and pass through." (Daniel 11:40)

Because the grammar is not quite clear as to whom "him" is referring, a division has arisen on how to interpret this verse. Two main theories have been developed; they are sometimes called the "three king theory" and the "two king theory."

On the one hand, the three king theory sees three subjects in verse 40: the Antichrist, the king of the North, and the king of the South. Using brackets to explain the pronoun referents, the three king theory would read as follows:

> "And at the end time the King of the South will collide with him [the Antichrist], and the King of the North will storm against him [the Antichrist]…and he [the Antichrist] will enter countries, overflow them, and pass through"

So, in this reading, the king of the South attacks the Antichrist, then the king of the North attacks him as well, but the Antichrist defeats them both.

The two king theory, the one that Richardson subscribes to, has only two subjects in view. This is because it sees the king of the North as the Antichrist, so the verse would read like this:

> "And at the end time the king of the South will collide with him [the king of the North/ the Antichrist], and the king of the North

[the Antichrist] will storm against him [the king of the South]…and he [the king of the North/ the Antichrist] will enter countries, overflow them, and pass through."[78]

In this reading, the king of the South (Egypt) attacks the king of the North (Antichrist), but the king of the North/Antichrist attacks the king of the South as well, and the Antichrist will be victorious.

One way to explain the difference is that in the three king view, the one that I, and most conservatives, believe, after the introduction of the Antichrist in verse 36, all the pronouns "him" or "his" are referring to the Antichrist, whereas the two king view (Richardson's view) has the pronouns going back and forth.

J. Paul Tanner has demonstrated that the Hebrew grammar is not much help for either view and both readings are technically possible.[79] So we will have to rely on other factors if we hope to fully understand this most critical verse. Tanner defends the three king theory in his paper "Daniel's 'King of the North': Do We Owe Russia an Apology?" I would direct anyone interested to read that paper, as he also interacts with the leading arguments against his theory.

The usage of "him" here to refer to different kings, back and forth without clarification (as in the two king view), is unprecedented in this chapter and would constitute an entirely new way to express who is fighting whom. Tanner sums it up this way:

> "In Dan. 11:10, the pronouns on the prepositions marking the recipient of the verbal action (עָלָיו and עִמּוֹ) are quite *out of keeping* with the way the hostilities between the two kings were previously described in the chapter. What I mean to say is that elsewhere in the chapter, whenever an assault by one of the kings against the other was mentioned, the one who was the object is

[78] *Vol. 35: Journal of the Evangelical Theological Society* Volume 35. 1992 (3) (319). Lynchburg, VA: The Evangelical Theological Society.
[79] *Vol. 35: Journal of the Evangelical Theological Society* Volume 35. 1992 (3) (317). Lynchburg, VA: The Evangelical Theological Society.

specified by his full title (not merely by a pronoun)...In light of this characteristic writing style of the author, the 'him' is more likely the same referent in this verse, namely, 'the king' of the preceding paragraph, i.e., the Antichrist. This favors the three-king theory."[80]

Tanner also notes that when referencing this king in verse 36, it simply calls him "the king," not using either "of the North" or "of the South." This is a particularly important point, considering that it would mark the only time in this chapter when this occurs (save verse 27, when it is referencing both kings).

I suggest that the three king theory is the most natural reading of the text, and that is why it is the majority view. Basically, after the Antichrist is introduced by the angel in verse 36, it quickly becomes obvious that the angel is again describing the same guy who has dominated Daniel's attention through the entire book, the Antichrist. So, when it becomes clear that the same guy, the main subject of three separate visions of Daniel, is again in view, it is only natural that from then on, the word "him" refers back to that dominating character. You can see the same basic pattern of pronouns in any of the other visions concerning the Antichrist in the book of Daniel.

Joel Richardson argues that in the three king view, the king of the North and the king of the South have become allies, a point he strongly disagrees with.

> "The kings of the North and South, who are enemies throughout the historical portion of the prophecy, are suddenly cast as allies together against the Antichrist."[81]

I have two things to say about this point. The first is this is not a necessary conclusion of the three king theory at all. Richardson quotes

---

[80] Observations on Daniel 11:40 - Two Kings or Three? - Dr. J. Paul Tanner
[81] Richardson, Joel (2012-06-08). *Mideast Beast: The Scriptural Case for an Islamic Antichrist* (p. 121). Joel Richardson. Kindle Edition.

Tim Lahaye, who theorizes that since the king of the North attacks the Antichrist and the king of the South attacks him, this is a coordinated attack of allies against their common enemy (the Antichrist). This view is simply assumed by Lahaye, but the text certainly does not say they are coordinated joint attacks against the Antichrist or that these two kings are allies in any way. In addition, we are not given the chronology of these attacks. How far apart is the attack of the king of the North from the attack of the king of the South? We are not told. It could be years between these attacks. It could simply be that the Antichrist is attempting to gain control over the entire region, and that these are isolated attempts of these countries at protecting themselves from the Antichrist.

The second point is that even if these countries make an alliance here against the Antichrist, it is not damaging to the three king theory at all. In fact, contrary to what Richardson says, such a thing has precedence in the historical portion of Daniel 11. For example, an alliance was formed in verse 6 between the king of the North and the king of the South. There is no biblical reason that these kings would not find it advantageous to form an end-times alliance in light of a mutual enemy of the magnitude of the Antichrist.

Another criticism of the three king view that Richardson makes is the following:

> "The three king view turns Antiochus into both a type of the Antichrist (throughout all of Daniel chapter 8 as well as Daniel 11:21-35) and a type of the Antichrist's greatest enemy [He says this because the Antichrist will defeat the King of the North which Antiochus was obviously a part of when that title referred to the Seleucid Empire]."[82]

Richardson first assumes that Antiochus is in view after verse 36, which almost every conservative scholar would disagree with. Antiochus cannot be said to have fulfilled anything past verse 36.

---

[82] Richardson, Joel. "Daniel 11:40-45 Two Kings or Three?" *Joel's Trumpet.* N.p., 29 Jan. 2013. Web.

By verse 36 a transition has been made that now describes someone wholly different and unconnected with Antiochus.

This particular genre of a "type," as seen with Antiochus IV and the Antichrist, where there is a complete divergence from the first individual, can also be seen in Ezekiel 28, where the first part of the chapter seems to be talking of an earthly king, the king of Tyre. Then there is a point where the actions of both the king of Tyre and Satan seem to overlap for a moment, and by the time we get to verse 12 of Ezekiel 28, it becomes clear that Satan is the only individual in view and the king of Tyre has absolutely nothing to do with what follows.

If Richardson's statement that the three king view turns Antiochus into "a type of the Antichrist's greatest enemy" is referring to the fact that the Antichrist fights Muslim countries, then it would be completely without merit. Such a claim only makes sense if you have already presumed, beyond any doubt, that the Antichrist is a Muslim, in which case the Antichrist destroying the Muslim world would be counterproductive. However, if the Antichrist is not a Muslim, then we simply accept the traditional view that the events in Daniel 11:40 describe the Antichrist's actions which include a destruction of the many Muslim nations. Only the people who have already determined to see the Antichrist as a Muslim are forced to explain away this passage.

Richardson believes that his two king view fits the theory that the Antichrist will be a Muslim, but even if we assumed his two king view, he still has to deal with the fact that the Antichrist conquers Egypt, a decidedly Muslim country, as well as chasing after, and clearly intending to destroy all the Muslim communities surrounding Israel (Moab, Edom and Ammon, verse 41, as well as Libya and Ethiopia, verse 43). The two king view still has the Antichrist defeating these Muslim nations regardless of what is done with the king of the North. In Richardson's book, it was not explained why the Antichrist would be so hostile to these Muslim nations and it seems that either the two or three king view of Daniel 11:40 is incompatible with the idea of an Islamic Antichrist.

Part 4

Chapter 14
The Dangers of the Islamic Antichrist Theory

I believe the Islamic Antichrist view is the most dangerous theory about the end times that has ever been proposed. I believe it surpasses all the other suspect views about the last days because it has the potential to be used so effectively by the Antichrist to convince both Jews and Christians that he is their savior. I should point out that this theory is only dangerous to those people who will live to encounter the Antichrist. It is not a dangerous belief for the average Christian; but for the people who encounter the Antichrist, it could be devastating.

To explain why I think the Islamic Antichrist theory is so dangerous, I will need to discuss some of my personal views about the Antichrist, which I intentionally avoided in the previous chapters. I don't expect many people to agree with my views, but I would ask that you at least suspend your disbelief for a while and be open to considering the disastrous course of events that would occur if my view is correct. I promise not to lead you down a path of quirky or unorthodox views about the Antichrist. In fact, the view I propose was the earliest view of the church and was the majority view of scholars up until the most recent times.[83]

In 2013 I wrote a book called *False Christ*, which explains my views in much greater detail than I will attempt to in this chapter. The basic thesis of the book is that the Bible seems to suggest the Antichrist will present himself as the Jewish Messiah and he will attempt to make it look like he is fulfilling all the prophecies the Messiah is supposed to fulfill in the last days.

Prophecies To Be Fulfilled by Jesus in the Last Days

- Destroying the enemies of Israel (Isaiah 13:6–22, Revelation 19:11–21)
- Making Jerusalem the capital city of the world (Isaiah 2:1–4)
- Personally ruling the world (Psalm 21:8–9; Psalm 89:23; Psalm 110:5–6; Isaiah 30:14; Isaiah 60:12; Jeremiah 19:11; Daniel 2:44; Matthew 21:44; Revelation 2:26–27; Revelation 12:5)
- Ruling the world as God from the Temple (Ezekiel 48:21)
- Starting animal sacrifices again (Ezekiel 45:13–46:15, Zechariah 14:16–18)
- Starting a worldwide pilgrimage system to Jerusalem to worship the Messiah (Isaiah 60:3–22; Isaiah 18:7; Zechariah 14:16–18)

For each one of these prophecies about the Messiah, there are corresponding prophecies about the Antichrist suggesting that he will attempt to make it look as though he is fulfilling each messianic prophecy, which suggests that he will want the world (especially Jews and Christians) to believe that he is their true Messiah.

The Antichrist Attempts to Fulfill Those Prophecies

- Destroying the enemies of Israel (Daniel 11:40–45)

---

[83] White, Chris (2014-07-06). *False Christ: Will the Antichrist Claim to Be the Jewish Messiah?* (p. 7). CWM Publishing. Kindle Edition.

- Making Jerusalem the capital city of the world (Daniel 11:45, 2 Thessalonians 2:4, Revelation 17:18)
- Personally ruling the world (Revelation 13:7, 15)
- Ruling the world as God from the Temple (2 Thessalonians 2:4)
- Starting animal sacrifices again (Daniel 9:27)
- Starting a worldwide pilgrimage system to Jerusalem to worship the Messiah (Revelation 13:15, Revelation 17–18)[84]

I wrote *False Christ,* leaving open the question of whether the Antichrist will claim to be the return of Jesus or will claim to be the true Messiah, as opposed to Jesus, giving credibility to his claims by seeming to fulfill all the prophecies that Jesus didn't in His first coming. Both are real possibilities, but I lean toward the view that he will claim to be the return of Jesus. (See Appendix 6 entitled *Will the Antichrist Claim to Be Jesus?*)

I will end the discussion of my view at this point since my intention is not to try to convince you of my theory but rather to invite you to suspend your disbelief for a moment and conduct a kind of thought experiment about what would happen if this theory were true.

How the Antichrist Will Win Hearts and Minds

A combination of factors have come together to make Christians and Jews fear the Muslim world as they do nothing else. Certainly it cannot be questioned that radical Islam is extremely dangerous and the religion of Islam is diametrically opposed to the teachings of the Bible. But because of acts of terrorism like 9/11, the rise of groups like ISIL, and the media's constant encouraging fear of the Muslim world (justified or not), the level of dread and hatred for Islam has never been higher. When you add the Islamic Antichrist theory into this mix, which is fast becoming the most prominent view of Christianity, the level of fear and hatred blossoms to apocalyptic proportions. After all, if Islam is the religion of the Antichrist, there is so much more reason to fear it, and

---

[84] See Appendix on Mystery Babylon.

hope desperately for its demise.

The high level of fear of the Muslim world puts both Jews and Christians in a psychologically vulnerable position. All the Antichrist has to do to be seen as their savior is destroy the enemies of Israel in a miraculous way during a war big enough to look like the battle of Armageddon. The scary thing is that this is exactly what the Bible tells us the Antichrist will do.

We have seen that the Antichrist's ability to fight wars is supernaturally empowered (Daniel 11:38-39, Revelation 13:2, 4), meaning that he will have the capability to wipe out any enemies he chooses in a way that makes the world worship him. In fact, we see them doing just that in Revelation 13:4:

> "So they worshiped the dragon who gave authority to the beast; and they worshiped the beast, saying, **'Who is like the beast? Who is able to make war with him?'"**

We also know that he turns his invincible military might on the Muslim enemies of Israel in Daniel 11:40-45. There we are told that the Antichrist destroys Egypt, Libya, and an Arab coalition that includes Iraq, Iran, Syria, Afghanistan, and others. We also see that when he enters the "Glorious land" to set up his throne in verses 41–45, his primary targets are those Muslim nations that surround Israel (Edom, Moab, and Ammon. He is never once said to attack Israel itself in that passage.

The concept that the Antichrist will seem at first to be a champion of Israel has not occurred to many people, and so it follows that they will be sitting ducks for this deception. I don't think many Christians have considered the possibility that the deception of the Antichrist would be to fool *them* into believing that he is the return of Jesus. I should note that I don't think the Antichrist will always appear to be the champion of Israel. Instead, toward the end of his allotted time, he seems to try desperately to destroy it, but by that time he will have such a powerful hold on the world that opposition to him will only end in death.

The rest of what we know from the Bible of the Antichrist's actions seems to suggest that after his conquest of the Muslim world, he sits in the temple as if he were God, in the same way Christians expect Jesus to do when he returns to rule during the Millennium. In essence, I am suggesting that the war against the Muslims that the Antichrist fights to gain credibility will be sold to the public as if it were the battle of Armageddon or perhaps the Gog-Magog war. Then Christians and Jews will be encouraged to believe that the beginning of the Kingdom Age, or the Millennium has begun and Jesus has returned. This is when the Antichrist makes Jerusalem the capital city of the world, institutes pilgrimages and worship, and all the other things that are supposed to occur when Jesus really does return But the difference is, The Antichrist is faking it.

The problem with the Islamic Antichrist theorists is they are telling Christians that when they see a man, who claims to be the Jewish Messiah, defeat the Muslim world (the Dajjal), then they should embrace him as their savior. If the Antichrist claims to be Jesus, which I tend to think he will, imagine the rejoicing among Christians when they hear that the Jews have accepted Jesus as their true Messiah. In fact, Richardson says this is the primary way we will be able to tell that the Dajjal is the real Jesus.[85] But the problem is that in this scenario, it would not be the real Jesus they have accepted as their Messiah, but rather the Antichrist. If Christians do not realize that the Antichrist could have such a sneaky trick up his sleeve, then they will be in great danger.

The Role of the Muslim World in the Antichrist's Plan

So what is the role of the Islamic world in this scenario? Unfortunately it seems that they are going to be used as little more than pawns in the Antichrist's game. He is planning on provoking the Islamic world to

---

[85]   Richardson, Joel (2009-07-28). *The Islamic Antichrist: The Shocking Truth about the Real Nature of the Beast* (p. 78). Midpoint Trade Books. Kindle Edition.

attack him, so that he can defeat them miraculously and appear to have fulfilled the prophecy of the final eschatological battle. This plan is quite complex, so I will take a bit of time to explain it here. It may help to read Appendix 5 about the seven-year covenant before you continue.

No group will be paying more attention to the monumental developments in Israel when the Antichrist makes his covenant with the Jews than the Muslims. A man who is claiming to be the Messiah, rebuilding the Jewish temple, and allowing Jewish sacrifices to begin again will enrage the Muslim people, who will almost certainly see him as the Dajjal.

Even if, as some believe, a way to construct the temple next to the Dome of the Rock without tearing it down is possible, there is no scenario in which the events that follow the covenant don't awaken the preprogrammed eschatological passions of the Islamic world.

The Temple Mount is currently controlled by the Muslims, even though Israel technically has sovereignty over the site. Today you can't be caught bringing a Bible or praying anywhere on the Temple Mount, let alone building an altar and sacrificing animals to Yahweh. Starting the daily sacrifice on the Temple Mount is not going to go over well at all with the Muslims.

I suspect that if the Jews really believe their Messiah has come, they also believe he is about to go to war with and conquer their enemies. So, The one thing that has prevented them from building the temple in the past— imminent war with all Muslims—will cease to be a problem, as they will believe the Messiah will protect them. They might even welcome the chance to defeat the Muslims in the epic war that building the temple will cause. If the Antichrist has a proven military background, which I believe the Bible says he will, this may add to their confidence about this impending war and make them feel free to build the temple.

It's not just the rebuilding of the temple that will guarantee a war with Islam. It is also the Islamic belief in a coming Dajjal (the false Jewish Messiah) that will inflame their passions to go to war with Israel en masse at this time. The Antichrist will be well aware of the consequences of these actions and will actually be counting on such a war. As far as Satan sees it, the bigger the number of Muslim armies that attack the Antichrist, the better, because he is attempting to make it seem like the Antichrist is fulfilling messianic prophecies of the destruction of Israel's enemies.

It is important to remember that that the war that follows, which I believe is described in Daniel 11:40-45, has the Muslim armies attacking the Antichrist, not the other way around. In a sense, you could say that the Antichrist has the moral high ground in these battles because he was attacked first by the Muslim world and he is not the aggressor. However, I suggest that in reality he is the aggressor because he knew his actions (building the temple, starting sacrifices, and declaring to be the Jewish Messiah) would force the Muslims to attack him. The great fear of the Muslim world by Jews and Christians will make him seem all the more like their savior when he defeats the Muslims.

To Christians—indeed, to many people in the secular world—there can be no return of the Messiah without a battle of Armageddon. This is one of those non-negotiable aspects of eschatology that spans almost all belief systems. If the Antichrist is going to try to deceive people in this way, he is going to have to fake the battle of Armageddon and win it to validate his messianic claims.

I am not sure whether the Antichrist will attempt to fake two separate wars (Gog-Magog and Armageddon) or if he will make it seem like the wars he fights, described in Daniel 11:40–45, are the fulfillment of both of these wars. Since there are so many similarities between the Gog-Magog war and the battle of Armageddon and since most Christians and Jews already see the two wars as being one and the same, I lean toward the view that he will make no distinction between them. I suggest that he will lead people to believe that when he defends himself and Israel from virtually the entire Middle East in a miraculous way, it should be seen as the fulfillment of all known eschatological wars and the Messianic Age has come.

Why Are Incorrect Views about These Wars Dangerous?

The belief that the Gog-Magog war will occur before the Millennium, a view I argued against in a previous chapter, is dangerous for a few reasons. First, it makes people believe that a war with the Muslim world is a necessary part of the end-time scenario. This is because, unlike the references to the battle of Armageddon where no specific nations are mentioned, the Ezekiel passages about the Gog-Magog war name certain nations like Persia in Iran and Turkey that are mostly Muslim nations today. It doesn't matter whether someone believes that Gog-Magog and Armageddon are the same event or are separated by a few years, the effect is still the same: It makes people believe a war with Islam is in the near future. This belief—that we are all to expect a war with the Muslims and the Messiah will emerge victorious from that war—will be exploited by the Antichrist, for reasons I will soon discuss.

As detailed previously, I also believe the Gog-Magog war will occur. But when it does take place at the end of the thousand-year reign (Revelation 20:7–8), it won't be with people who believe in the Islamic faith. It is impossible to know the mindset of the people who will attack Israel after the millennium, but one thing is certain: Islam will not be a viable religion during the thousand-year reign of Christ. And it's unlikely that it will be revived when Satan is released from the pit after the thousand years, given the fact that all the major tenets of Islam will have been unquestionably refuted one thousand years prior to the event. In addition, Islam will not play a role in the battle of Armageddon because the people who fight in that war will be firm adherents to the religion of the Antichrist, which requires them to worship a man who had recently fought a war with the Islamic world and is sitting in the Jewish temple as God. These things simply cannot be reconciled with Islam in any form. In other words, neither the battle of Armageddon nor the Gog-Magog war will have anything to do with Islam; yet, this has become a prevailing belief among some prophecy teachers. What is the problem with that thinking? And how could it be exploited by the Antichrist?

As discussed earlier, the Antichrist will easily be able to manipulate the Muslim world into attacking him by claiming to be the Messiah, whom it will see as the Dajjal. His rebuilding the temple and starting the daily sacrifices will also incite the Muslim world to attack him. If Christians can be convinced that the Muslims are the enemy that needs to be defeated to usher in the messianic age, then they will reflexively see the wars that the Antichrist fights against the Muslims as the Gog-Magog war, the war of Armageddon, or both. The obvious problem is that since the Antichrist wins the wars in Daniel 11 and Scripture says God wins the wars of Gog-Magog and Armageddon, the Antichrist will be seen as God by Christians and Jews when he emerges victorious from the wars. Essentially, the Antichrist will be creating an artificial Gog-Magog/Armageddon war long before any of these wars actually take place to convince people that the reign of the Messiah has come.

The following chart shows the chronology of these events:

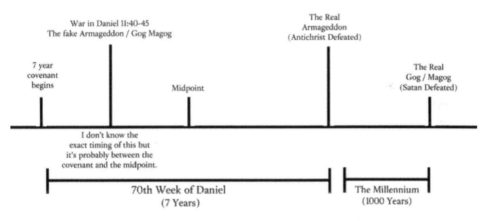

It should be said that the illustration depicts my best guess. By their very nature, the deceptions of the Antichrist are difficult to anticipate, and I am not dogmatic that it must play out exactly as I suggest. Regardless of the details, however, the fact that that the Antichrist is attacked by the Muslim world and then defeats it before making his claim to be God and starting a fake messianic age should suggest that he will attempt to look like the savior of Israel. Many modern prophecy teachers, especially the Islamic Antichrist proponents, are telling their students that when they see an attack by the Muslim world and then see it defeated, they will know that the person who does that is God. This should be seen as the terrible danger that it is. The Islamic Antichrist theorists, by suggesting that Christians should embrace the Dajjal as Jesus simply because he defeats the Muslim world and convinces the Jews that he is their Messiah, are unbelievably reckless, because these are the same things the Bible says the Antichrist will do.

My sincere hope is that this book will be a wake-up call to Christians. I don't expect many people to believe my own theories about the end times, and as a result, I don't expect them to fully appreciate why I consider the Islamic Antichrist doctrine so dangerous. I do, however, hope the first part of this book, which argues against the Islamic Antichrist theory, will be of some use to the body of Christ in slowing down or even stopping the spread of the Islamic Antichrist theory, if for no other reason than because it is wrong.

Appendix 1
The Revived Roman Empire Revisited

In Daniel 2 we find Nebuchadnezzar's dream of the statue. I will attempt to establish that while the last empire being spoken of in this chapter is indeed Rome, the Babylonian king's vision was not intended to give us information about the end times. Unlike Daniel's vision in chapter 7, Nebuchadnezzar's vision was intended to be a prophecy of the first coming of Jesus Christ and the establishment of the kingdom of God that would one day grow to encompass all the earth—a kingdom that Jesus said was established during the days of his earthly ministry during the Roman Empire (Matthew 12:28, 13:31–33 Luke 17:20–21, Mark 1:15).

Let's first study the last part of Daniel 2 to show the strong biblical support for this view that Nebuchadnezzar's dream is a self-contained unit not intended to be seen as a prophecy of the end times. .

Nebuchadnezzar's Vision of a Statue

Daniel 2:40: "And the fourth kingdom shall be as strong as iron, inasmuch as iron breaks in pieces and shatters everything; and like iron that crushes, that kingdom will break in pieces and crush all the others."

Daniel 2:41: "Whereas you saw the feet and toes, partly of potter's clay and partly of iron, the kingdom shall be divided; yet the strength of the iron shall be in it, just as you saw the iron mixed with ceramic clay."

Daniel 2:42: "And as the toes of the feet were partly of iron and partly of clay, so the kingdom shall be partly strong and partly fragile."

Daniel 2:43: "As you saw iron mixed with ceramic clay, they will mingle with the seed of men; but they will not adhere to one another, just as iron does not mix with clay."

Daniel 2:44: "And in the days of these kings the God of heaven will set up a kingdom which shall never be destroyed; and the kingdom shall not be left to other people; it shall break in pieces and consume all these kingdoms, and it shall stand forever."

I agree that these feet and toes are somehow a part of the Roman Empire. While different, the feet and toes mixed with iron and clay are not a part of a new kingdom, but are a part of the legs of iron, which indicates the Roman Empire—just a chronologically later part of it, (i.e., the end). Most conservative scholars tend to agree with this interpretation, but with some of the following variations:

1. The feet and toes represent the final period of the Roman Empire being divided, weak, and trying to cleave its divided empire together but failing.

2. The feet and toes represent the final kingdom of the Antichrist in the last days.

3. The feet and toes represent a nephilim[86] hybrid kingdom in the last days.

I agree with conservative scholar Stephen Miller that, in addition to your view of Daniel 2 and 7, your view about the rock that destroys this statue

---

[86] The nephilim were offspring of the "sons of God" and the "daughters of men" before the Deluge, according to Genesis 6:4. The name is also used in reference to giants who inhabited Canaan at the time of the Israelite conquest of Canaan according to Numbers 13:33.

is the key to interpreting this passage. I ask you to withhold your judgment on this matter until we get to those verses.

The Kingdom Shall Be Divided

A very important part of this discussion is that at some point the last kingdom will be divided. Since most views rightly presume that the feet and toes represent a chronologically later point of Rome, we can safely say this indicates that Rome will be divided toward the end of its existence, whether we believe that its end *was* in the past or *will be* in the future.

Here we have a few problems for the revived Roman Empire view. The first is that we have an unambiguous fulfillment of this passage in the history of the fall of Rome. We know that Rome was divided into several parts before its fall, eventually settling into just two parts: the east and west empires. The second major problem here for the revived Roman Empire view is that forcing this prophecy to the end times means we have to hold the view that the Antichrist has a divided, weak kingdom in the end times.

The descriptions of the Antichrist's kingdom in the Bible do not give the impression that it will be weak or divided, but rather that the Antichrist will have absolute power and those who do not worship him will be killed. This does not sound like a weak or divided kingdom.

If we look up the phrase, "the crisis of the third century," we learn about a hundred-year-or-so period in Roman history when the empire almost lost everything. It was the first time in Rome's history that it started to show weakness. All the years of Roman dominance and iron-fisted—or should I say "iron-legged"—rule was starting to slow down during this time.

In AD 285, Diocletian split the empire into four parts called the tetrarchy, but it didn't last. It briefly was united again under Constantine, but after his death it quickly split again into three divisions. It was total chaos, everyone claiming to be emperor for a few years.

Eventually, when all the dust settled, there were only two divisions of Rome: the eastern half and western half. That is how it would stay until Rome fizzled out of existence. Rome would never again rise to the prominence it once had, and it will grow less and less powerful until it is a shadow of its former self, constantly sacked by invading barbarians, penniless, and powerless. The exact date of Rome's fall varies because of the death-by-a-thousand-cuts nature of its decline, but most historians put its fall at about AD 480, a mere one hundred years after the division of east and west was solidified.

I'm trying to establish that the end of Rome is characterized by weakness and division, and, as noted before, the one thing both sides of the argument about the feet and toes made of iron and clay agree on is that this passage is saying the end of the Roman Empire will be characterized by weakness and division. The only difference is that some say the end of the Roman Empire is in the past, and others say we need to "revive" a Roman Empire first, and *then* watch its end be characterized by weakness and division.

The Kingdom Shall Be Partly Strong and Partly Fragile

Again, this is a terrific description of the last three hundred or so years of the Roman Empire. There were times during this period, often called "the decline of the Roman Empire," in which Rome was **partly strong** in some ways, but **partly fragile** in others.

We have seen already to an extent, and will see again in the next verse, that it is grammatically necessary to see that the clay and iron represent the *two divisions* of the empire, in this case, the east and the west empires. So, in order for this interpretation to be a perfect match, we need to see a clear description in history of one of these divisions being much weaker than the other.

The so-called "final split" of the Roman Empire occurred when it was becoming clear that the Western Empire was going to be a lot more dangerous place to live than the east. This is when Constantine moved the capital from Rome to Constantinople. Eventually, Rome would be sacked by Alaric in AD 410, while Constantinople would not be sacked until the late Middle Ages.

Here are what some scholars have said about the weakness of the Western Empire compared to the Eastern.

> "The East, always wealthier, was not so destitute, especially as Emperors like Constantine the Great and Constantius II had invested heavily in the eastern economy. As a result, the Eastern Empire could afford large numbers of professional soldiers and augment them with mercenaries, while the Western Roman Empire could not afford this to the same extent. Even in major defeats, the East could, certainly not without difficulties, buy off its enemies with a ransom."
>
> "The political, economic and military control of the Eastern Empire's resources remained safe in Constantinople.... In contrast, the Western Empire was more fragmented. Its capital was transferred to Ravenna in 402 largely for defensive reasons."
>
> "The Western Empire's resources were much limited, and the lack of available manpower forced the government to rely ever more on confederate barbarian troops operating under their own commanders, where the Western Empire would often have difficulties paying. In certain cases deals were struck with the leaders of barbaric mercenaries rewarding them with land, which led to the Empire's decline as less land meant there would be even less taxes to support the military.... As the central power weakened, the State gradually lost control of its borders and provinces, as well as control over the Mediterranean Sea."

The divided parts of this kingdom were noticeably different in strength. As mentioned, the Eastern Empire would survive in some capacity for hundreds of years after the West had long disappeared.

> **"As you saw iron mixed with ceramic clay, they will mingle with the seed of men; but they will not adhere to one another, just as iron does not mix with clay." (Daniel 2:43)**

There is a lot of confusion about this verse, which I think is due to the English translation of the Aramaic. This section of Daniel is written in Aramaic, not Hebrew. Other translations, such as the ESV, render the underlying Aramaic phrase this way:

> "As you saw the iron mixed with soft clay, so they will **mix with one another in marriage**, but they will not hold together, just as iron does not mix with clay." (emphasis added)

Instead of "mingle with the seed of men," the phrase reads, "mix with one another in marriage." So the question is: Is the ESV capturing the intent of the Aramaic here? Let's first look at the word translated as "mingle."

The word translated as "mingle" is the Aramaic word "Arab" (ar-av), which corresponds to the Hebrew "Arab." This word, if you look it up, will be in Aramaic, and its only use is right here in Daniel, because Aramaic is very rare. However, most Aramaic words correspond directly to ancient Hebrew words, and that is the case here. In fact, the Aramaic and Hebrew for "mingle" are even pronounced the same. The Hebrew "Arab" means "to pledge, exchange, mortgage, engage, occupy, undertake for, give pledges, be or become surety, take on pledge, give in pledge."[87] For example, in Genesis 43:9, when Judah was begging his

---

[87] The *KJV Old Testament Hebrew Lexicon.*

father to let him take Benjamin to Egypt as per Joseph's request, Judah says that he will become "surety" for Benjamin. The word "surety" is where we get the word "mingle." "I myself will be **surety** for him; from my hand you shall require him. If I do not bring him back to you and set him before you, then let me bear the blame forever" (Genesis 43:9, emphasis added).

Another example of the use of this word is in 2 Kings 18:23, where the word "pledge" is the word translated "mingle" in our passage: "Now therefore, I urge you, give a **pledge** to my master the king of Assyria, and I will give you two thousand horses—if you are able on your part to put riders on them!" (2 Kings 18:23).

But the same word for "mingle" also can mean "to mix together." And in fact, of the two times it's used that way in the Bible, it is speaking of the intermarriage of Jewish and pagan tribes:

> "For they have taken of their daughters for themselves, and for their sons: so that the holy **seed** have **mingled** themselves with the people of those lands: yea, the hand of the princes and rulers hath been chief in this trespass." (Ezra 9:2, emphasis added)

Here we have a very similar phrase to the one in our verse. I think this shows some precedent that the translators of the KJV believed that mingling seed was referring to intermarriage with two groups: "But they **mingled** with the Gentiles and learned their works" (Psalm 106:35).

I think you can see that the ESV has a pretty decent rendering of this phrase when it says "mix with one another in marriage." Even if that is true, we still have to determine who "they" are, and with whom "they" are trying to intermarry.

I suggest the simple method of sentence structure and basic grammar to find out who "they" are. If we look in verse 41, we see that Daniel says the feet and toes of clay and iron represent a divided kingdom. The next three verses repeatedly refer to these two divisions of the kingdom as iron and clay. Grammatically, there is no other possible plural subject other than the separate, divided parts of the kingdom represented by the iron and clay. This is confirmed in verse 44, which says "in the days of *these kings*," making it clear that the plural subject in view in verse 43 must be referring to the kings of the divided kingdom in verse 41. So, this verse is saying that the divided parts of the empire (the iron and the clay) will pledge their offspring to one another in an attempt to become strong again, but it will not work.

It would be one thing if we had to look for some obscure fulfillment of this in Roman history, but the strength of this interpretation is the unambiguous fulfillment of it in the history of Rome, which gives the interpretations a great deal more credibility. In order for this to be true, we can't just go picking any arranged marriages of emperors in Ancient Rome. Almost every senator, general, prefect, or any other person with imperial ambitions had arranged marriages to secure their legitimacy to the throne. I'm only slightly exaggerating when I say that we can't look at a single page in the entire history of Rome without reading about an arranged political marriage to solidify alliances. But we are looking for a very specific type of political marriage here. It has to be toward the very end of Rome's existence, and because it is regarding the feet and toes, it has to be between the Eastern and Western Empires. In addition, the two kings of the divided kingdom need to pledge their offspring to one another for the specific purpose of trying to unify Rome and prevent its demise. That should narrow the search quite a bit.

There are two instances of this exact thing happening at the end of the Roman Empire. The first occurred in AD 467, only about nine years before the last Roman emperor. This is when the Vandals were posing a major threat to Rome and Leo was reigning strongly in the East. There had not been an emperor in the West for a few years because a man named Ricimer, who had been ruling behind the scenes for many years by manipulating puppet emperors, had not appointed another puppet emperor and was hoping no one would care or that people would just accept him as the default emperor. This became a problem in the Eastern Empire because of the threat of imminent war with the Vandals. Leo needed to find a way to unite the divided empire to defend itself from destruction. He decided to choose an emperor of the West for the West.

He chose a guy named Anthemius and sent him to the West with a big army so that Ricimer would have no choice but to agree.

Here is the marriage connection: The emperor of the east, Leo, gave his daughter, Leontia, to Anthemius's son, Marcian, to legitimize the reign of his new appointee to the West, essentially saying, "OK, East and West, we are all one big happy family now. So let's go fight the Vandals or we are all in big trouble." In addition, Anthemius also gave his only daughter, Alypia, to Ricimer, which also made Anthemius, a Greek-speaking foreigner to the west, acceptable to the Latin-speaking Romans, of which Ricimer had become a kind of ringleader. This plan actually might have worked, too, but the battle with the Vandals went very badly, and Anthemius would soon be killed, putting all of them right back where they started.

This brings us to the second attempt to cleave together the East and the West through marriages. This time it occurred in AD 474, just two years before the last Roman Emperor, with Julius Nepos. Many people argue that Nepos was the last Roman Emperor, choosing not to count the child Romulus Augustulus, who "ruled" for about a year after Nepos was exiled. This time, Leo married off his niece to Nepos. The surname "Nepos" actually means "nephew." He took the surname "nephew" as his title, referring to his newly acquired nephew status to Leo in the East. This alone should show the importance of that marriage in the attempt to unify the East and the West. This effort to save the Roman Empire failed as well. It was just too late for Rome; too many problems were converging to cause its destruction. Just like this verse in Daniel says, these two divisions of the final kingdom did not adhere to one another, and the fall of the Western Roman Empire is placed somewhere around this time, between AD 476–480.

> **Daniel 2:44:** "And in the days of these kings the God of heaven will set up a kingdom which shall never be destroyed; and the kingdom shall not be left to other people; it shall break in pieces and consume all these kingdoms, and it shall stand forever."

Daniel 2:45: "Inasmuch as you saw that the stone was cut out of the mountain without hands, and that it broke in pieces the iron, the bronze, the clay, the silver, and the gold—the great God has made known to the king what will come to pass after this. The dream is certain, and its interpretation is sure."

Here we come to the most crucial part of our study of this vision: the identification of this stone. Let's briefly recall what happened with this stone in Nebuchadnezzar's dream in verses 34–35:

"You watched while a stone was cut out without hands, which struck the image on its feet of iron and clay, and broke them in pieces. Then the iron, the clay, the bronze, the silver, and the gold were crushed together, and became like chaff from the summer threshing floors; the wind carried them away so that no trace of them was found. And the stone that struck the image became a great mountain and filled the whole earth." (Daniel 2:34–35)

So this stone strikes the statue on the feet, and it eventually grows to fill the whole earth.

A Kingdom

This stone in Daniel 2:44 is a kingdom God will institute during the Roman Empire that will eventually grow to encompass the entire world. Some would say this has to be speaking of Jesus, not of a kingdom, because of Ephesians 2:20 which says He is a "cornerstone"; but that would offend the explicit teaching in this verse that this rock is a "kingdom" just as the parts of the statue were kingdoms.

This rock is representative of what is known throughout the Bible as the "kingdom of God." Let's look at a few verses to demonstrate two points:

1. Jesus Christ begins the kingdom of God in his day (during the Roman Empire).

2. The kingdom of God is supposed to start small and then grow large (typified by starting with the apostles and spreading to all those who will ever be saved).

Jesus Christ begins the kingdom of God in His day:

> "But if I cast out demons by the Spirit of God, surely **the kingdom of God has come upon you."** (Matthew 12:28, emphasis added)
>
> "Now at one point the Pharisees asked Jesus when the kingdom of God was coming, so he answered, 'The kingdom of God is not coming with signs to be observed, nor will they say, "Look, here it is!' or 'There!" **For indeed, the kingdom of God is in your midst.'"** (Luke 17:20–21, emphasis added)
>
> "And saying, 'The time is fulfilled, and **the kingdom of God is at hand**. Repent, and believe in the gospel.'" (Mark 1:15, emphasis added)

It should be noted here that there seems to be a present and future sense of the kingdom of God, in the sense that the ultimate fulfillment of the kingdom of God is not here or in this world, but rather in the future. But I believe it can also be shown with certainty that Jesus considered the kingdom of God to have been established with Him on earth during His teaching ministry.

The kingdom of God is supposed to start small and then grow large.

> "Another parable He put forth to them, saying: 'The kingdom of heaven is like a mustard seed, which a man took and sowed in his field, which indeed is the least of all the seeds; but when it is grown it is greater than the herbs and becomes a tree, so that the birds of the air come and

nest in its branches.' Another parable He spoke to them: 'The kingdom of heaven is like leaven, which a woman took and hid in three measures of meal till it was all leavened.'" (Matthew 13:31–33)

These two parables describe the small and then growing large aspect of the kingdom of God. So this is, in a sense, a prophecy for all ancient peoples pointing toward a general time the Messiah will come; that is, the kingdom of God would be established sometime during the Roman Empire. This may be one reason messianic expectations were so high in Jesus' day.

At this point, we've only looked at one aspect of the argument that the revived Roman Empire idea is a modern, unbiblical tradition. We have seen that there is no reason to believe the last empire in Nebuchadnezzar's dream of the statue is speaking of an end-times kingdom. But to complete this argument, we need to study Daniel's vision of the four beasts in Daniel 7 to see for certain that these two chapters are unrelated. This will help us more clearly understand what the world will look like when the Antichrist rises to power.

Daniel's Vision of the Four Beasts—Daniel 7

In Daniel 7, Daniel has a vision of four beasts: a lion, a bear, a leopard and a "diverse beast." These beasts are identified as kings and/or kingdoms by the angel who interprets Daniel's dream, starting in verse 17.

The question is which kingdoms are being referred to with these beasts? As I said in an earlier chapter, most conservatives believe Daniel 7 is simply a retelling of Daniel 2. In other words, the dream Nebuchadnezzar had in Daniel 2 of a multi-metal statue that represented the four kingdoms of Babylon, Medo-Persia, Greece, and Rome are again described here in Daniel 7. I don't agree with that view, but I do agree that the fourth beast in Daniel 7 is the kingdom of Antichrist.

In the traditional view, the beasts of chapter 7 are succeeded in time by the next beast. For example, the lion, the first beast (representing Babylon) would be followed after much time by the bear (representing Medo-Persia), since Babylon was conquered by Medo-Persia, and then the leopard (Greece) would conquer the bear after that, and so on. I believe there are significant reasons to challenge this view of the kingdoms being in temporal succession of one another.

I propose that this vision of the four beasts in Daniel 7 is not simply a picture of four kingdoms that have come and gone in the past, but rather of the four kingdoms that will be on the earth *at the same time* when the Antichrist begins his reign in the end times. This means the fourth beast in Daniel 7 is not necessarily Rome.

Daniel 7:11–12 describes the Antichrist, who is thrown into the lake of fire after his reign is completed. Few conservatives would debate this point. However, after he is thrown into the lake of fire, the mentioning of the previous three beasts shows that they are *still around* at that time. In fact, Daniel says specifically that they are allowed to live on after that.

> "I watched then because of the sound of the pompous words which the horn was speaking; I watched till the beast was slain, and its body destroyed and given to the burning flame. As for the rest of the beasts, they had their dominion taken away, yet their lives were prolonged for a season and a time." (Daniel 7:11–12)

In what sense can Neo-Babylonia or Medo-Persia be spoken of as living on after the Antichrist is destroyed? Most scholars give no compelling explanations for their presence and prolonging of their lives at this point. I will show why the contemporaneous view explains this verse, with many confirmations from the text. Additionally, several grammatical and contextual indications make it plain that these kingdoms exist at the same time in history. The following is an overview of the key points we will find in this vision as understood by what I call the "contemporaneous beast view."

There is a dividing of the world into four parts in the time just before the Antichrist begins his rule (figure 1). The Antichrist eventually takes control of one of those four kingdoms, which has ten rulers (figure 2). He eventually conquers all four kingdoms through war and effectively rules the entire world in a new, amalgamated beast, as seen in Revelation 13:1–2 (figure 3).

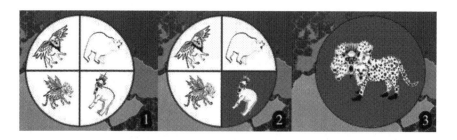

This view suggests that Daniel 11:36 and following essentially links Daniel 7 with Revelation 13. Let me explain what I mean by all that.

Daniel 11:36–45 describes how the Antichrist will conquer all kinds of lands and kingdoms; then at some point, he will declare himself to be higher than God Himself in the "Holy Place" in Jerusalem. At that point, the last three-and-a-half years of his reign will begin. But before this, he is busy making war, conquering other kingdoms, and establishing his domain. This is perhaps why the book of Revelation says that one of the reasons the world marvels at the Antichrist is because of his war-making capability: "So they worshiped the dragon who gave authority to the beast; and they worshiped the beast, saying, 'Who *is* like the beast? Who is able to make war with him?' (Revelation 13:4).

Arguably, the chapter that gives the most detail of the Antichrist is Revelation 13. The first two verses of that chapter say:

> "Then I stood on the sand of the sea. And I saw a beast rising up out of the sea, having seven heads and ten horns, and on his horns ten crowns, and on his heads a blasphemous name. Now the beast which I saw was like a leopard, his feet were like *the feet of* a bear, and his mouth

like the mouth of a lion. The dragon gave him his power, his throne, and great authority." (Revelation 13:1–2)

This is an unambiguous reference to our chapter, Daniel 7. The fact that we have a lion, a bear, and a leopard in the same place—all in the context of the Antichrist—is enough to make us pay attention, but when we see that this beast has seven heads and ten horns, plus a direct correlation to Daniel 7, the possibility of this being coincidental is not reasonable.

Why is this significant? If we take the beasts in Daniel 7—a lion with wings, a bear, a four-headed leopard, and a ten-horned beast—and combine them into one, we would have a seven-headed, ten-horned beast with the characteristics of a bear, a leopard, and a lion—exactly what we see in Revelation 13.

In other words, I am proposing that what we are looking at in the first few verses of Revelation 13—when a seven-headed, ten-horned lion/leopard/bear beast comes out of the sea—is the Antichrist, who is now finished with his conquest of the other three world powers and is the uncontested ruler of the world.

So, turning back to what I said earlier: The contemporaneous-beast view, that I promote, suggests that Daniel 11:36–45 (which describes the wars of Antichrist) essentially links Daniel 7 (the Antichrist pre-wars in which he is only one of four powers) with Revelation 13, in which he is the uncontested ruler of all world powers. These three chapters, spread out all over the Bible, more or less provide before-, during-, and after-conquests snapshots of the Antichrist.

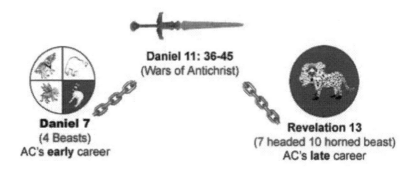

Daniel 11: 36-45
(Wars of Antichrist)

Daniel 7
(4 Beasts)
AC's **early** career

Revelation 13
(7 headed 10 horned beast)
AC's **late** career

Daniel 7 gives us details on what to look for in the world just prior to and during the beginning of the Antichrist's ascent to power. Daniel 11:36–45 gives what his conquests of the other powers will look like. And Revelation 13 tells what it will look like once he has gained complete control.

Let's study Daniel 7 to see if there are significant reasons to challenge the idea that Daniel's vision is simply a mirror image of Nebuchadnezzar's vision of the statue.

"The first was like a lion, and had eagle's wings. I watched till its wings were plucked off; and it was lifted up from the earth and made to stand on two feet like a man, and a man's heart was given to it." (Daniel 7:4)

The traditional view has this beast being Babylon, and specifically, Nebuchadnezzar. For example, traditionalists say that wings being plucked off and being made to stand on two feet and given a heart of a man refers to the humbling experience God gave Nebuchadnezzar in chapter 4. The king was forced to act like an ox for several years until he recognized the sovereignty of God; he was then was restored to his right mind.

The picture painted by the traditional view is that the lion represents Nebuchadnezzar when he was forced to act like a beast; the plucking of the lion's wings, making it stand on two feet, and giving it a man's heart is symbolic of God's restoring Nebuchadnezzar to his right mind at the end of Daniel 4. This suggests that the four beings were described as "beasts" because of situations that were similar to Nebuchadnezzar's. Are we to understand, then, that the kings of Medo-Persia, Greece, or Rome are also described as beasts, because they, too, were forced by God to act like beasts? If so, they were apparently not restored to sanity as Nebuchadnezzar was, since no man's heart was given to them.

The description of the first beast in Daniel 7 doesn't even fit what happened to Nebuchadnezzar in chapter 4. The clear intent in Daniel 7 is that the lion was always a lion, but was given a "man's heart" and thus changed. The lion was not restored to its natural state by the plucking of its wings and making it stand on two feet. It was permanently transformed, and the intent of the text, as we will see, is that it was a downgrade for the lion, not an upgrade. Nebuchadnezzar's situation was exactly reversed if we analyze this closely.

The traditional view also asserts things like "the winged lion is the traditional symbol for Babylon; evidence of this can be seen on the Ishtar Gate from Babylon." Citation? Footnote? To start with, there is no evidence to suggest that winged lions were considered a symbol of Babylon. Lions in general, regardless of wings, were associated not with Babylon, but with the goddess Ishtar. This is partly because of the reference to her loving lions in the *Epic of Gilgamesh*, which states of Ishtar: "Thou has loved the lion, mighty in strength." Citation?

Ishtar was often depicted with lions in sculptures and reliefs; only occasionally are the lions winged, for reasons we will get to later. This is why lions appear on the famous Ishtar gate of Babylon because of their association with Ishtar, but Ishtar was not even the main goddess of Babylon. However according to some traditions, she was considered to be married to Marduk, the primary god of Babylon, thereby making Ishtar the queen of Babylon by marriage.

There are other winged animals on the gate, like the bull, though most of the bulls do not have wings. In fact, the other two animals depicted on the gate (bulls and dragons) vastly outnumber the lions. There were 120 lions compared to 575 dragons and bulls. Incidentally, Nebuchadnezzar was really proud of the bulls and dragons on the front of the gate (where we won't find any lions). He even mentions them specifically in his inscription about why he built the gate, but he doesn't mention the lions at all.

All that to say that many commentators who try to make the point that winged lions are symbols of Babylon do so despite the historical evidence that winged lions are quite simply not symbols of Babylon at all and when they do show up in Babylon, they are exceedingly rare.

People trying to make this winged lion in verse 4 be Babylon are often thinking of the so-called *Lamassu*. A *Lamassu* is a representation of a protective deity, not from Babylon, but rather thousands of years before this in the Akkadian and then Assyrian kingdoms, who were enemies of Babylon. Although there are occasions when *Lamassu* have been depicted with lions' bodies, the vast majority are with bulls' bodies. There is some evidence that the Assyrian tradition of putting *Lamassu*, their protective deities, on city gates was why certain animals on other gates in later periods were given wings, as a tip of the hat to the older Akkadian traditions regarding these protective deities.

This interpretation causes a hermeneutical problem as well. If we are going to say we should look for a culture's symbol for itself to decipher the following beast kingdoms, then how are we to deal with the rest of the beasts? There is not a shred of evidence that, for example, the Medo-Persians symbolized themselves with a bear. I don't even think any traditional commentators try to suggest this. Greece did not make statues or reliefs symbolizing itself as a leopard, nor did Rome depict itself with the odd beast Daniel describes. If we're going to say we can decipher the beasts/kingdoms in Daniel 7 by looking at the artwork and symbols of the kingdom in question, then it needs to be consistent.

There is a similar problem with the next point, brought up by proponents of the traditional view that Nebuchadnezzar is called both a lion and an eagle in Scripture. This is the best of the points offered by the traditionalists in favor of their view that the four beasts of Daniel 7 are the same as the nations in Daniel 2. Even so, it should be considered that Scripture also calls Shalmaneser, the king of Assyria, a lion and an eagle in Hosea 8:1 and Jeremiah 50:17. A simple study of the usage of lions, eagles, or any other beast in Scripture reveals that they are used to designate characteristics and are often widely interchangeable among individuals or nations—as long as the individuals or nations display the characteristics of the animal described in Scripture. For example, when used in a negative sense, lions are, among other things, strong (Proverbs 30:30), fearless (Proverbs 28:1, 30:30), stealthy (Psalm 17:12), frightening (Ezra 19:7; Hosea 11:10; Amos 3:8), destructive (1 Samuel 17:34; Micah 5:8) and territorially protective (Isaiah 31:4).

Similarly, eagles are used to depict specific characteristics of individuals or nations throughout Scripture. According to one Bible encyclopedia, an eagle is "referred to for its swiftness of flight (Deut. 28:49; 2 Sam. 1:23), its mounting high in the air (Job 39:27), its strength (Psalm. 103:5), its setting its nest in high places (Jeremiah 49:16), and its power of vision (Job 39:27-30)." Referred to in the article cited as a "ravenous bird," it "is a symbol of those nations whom God employs and sends forth to do a work of destruction, sweeping away whatever is decaying and putrescent (Matthew 24:28; Isaiah 6:11; Ezekiel 39:4; Deuteronomy. 28:49; Jeremiah 4:13; 48:40).[88]

So consider that when lions or eagles are used to describe kings, the imagery is used of different kings and often different kingdoms, but the unifying factor is that they are instruments of God in the judgment of Israel and display the characteristics of the animals laid out in Scripture.

Again, the traditional view would fail at applying this hermeneutic to the other three beasts. For example, there is no reference in Scripture to Alexander the Great or Greece as a leopard or to Cyrus or Medo-Persia as a bear.

I suggest that we should attempt to interpret the first beast the same as

---

[88] http://christiananswers.net/dictionary/eagle.html.

we would the others. The most scriptural way to do that is by understanding the symbolism of the beasts by the different characteristics of that particular animal provided in Scripture.

The first was "like a lion, and had eagle's wings." A kingdom that is like a lion and has wings like an eagle suggests a strong and swift nation. Second Samuel 1:23 says:

> "Saul and Jonathan were beloved and pleasant in their
> lives,
> And in their death they were not divided;
> They were swifter than eagles,
> They were stronger than lions. " (2 Samuel 1:23)

We could apply the other characteristics of these two animals to these beasts for more clarity, but the important part in terms of interpretation comes with the following lines:

"I watched till its wings were plucked off; and it was lifted up from the earth and made to stand on two feet like a man, and a man's heart was given to it." (Daniel 7:4)

Both the wings being plucked off and the lion being forced to act like a man are to be understood as a bad thing, not a good thing, for this kingdom. The wings being plucked is pretty obvious: If the kingdom was swift like an eagle, but its wings were plucked, it would not be to the nation's advantage.

The act of giving the creature a man's heart should be understood as having its lion's heart changed into a weaker heart. Scripture is clear that a lion's heart is better than a man's with regard to boldness or fearlessness.

- "And even he who is valiant, whose heart is like the heart of a lion, will melt completely. For all Israel knows that your father is a mighty man, and those who are with him are valiant men." (2 Samuel 17:10)

- "The wicked flee when no one pursues, But the righteous are bold as a lion." (Proverbs 28:1)

If I were looking for this kingdom, I would look for one that was strong and fast, but that had its swiftness removed and demonstrated less boldness than it once had.

"And suddenly another beast, a second, like a bear. It was raised up on one side, and had three ribs in its mouth between its teeth. And they said thus to it: 'Arise, devour much flesh!'" (Daniel 7:5)

The next beast Daniel describes is "like a bear." In the traditional view, this is Medo-Persia, because, again those who hold the traditional view believe that this is a retelling of Daniel 2 in which the second part of the statue is indeed Medo-Persia.

As we have already noted, none of the ideas applied by traditional-view proponents to the lion work for the bear. There is nothing to indicate any Medo-Persian king had a humbling experience that made him think like a beast, nor is there any indication whatsoever that the Medo-Persian empire identified itself symbolically or any other way with a bear—and there is never a reference to a Medo-Persian king as a bear in Scripture.

"It was raised up on one side."

Proponents of the traditional view say that the bear being raised up on one side is symbolic of the uneven relationship between the Medes and Persians in their coalition. The Medes were initially the dominant party, but later, the Persians were the more dominant of the two parts of this empire.

Note that the phrase "raised up" here is passive; that is, the bear was raised up on one side by an outside force—not of its own doing. Much like the lion having its wings plucked and being stood up, etc., this bear is being raised up on one side by another party, probably by the group that is also ordering it to "devour much flesh." The verse says: "And they said thus to it: 'Arise, devour much flesh!'" The "they" could be a reference to the winds of the earth that stir up the sea in verse 1.

"And had three ribs in its mouth between its teeth."

The three ribs in the bear's mouth, according to the traditional view, represent three notable conquests of the Medo-Persian Empire. But because there are more than three notable conquests of the Medo-Persian Empire, there is much argument among those holding this view as to which three should be considered the most important. I, of course, don't think this has anything to do with the Medo-Persian Empire and so believe we should not concern ourselves with why this is not a perfect description of its military conquests—because it isn't.

One interesting verse is found in Hosea 13:7–8, in which God describes Himself as all of the beasts in this chapter. This is the only time these beasts are found together other than in Revelation 13, and that passage gives us an idea of what these ribs are:

> "So I will be to them like a lion;
> Like a leopard by the road I will lurk;
> I will meet them like a bear deprived *of her cubs;*
> I will tear open their rib cage,
> And there I will devour them like a lion.
> The wild beast shall tear them." (Hosea 13:7–8)

The bear is described here as tearing open a rib cage, so the basic hermeneutic applied to the bear by the traditional view is correct: the ribs represent initial conquests by this kingdom that are three in number.

Also note that almost every time a bear is figured in Scripture, the idea of it being, as it says here, "deprived of her cubs," is mentioned. That is, the biblical bear is the most ferocious when its offspring are threatened. This is such a consistent theme that I would be surprised if the nations the bear represents are not acting out of a real or perceived sense of defense.

"And they said thus to it: 'Arise, devour much flesh!'"

This phrase is very important as it weakens the case that this beast represents Medo-Persia. After the conquests of Cyrus the Great and his son Cambyses II, which occurred relatively quickly and very early in the Medo-Persian history, there were two hundred years of no conquering at all until the empire was defeated by Alexander the Great. The empire spent most of its existence simply struggling to maintain the lands that were initially conquered by Cyrus and his son. So, if this bear, already with the main conquests in its mouth, is supposed to be Medo-Persia, then it either chose not to devour any more flesh, as it was ordered to, or the image simply is not referring to the Medo-Persian Empire.

"After this I looked, and there was another, like a leopard, which had on its back four wings of a bird. The beast also had four heads, and dominion was given to it." (Daniel 7:6).

In the traditional view, the leopard with four bird wings and four heads is the Greek Empire. Again, this theory has the same problems as the bear, since Alexander the Great was not humbled by having his mind turned into a beast's mind. The symbol of the leopard is not associated with the Greek Empire, nor is Alexander the Great or Greece referred to as a leopard in the Bible. I would agree, however, that the four wings on the leopard probably represent a very fast-moving empire.

One of the biggest problems with this view is the four heads of this beast. The traditional proponents say that these heads represent the four generals to whom Alexander the Great gave his empire after he died. The traditional view, then, has Scripture attributing the fast and ferocious conquests of the Grecian Empire to the four generals; no mention of Alexander is present. This is problematic, to say the least. Even if we were to assume that Alexander was somehow involved (perhaps he was the torso), to give such prominence to the generals is inconsistent with history and the way Scripture uses the head/kingdoms motif.

How does Scripture speak of leopards? They tear into pieces (Jeremiah 5:6), they are swift (Habakkuk 1:8), and they lie in wait for their prey (Jeremiah 5:6, Hosea 13:7).

We are looking for an exceedingly fast coalition of four end-times kings or kingdoms or even four leaders of the same kingdom. And, because of the consistent use in Scripture, this kingdom will have some quality that can be described as "lying in wait" or "being patient before striking."

Mention of the leopard is found only about six times in Scripture. The only time the term seems to apply to any nation or king is in Revelation 13, where we see that all four of the beasts have been combined as they rise out of the sea for the final three-and-a-half years of Antichrist's rule. This suggests again that we are to understand these kingdoms in Daniel 7 as somehow being represented again in Revelation 13.

> **Daniel 7:7:** "After this I saw in the night visions, and behold, a fourth beast, dreadful and terrible, exceedingly strong. It had huge iron teeth; it was devouring, breaking in pieces, and trampling the residue with its feet. It *was* different from all the beasts that *were* before it, and it had ten horns."
>
> **Daniel 7:8:** "I was considering the horns, and there was another horn, a little one, coming up among them, before whom three of the first horns were plucked out by the roots. And there, in this horn, *were* eyes like the eyes of a man, and a mouth speaking pompous words."

Here the traditional view has Rome in sight. The reasons for this—strength and fearfulness because of its might—are very general and can apply to any of the previous kingdoms. Any world empire would be able to claim these characteristics. The idea that Rome was "different" from the previous kingdoms can also apply to any kingdom on the list, depending we how you define "different."

There are major differences in the fourth empire described here and the last empire described in the statue vision in Daniel 2. For instance, in this verse, the strength of the empire is clearly the main focus; not a hint of weakness is detected. Contrast that with the last part of the last empire of Daniel 2, in which the Bible spends verse after verse describing the divided nature and inherent weakness of that kingdom. I would call that a very big difference. The kingdom in Daniel 2 is divided and weak, and the kingdom in Daniel 7 is described as invincible.

The main point seen as the clincher for the traditional view is the reference to the ten horns, which are said to correspond to the ten toes in Daniel 2. But I beg the reader to realize that there is no mention of ten toes in Daniel 2. That idea has been read back into the text by people who assume these two chapters are the same.

In chapter 2, the feet and toes are one unit, a fact easily demonstrated, not just by the descriptions of them being one unit in the text, but also by the rock striking the feet—not the toes—to destroy the statue. If the biblical writer wanted to make a big deal out of the ten toes, he would have said, "By the way, there are ten toes," but he does not. There is no mention of the number of toes in the text. For example, I believe we are supposed to pay attention to the number of ribs in the bear's mouth (three), and, in the next chapter, the number of horns on the ram's head and even the number of horns on this beast's head (ten). But when a number is not mentioned, we shouldn't read one into the text. No one tries to draw attention to the ten fingers on the hands of the statue that represents Medo-Persia because there is no correlation there; it takes the analogy too far. We wouldn't note the two eyes and two ears on the head, either. When the Bible is silent, we should be too.

That being said, I do have some agreement with the traditional view at this point. I think the kingdom the Antichrist comes from will have ten kings because of this passage in Daniel 7 and because of its interpretation by the angel, which we will get to later. The Antichrist indeed seems to arise from some kind of ten-nation/king confederacy, and he will subdue three of them before ultimately talking over the whole organization.

Two grammatical clues in Daniel 7:7 support the overall premise that the four beasts are contemporaneous and not successive. The first is the use of the word "before" in verse 7: "It *was* different from all the beasts that *were* before it."

The word "before" here is the Aramaic word *qodam, which is only used in a spatial sense and never in a temporal sense. It is never used in the time sense, like "he tied his shoes before he ran." It is only used in the sense of being in front of something, like "I put some food before the king."*

One example of how this word is used is in Daniel 2:25:

> "Then Arioch quickly brought Daniel before the king, and said thus to him, "I have found a man of the captives of Judah, who will make known to the king the interpretation." (Daniel 2:25)

A different word would be used to speak of something happening before something else in time. So when the verse says, "It *was* different from all the beasts that were **before** it," it must mean that the other beasts are spatially in front of it, indicating that these beasts must be on the earth at the same time.

This brings us to the second grammatical clue in verse 7. The phrase, "trampling the residue with its feet," also supports the idea that these beasts are contemporaneous.

> Biblical scholar Charles Cooper says the following on this point: 'The importance of the translation of this verse is evident by examining several Bible translations:
> 'A fourth beast, dreadful and terrifying and extremely strong; and it had large iron teeth. It devoured and crushed and trampled down the remainder with its feet.'(NASB)
> 'A fourth beast, terrifying and dreadful and exceedingly strong. It had great iron teeth; it devoured and broke in

pieces and stamped what was left with its feet.'(ESV)

'A fourth beast, dreadful and terrible, and strong exceedingly; and it had great iron teeth: it devoured and broke in pieces, and stamped the residue with the feet of it.' (1895-KJV)

'A fourth beast—terrifying and frightening and very powerful. It had large iron teeth; it crushed and devoured its victims and trampled underfoot whatever was left.' (NIV)

"The reader should discern that the translations, with the exception of the NIV, place the final clause as the object of all three verbs. Does 'what was left' go with the final verb to stamp or with all three verbs: to devour, to break in pieces, and to stamp? The answer to this question along with the question regarding the meaning of the clause 'what was left' support our contention that the four kings/kingdoms of Daniel 7 reign upon the earth at the same time. If the clause "what was left" applies only to the verb to stamp, we would have to conclude that the clause refers to the things the beast did not devour or break in pieces. In other words, 'what was left' is everything else the beast is not able to devour or break in pieces. If the beast could not 'eat' it or 'break' it, he stamped on it.

"The other option is to take 'what was left' as the object of all three verbs: to devour, to break in pieces, and to stamp, which is reflected in most translations. Taken in this sense, "what was left" represents everything the first three beasts do not control. In other words, the four kings/kingdoms divided the world up between them. The lion-king, the bear-king, the leopard king, and the diverse-king each get a fourth. In context, 'what was left' is best taken to refer to that part of the earth that did not fall under the control of the first three beasts/kings/kingdoms."[89] Assuming that all this is quoted from Charles Cooper

Daniel 7:9–11

> **Daniel 7:9:** "I watched till thrones were put in place, And the Ancient of Days was seated; His garment *was* white as snow, And the hair of His head *was* like pure wool. His throne *was* a fiery flame, its wheels a burning fire;"
>
> **Daniel 7:10:** "A fiery stream issued And came forth from before Him. A thousand thousands ministered to Him; Ten thousand times ten thousand stood before Him. The court was seated, And the books were opened."
>
> **Daniel 7:11:** "I watched then because of the sound of the pompous words which the horn was speaking; I watched till the beast was slain, and its body destroyed and given to the burning flame."

Daniel now shifts his attention to a new character in the vision: the Ancient of Days. This is a reference to YHWH, though the same description is applied to Jesus in Revelation. Later we will see the Son of Man whom Jesus identified with, interacting with the Ancient of Days.

Daniel is now going to watch the Ancient of Days destroy the beast with the little horn by giving it to the burning flame. These verses are very important for our discussion, because they correspond directly to events in the book of Revelation. If we compare the two books, we will see that Daniel is giving us very specific information about the timing of the events being described in this chapter.

---

[89] Charles Cooper. "Daniel 2 and 7: Equal or Not Equal Part 4", n.d. http://www.prewrathrapture.com/Daniel%202%20and%207%20-%20Equal%20or%20Not%20Equal%20-%20Part%204.pdf.

Let's start with the first phrase: "I watched till thrones were put in place."

I will quote from the last part of Revelation 19 to the first part of Revelation 20. First you will see the Antichrist is cast into the lake of fire, just as it happens in our passage:

> "Then the beast was captured, and with him the false prophet who worked signs in his presence, by which he deceived those who received the mark of the beast and those who worshiped his image. These two were cast alive into the lake of fire burning with brimstone." (Revelation 19:20)

We then read that thrones are set up after that, which corresponds with Daniel as well:

> "And I saw thrones, and they sat on them, and judgment was committed to them." (Revelation 20:4a)

This shows that there is a direct chronological match with the events of Daniel 7 and Revelation 19 and 20.

The comparisons to the time just before the millennial reign of Christ are very important, and Daniel will continue to make unambiguous references to it. One reason I address this is because it helps to explain the next verse.

"As for the rest of the beasts, they had their dominion taken away, yet their lives were prolonged for a season and a time." (Daniel 7:12)
"As for the rest of the beasts": There is no doubt that the other beasts of Daniel 7 are in view here—that is, the lion, the bear, and the leopard. Their dominion is taken away, but their lives are prolonged for a time.

This verse is very difficult to get around for those who still hold the

246 | T h e   R e v i v e d   R o m a n   E m p i r e   R e v i s i t e d

traditional view because the other beasts are long gone by this point. Stephen Miller, author of the commentary on Daniel for the *New American Commentary* who holds to the traditional view, offers the following to explain this most serious problem:

> "How could these beasts lose their authority and still exist? The explanation is that their dominance ceased, but they continued to live because they were absorbed into the next empire. For example, Greece was conquered by Rome; and although Greek dominance came to an end, the nation continued to live by being absorbed into another one of the earthly kingdoms, the Roman Empire."[90]

So according to Miller, when Daniel says, "As for the rest of the beasts, they had their dominion taken away, yet their lives were prolonged for a season and a time," he means there would still be Neo-Babylonian or Medo-Persian blood on the earth in the last days. This presumes that the Bible sees kingdoms in a purely ethnic sense, which is very difficult when dealing with kingdoms like the Romans, who were very ethnically diverse.

I have another explanation for this problem. After the Antichrist is destroyed at Armageddon, there will still be people and indeed nations on earth who will populate the thousand-year period after the sheep and goat judgment. This has explicit biblical support. We know there will be specifically identifiable nations in the Millennium. For example, in Zechariah 14:16–19, Egypt is mentioned. In fact, that same passage specifically states that some of the nations that were a part of the final battles would be serving the Lord during this time:

> "And it shall come to pass, that **every one that is left of all the nations** which came against Jerusalem shall even go up from year to year to worship the King." (Zechariah 14:16, emphasis

---

[90] Stephen B. Miller. "Daniel." In *New American Commentary,* 18, 206, n.d.

added)

So the nations involved in this vision are allowed to continue into the Millennium, based on the context. This is very difficult to say of Neo-Babylonia or Medo-Persia, but it makes sense if these four beasts are last-days kingdoms controlled by the Antichrist.

For a complete study on this chapter in Daniel, see my commentary on the book of Daniel entitled *Daniel—A Commentary,* available on www.Amazon.com.

I hope readers will consider the possibility that Daniel 2 and Daniel 7 are not speaking of the same events. While I don't regard this as an absolutely crucial doctrine to understanding the end times as a whole, I do think that by believing them to be the same, thereby causing a revived Roman Empire view to exist, we set ourselves up to be confused when the Antichrist does appear.

Appendix 2
The Resurrection of the Antichrist

"Was, and is not; and shall ascend out of the bottomless pit, and go into perdition…"

This phrase gives people a great deal of difficulty, and so we will spend a bit of time on it. I intend to show that this idea of "was, and is not, and coming out of the bottomless pit" is a title referring to the Antichrist, having been miraculously healed or resurrected from the dead.

The last phrase in this verse; "…**the beast that was, and is not, and yet is…**" is another way to say the same thing, that is he lives, he dies, he seems to rise again, and he will ultimately go to destruction or perdition. It's sort of a chronology of his entire career on earth, and it functions as a title on several occasions in the book of Revelation.

Before I begin to explain the details of this, we need to refresh our memories to the significance that the Bible puts on the seeming resurrection of the Antichrist from the dead.

Let's review Revelation 13, which is primarily about the Antichrist, to make sure we understand this preliminary idea. The relatively short chapter of Revelation 13 mentions the Antichrist's fatal wound that was healed three times. The first instance is in verse 3:

> "And I saw one of his heads as it were **wounded to death; and his deadly wound was healed: and all the world wondered after the beast**. And they worshipped the dragon, which gave power unto the beast: and they worshipped the beast, saying, 'Who is like unto the beast? Who is able to make war with him?'" (Revelation 13:3–4)

This passage seems to imply that the world's worship of the beast is directly connected to his deadly wound being healed. It says that they "wondered after him saying "Who can make war with him?" This is the exact same word **"wondered"** used in our current verse. It is also in the exact same context (i.e. wonder from the earth dwellers, associated with worship, and the Antichrist's apparent resurrection from the dead).

This is one of the first descriptions of the Antichrist given in Revelation 13, right after the symbolic imagery of verses 1 and 2. The first thing that we are told about the beast is that he has a deadly wound that is healed. The Bible, as we will see, considers this event very important.

By the second reference of this event in verse 12, the idea of a healed deadly wound has become a title, or an identifying description, of the beast. Here, it distinguishes the first beast from the second by adding the clarification: **"whose deadly wound was healed."**

> "And he [false prophet] exerciseth all the power of the first beast [Antichrist] before him, and causeth the earth and them which dwell therein to worship the first beast, **whose deadly wound was healed."** (Revelation 13:12)

In the third reference in Revelation 13:14, we see that the healed deadly wound is used again as a title or distinguishing characteristic of the Antichrist beast. Here it says:

> "And [the false prophet] deceiveth them that dwell on the earth by the means of those miracles which he had power to do in the

sight of the beast; saying to them that dwell on the earth, that they should make an image to the beast, **which had the wound by a sword, and did live."** (Revelation 13:14)

So, we see again this idea of a resurrection being used as a type of title to distinguish which beast is in view. Therefore, this phrase "was, and is not; and shall ascend out of the bottomless pit" is basically just another way of saying the same thing. It is an identifier as to which beast we are talking about, the one that was (lived), is not (died), and shall ascend out of the bottomless pit (come back from the dead).

Arthur Pink, an early English Bible scholar who wrote extensively on the Antichrist, agrees, saying the following:

> "A further reference to the resurrection of the Antichrist, his coming forth from the Bottomless Pit, is found in Rev. 17:8.... It is to be noted that the earth-dwellers wonder when they behold the Beast that was (alive), and is not (now alive), and yet is (raised again). The world will then be presented with the spectacle of a man raised from the dead."

Pink, as well as many other people, associate the phrase "coming out of the bottomless pit" in Revelation 17:8 with the apparent resurrection of the Antichrist in Revelation 13. We will see explicit biblical proof of this interpretation in just a moment.

The Bible uses the word, "abyss," which is here translated as "bottomless pit," in many different ways: It is a prison for spirits in Mark 5, and it is almost synonymous with the abode of the dead. "Abyss" is also the same word the apostle Paul uses to describe where Jesus went during at least part of the three days in which He was dead before He resurrected.

> "But the righteousness which is of faith speaketh on this wise, 'Say not in thine heart, "Who shall ascend into heaven? (that is, to bring Christ down from above:) Or, "Who shall descend into the **deep?** [Abyss] that is, to bring up Christ again from the dead." (Romans 10:6–7)

So this same word for "bottomless pit" or "abyss" is also the place out of which Christ came when He resurrected.

We find more detail on this event in Acts 2:27–32 where Peter starts off by quoting from the Old Testament:

> **"Because thou wilt not leave my soul in hell [hades],** neither wilt thou suffer thine Holy One to see corruption. Thou hast made known to me the ways of life; thou shalt make me full of joy with thy countenance. Men and brethren, let me freely speak unto you of the patriarch, David – that he is both dead and buried, and his sepulchre is with us unto this day. Therefore being a prophet, and knowing that God had sworn with an oath to him, that of the fruit of his loins, according to the flesh, he would raise up Christ to sit on his throne; He seeing this before spake of the resurrection of Christ, **that his soul was not left in hell [hades],** neither his flesh did see corruption. This Jesus hath God raised up, whereof we all are witnesses." Act 2:27–32

Now, this is interesting because the word "hades" here was mentioned by Peter as the place where Jesus' soul went when He died, when Paul says that it was the abyss. But we can see that contextually, they are both talking about the place where Jesus' soul went during His death.

My point is not to do an exhaustive study on this subject but only to show that Jesus went to the abyss at some point during His death. He may have also gone to other locations in hades such as paradise and even "*tatarus.*" There are more references to this event which I will leave for you to study further: Ephesians 4:8–10, 1 Peter 3:18–20, 2 Peter 2:4–5, Matthew 12:38–45, and Luke 23:43.

My only point is that coming up from the "abyss" can be shown from Scripture to mean resurrection from the dead.

So, these phrases are used like a title referring to the Antichrist's apparent resurrection from the dead, as if it is a chronology of his career and a title all at the same time. He is the beast that lives, dies, resurrects, and ultimately meets his doom in perdition or the lake of fire in Revelation 19:20.

I would suggest that the following phrases are all referring to not only the same person, the Antichrist, but the same identifying event in that person's life—his apparent resurrection.

- The beast that was, and is not, and yet is.
- The beast that was, and is not; and shall ascend out of the bottomless pit, and go into perdition.
- The first beast, whose deadly wound was healed.
- The beast, which had the wound by a sword, and did live.
- The beast that ascendeth out of the bottomless pit.

Back in Revelation 17:8, the angel is about to explain some very interesting details to John about the seven-headed beast that John saw, but this entire verse is basically preliminary. It is simply the restating of the characteristics of the beast of Revelation 13 to clarify that the beast he saw is the same one he saw in a previous vision.

Before we get to new information about the beast, there is one more aspect of this verse that must be covered. There are many interpretations that, even while understanding that phrases like "**the beast that was and is not and yet is**" are referring to the Antichrist's resurrection, will say that the tense of some of the words in these verses require the Antichrist to have lived before the time of John. They will say that since John wrote in the late first century, the past tense of the word "**was**" in the first part of the phrase (i.e., "**the beast that was**") means the beast that will come to live in the future as Antichrist and must have lived sometime before the time of John.

Common candidates for the Antichrist proposed in this scenario are Hitler, Judas, or even Nimrod. Again traditional views are saying the beast that is "yet to come" must have been dead already when John was writing. This view can lead to any number of wrong conclusions about the identity of the Antichrist.

The traditional interpreters fail to see that John consistently uses these phrases like **"the beast that was, and is not, and yet is"** as a title for the beast of his visions—visions in which he sees all the way to the end of knowable time in some cases. Yet he never ceases to refer to everything he sees as having happened in the past. Even the New Jerusalem's descent in Revelation 21, which is almost universally considered to be a future event, must have already occurred in the first century, if this is the correct way to view the text because John said, "And I John **saw** [past tense] the holy city, new Jerusalem, coming down" (verse 2).

More to this specific point about phrases like **"was and is not and yet is,"** if you applied it consistently to the other titles that refer to the Antichrist's resurrection, the theory that the beast must have already existed like Judas or Nimrod would quickly break down.

- The beast that was, and is not, and yet is.
- The beast that was, and is not; and shall ascend out of the bottomless pit, and go into perdition.
- The first beast, whose deadly wound was healed.
- The beast, which had the wound by a sword, and did live.
- The beast that ascendeth out of the bottomless pit. Again— quotes and Scripture reference?

So, if we applied this first century tense idea to these other passages, we must also conclude that the Antichrist not only has lived and died by the time of John, but that his wound had to have already been healed in the first century as well, because John also refers to it in the past tense.

This would, of course, not be agreed upon by those making this claim. They would not say this pre-John character has risen from the dead yet; they would only say that he would have already died before John's time.

The answer here is to realize that phrases like "the beast that was, and is not, and yet is," "the beast, which had the wound by a sword, and did live," or "the first beast, whose deadly wound was healed" have the same function as a way to refer to the Antichrist. They can even be used to refer to the defining event of his life and also the entire end times course of events. The tense used is the exact tense you would expect from someone who was trying to refer back to an event he saw in a vision consisting of future events. In theology it is called the "prophetic perfect tense."

It is also notable that the words in the phrase are in the exact order one would expect to see if this were true. For instance, "coming out of the abyss" would seem to be the first thing mentioned in this phrase if it were, in fact, referring to where he initially comes from; but instead we see it being consistently placed precisely after he was "**not**" or after he dies, exactly where we would expect to see a reference to his resurrection.

I will show what I believe to be proof of this idea.

"And the beast that was, and is not, even he is the eighth, and is of the seven, and goeth into perdition." (Revelation 17:11)

This verse is where we will find confirmation of the view that the beast's coming out of the bottomless pit in verse 8 is a reference to the Antichrist's resurrection.
Notice first the similarity to this phrase in verse 11 and the one we looked at earlier in Revelation 17:8:

> "The beast that thou sawest was, and is not; **and shall ascend out of the bottomless pit**, and go into perdition." (Revelation 17:8)

> "And the beast that was, and is not, **even he is the eighth, and is of the seven**, and goeth into perdition." (Revelation 17:11)

The difference here is found in the middle of these two verses (the part about the resurrection.) In 17:8 the resurrection is described as "ascending out of the bottomless pit." In verse 11, the part that says "even he is the eighth and is of the seven" is not only is being used to convey the same thing (that is the resurrection portion of his chronology) but as we will see, it is also giving us more information about this king.

The phrase "**even he is the eighth, and is of the seven**" is saying that though there are only seven kings, there will be eight reigns. That is, one of these kings will rule twice. The resurrection of Antichrist explains how there can be eight reigns and only seven kings. This is almost universally considered to be speaking of a resurrection of one of the dead seven kings to rule twice. In other words, he will be the eighth king while never ceasing to be the one of the seven kings.

This provides great credibility to the earlier interpretation that this phrase is a technical title of the beast in Revelation 13 and the "bottomless pit" in verse 8 is a reference to the beast's resurrection. Just as the phrase "even he is the eighth, and is of the seven" is a reference to the resurrection. All of it is packaged in an identical word structure, so we can be confident of our interpretation that this is a title of the Antichrist referring to his most identifiable trait, his apparent resurrection.

Appendix 3
Mystery Babylon

Some popular teachers assert that Mystery Babylon is metaphorical; in other words, it is not an actual city but symbolic of something else, possibly a worldwide pagan religious/financial system. They say this despite the fact that in Revelation 17:18, the angel, while interpreting John's vision, refers to the "woman" as a "city": "And the woman which thou sawest **is that great city**, which reigneth over the kings of the earth" (emphasis added).

Mystery Babylon is referred to as a "city" eight times in the book of Revelation, and many of the things that happen to it in the narrative seem to be talking about a literal city. For instance, the city is burned down and the smoke can be seen from the nearby sea; merchants sell items to it; and it experiences famine. These, plus many other factors we will soon see, cause many to believe that it is in fact a literal city, just as the angel said.

Those who see Mystery Babylon as a literal city have proposed several candidates for the identity of the city, including:

1. Rome or Vatican City. Many early reformers saw

Mystery Babylon as Rome. Somewhat ironically, the Catholic Church, on the Vatican website, also teaches that it is Rome[91]—though it is referring to ancient pagan Rome, whereas Protestant reformers would say that it was the Rome of the Catholic Church.

2. **Babylon.** Some suggest Mystery Babylon is the actual city of Babylon in Iraq. In this scenario, the city will be rebuilt in the future.

3. **Mecca or some other Arab cities.** This view has been especially popular recently.

4. **Jerusalem.** This is the view that will be defended in this chapter.

5. **New York City**, as well as a long list of other, less popular candidates.

I believe Mystery Babylon is the last-days city of Jerusalem. I choose my words very carefully in this description. In other words, it's not referring to any previous Jerusalem, or even to Jerusalem today; it is the Jerusalem of the end times, when the people of that city make the temporary mistake of accepting the Antichrist as Messiah and promote his worship to the rest of the world—the Jerusalem that becomes the capital city of the world under the Antichrist's authority.

We know the Antichrist will choose Jerusalem as the place to declare himself to be God (2 Thessalonians 2:4; Matthew 24:15; and Daniel 11:31–32). We know the greatest religious persecution of all time, prompted by the abomination of desolation, will happen in the city of Jerusalem (Matthew 24:15–21) and the Antichrist seems to set up his headquarters in the city itself (Daniel 11:45). So, we already understand that there is a relationship between the Antichrist and the city of Jerusalem in the last days. We have also seen the Antichrist is attempting to fulfill Messianic prophecies, and we know the most important of those prophecies include setting up Jerusalem as the capital city of the world

---

[91] http://www.vatican.va/archive/ENG0839/_P12J.HTM.

(Isaiah 2:1–4) as well as setting up a worldwide pilgrimage system enabling Gentiles to flow into Jerusalem (Isaiah 60:3–22; Isaiah 18:7; Zechariah 14:16–18). We will see that these things are taking place in Mystery Babylon, and we will look at what I believe are scriptural proofs that the term refers to the last-days Jerusalem.

Basics of Mystery Babylon

Before we get into specifics, it will be helpful to go over some of the basics about what John saw in his vision about Mystery Babylon.

John saw a vision of a woman riding a seven-headed, ten-horned beast— the same beast seen earlier in Revelation 13, which is by this time an established reference to the Antichrist. As I mentioned, we are told specifically by an angelic interpreter in Revelation 17:18 that the woman is a city. So, the basic idea is that John saw a city riding the Antichrist. We know that the city is deceived because she says she has found her husband and her king (Revelation 18:7). She is extremely happy with the beast she is riding at first, but she finds later on, at the very end, that the beast turns on her and tries to destroy the city (Revelation 17:16–17).

We also know that the city is responsible for the promotion of the Antichrist's worship to the rest of the world because of verses like Revelation 17:2b, which says:

> "The inhabitants of the earth were made drunk with the wine of **her fornication**" (emphasis added).

> Or, as Revelation 18:3 puts it, "For all nations have drunk the wine of **the passion** of her [fornication]" (ESV, emphasis added).

The idea is that Mystery Babylon herself is so deceived by the Antichrist that she is passionately worshiping him as her long-awaited king and husband. So intense is the passion of her fornication that the entire world is drawn in (made drunk) and deceived into doing this with her.

Now, a few biblical reasons to validate this theory.

Blood of the Prophets

The last verse of Revelation 18 makes a very impressive statement: "And in her was found the blood of prophets and saints, and of all who were slain on the earth" (verse 24). I submit that the only city this can apply to is Jerusalem. Let's take each part separately to see why.

The idea that the blood of prophets was found in this city is interesting, because there is only one place that the prophets were ever killed in Scripture: Jerusalem. In fact, Jesus actually says that it is *impossible* for a prophet to be killed anywhere except Jerusalem!

> "The same day there came certain of the Pharisees, saying unto him, 'Get thee out, and depart hence: for Herod will kill thee.' And he said unto them, 'Go ye, and tell that fox, behold, I cast out devils, and I do cures today and tomorrow, and the third day I shall be perfected. Nevertheless I must walk today, and tomorrow, and the day following: **for it cannot be that a prophet perish out of Jerusalem.**'" (Luke 13:31–33, emphasis added)

He reiterates this point in the next verse: "O Jerusalem, Jerusalem, which killest the prophets" (Luke 13:34a).

That should end the discussion about which city is responsible for killing the prophets, but what do we make of the next part of the verse in Revelation 18:24, which says "the blood of **all who were slain on the earth**" is found in this city? You might think we need to go looking for somewhere other than Jerusalem to find a place responsible for *all* the blood of the slain, but Jesus actually said that Jerusalem would be blamed for all the righteous blood shed on the earth, not just for the people who were killed there.

"Therefore, indeed, I send you prophets, wise men, and scribes: some of them you will kill and crucify, and some of them you will scourge in your synagogues and persecute from city to city, **that on you may come all the righteous blood shed on the earth, from the blood of righteous Abel to the blood of Zechariah**, son of Berechiah, whom you murdered between the temple and the altar." (Matthew 23:34–35, emphasis added)

No other city in Scripture is said to have this kind of blame put on it; therefore, passages like Revelation 18:24 about Mystery Babylon being blamed for the blood of the prophets, etc., must be intended to point directly to Jerusalem because we have explicit references from the Lord Himself about this very issue.

Harlot

Consider the very idea of a city being a harlot: Jerusalem is specifically called a "harlot" hundreds of times in Scripture, and always in a spiritual context—the harlotry of following false gods and killing prophets. Just a small sampling of this can be found in Isaiah 1:21: "How is the faithful city become an harlot! It was full of judgment; righteousness lodged in it; but now murderers."

Ezekiel 16 is devoted entirely to this subject. The chapter starts: "Again the word of the LORD came unto me, saying, Son of man, cause Jerusalem to know her abominations."

In fact, Ezekiel spends the whole chapter saying things like:

"But thou didst trust in thine own beauty, and playedst the harlot because of thy renown, and pouredst out thy fornications on every one that passed by; his it was. And of thy garments thou didst take, and deckedst thy high places with divers colours, and playedst the harlot thereupon: the like things shall not come, neither shall it be so." (Ezekiel 16:15–16)

Mystery Babylon is called the "Mother of Harlots." Some try to make this phrase more than the text makes of it. They see it requiring the city to be the source of all the world's evil from time immemorial, but that is not what I believe the text is intending. I believe this is talking about Jerusalem, which is, at this point, committing the worst kind of adultery (because she, of all cities, should know better than to be worshipping a false god like the Antichrist). Also, a consistent idiom in Scripture conveys the idea that cities have children, which are often referred to as "daughters," "sons," or simply "children." So "harlots," as in "mother of harlots," simply refers to Jerusalem's inhabitants. One example of the use of this concept can be seen when Jesus was on the road to be crucified:

> "But Jesus turning unto them said, '**Daughters of Jerusalem**, weep not for me, but weep for yourselves, and for your children. For, behold, the days are coming, in which they shall say, "Blessed are the barren, and the wombs that never bare, and the paps which never gave suck."'" (Luke 23:28–29, emphasis added)

Isaiah 4:4, when speaking of the institution of the millennial kingdom, says:

> "When the Lord has washed away the filth of the **daughters of Zion**, and purged the blood of Jerusalem from her midst, by the spirit of judgment and by the spirit of burning." (Isaiah 4:4, emphasis added)

Here is yet another example of the inhabitants of a city being referred to as "children" of that city:

> "O Jerusalem, Jerusalem, the one who kills the prophets

and stones those who are sent to her! How often I wanted to gather **your children** together, as a hen gathers her chicks under her wings, but you were not willing! See! Your house is left to you desolate." (Matthew 23:37–38, emphasis added)

Jerusalem is constantly warned in Scripture that if it does not turn from its harlotries, it will be judged. As we go through Revelation 17–18, we find that the specific judgments Mystery Babylon gets are the exact same as those promised to Jerusalem because of its spiritual harlotry. Jerusalem is judged in the end times for the purpose of ending this harlotry as a means of purification, and it is clear that this happens just before the Millennium. The following is just one example from Ezekiel 43 where Ezekiel talks to God while looking at the millennial temple. God talks about the things that will happen just before the temple He is showing Ezekiel will be able to be built:

> "And he said to me, 'Son of man, this is the place of my throne and the place of the soles of my feet, where I will dwell in the midst of the people of Israel forever. And the house of Israel shall no more defile my holy name, neither they, nor their kings, **by their whoring** and by the dead bodies of their kings at their high places, by setting their threshold by my threshold and their doorposts beside my doorposts, with only a wall between me and them. They have defiled my holy name by their abominations that they have committed, **so I have consumed them in my anger. Now let them put away their whoring** and the dead bodies of their kings far from me, and I will dwell in their midst forever.'" (Ezekiel 43:7–9, emphasis added)

The judgment of Jerusalem for the purpose of purification that occurs just before the Millennium is mentioned in several other places (Zechariah 14:1–5, 13:1–9; Revelation 16:18–21; Zephaniah 1:4–18).

Items Sold to Mystery Babylon

Most people with differing theories about Mystery Babylon have to view the twenty-nine items in Revelation 18 sold to Mystery Babylon by merchants as symbolic (an allegory of economic wealth). This is because the items listed are kind of odd and don't seem like things that any modern city would be purchasing in large quantities. But as I show in my book, each of the items brought to Mystery Babylon has some explicit use in the temple system, whether to do with offerings that are to be made at the temple or with building up the fake millennial Jerusalem. Why are the merchants getting so rich? Let's look at some of examples, and I will show you.

The first items mentioned are "gold and silver, precious stones." The *only* other place this *exact phrase* is used is in describing the specific offerings needed to worship the Antichrist's god in Daniel 11: "But in their place he shall honor a god of fortresses; and a god which his fathers did not know he shall honor with **gold and silver, with precious stones** and pleasant things" (Daniel 11:38, emphasis added).

This can't be a coincidence. We also know that the place where the Antichrist demands worship of both himself and the image of the beast is in the temple in Jerusalem. Therefore, we can easily conclude that the items needed to be brought by the people of the world to worship the image of the beast in Jerusalem are gold, silver and precious stones.

So, consider that the Antichrist has demanded worship, and the way he says to worship is by offering gold, silver, and precious stones. Can you even imagine what that would do to the cost of these items in the global economy? If the money changers and the people selling birds for sacrifice in the temple were bad, wait until they sell gold, silver, and precious stones to pilgrims. Like I said, this will make the merchants richer than anyone ever has been.

Another group of goods mentioned as being sold to Mystery Babylon in Revelation 18 includes cinnamon, incense, fragrant oil, and frankincense.

Each of these words is extremely rare in the Bible, and they are only grouped together in one other context: They are the exact items God said to be used to make holy anointing oil to consecrate the temple and all the items in it. The oil was also to be used to anoint the priests and served an important role in temple services. The compound made from these items was so holy that God warned against anyone making it for any purpose except for temple services; those who did so would be "cut off."

The next list of items in Revelation 18 is even more amazing: wine and oil, fine flour and wheat, cattle and sheep. These are the specific items needed to start the so-called daily sacrifice, a twice-daily sacrifice described in Exodus 29. Daniel 11 and 12 state that this particular sacrifice will again be started in the end times.

So you can see that when we take this section seriously, all of these items are clues that point to one thing: the temple and its services in Jerusalem. In my book, I go through all twenty-nine items that are sold to Mystery Babylon in the last days. It's amazing to see how each of them points to this conclusion.

What Mystery Babylon Is Wearing

Even the items worn by the woman/city are far from random: "Alas, alas, that great city that was clothed in **fine linen, purple, and scarlet**" (Revelation 18:16a, emphasis added). These are the specific colors to be worn by the high priest. This exact phrase is used dozens of times in Scripture. Even the idea that Mystery Babylon has a name written on her forehead is taken from the very same place where we find the description of the high priest's attire in Exodus 28. The high priest had a name written on his forehead, too, but it read "Holiness to the Lord." Mystery Babylon, on the other hand, has the name "Mother of Harlots" written on her forehead.

The idea is that the city of Jerusalem is being pictured as a harlot-high priest, promoting the Antichrist as if he were their true God, causing the whole world to worship the Antichrist in the same way a high priest should promote the worship of the true God.

Common Objections

Objection 1—What about the Seven Hills?

Many people say that Mystery Babylon sits on "seven hills," derived from their interpretation of Revelation 17:9–10:

> "Here is the mind which has wisdom: The seven heads are seven mountains on which the woman sits. There are also seven kings. Five have fallen, one is, and the other has not yet come. And when he comes, he must continue a short time." (Revelation 17:9–10)

Many people say that this city on seven "hills" is Rome, which is famous for its seven hills. But that doesn't stop those who think Mystery Babylon is Mecca or even Jerusalem from claiming that their city also sits on seven hills. That all may be true, but the problem is this is not what the verse is talking about.

There are many ways to show the interpretation of this passage I am about to suggest is true: grammatically, contextually, logically, and by comparing Scripture with Scripture. Let's start with grammar.

Revelation 17:9-10

(KJV) And here *is* the mind which hath wisdom. The seven heads are seven mountains, on which the woman sitteth. **And there are seven kings:** five are fallen, and one is, *and* the other is not yet come; and when he cometh, he must continue a short space.

(ESV) This calls for a mind with wisdom: the seven heads are seven mountains on which the woman is seated; **they are also seven kings,** five of whom have fallen, one is, the other has not yet come, and when he does come he must remain only a little while.

The key is the phrase "and there are seven kings." The excerpt indicates how the passage reads in the KJV. Other versions render this with a very important distinction. They say that the seven heads of the beast are seven mountains; however, the angel then further defines these mountains as being "seven kings": "They [the mountains] are **also** seven kings, five of whom have fallen, one is, the other has not yet come" (ESV, emphasis added).

We can see the difference. The KJV gives the idea that the angel begins to talk about a totally separate thing when he talks about the seven kings, whereas the ESV defines the seven mountains as *being* seven kings.

The difference in translations here is not an issue with the Greek texts, like the *Textus Receptus* or the *Critical Text*. The Greek manuscripts say the same thing here, so it's not one of *those* issues. This is simply a matter of translator choice.

There is near universal agreement among Bible translators that the seven mountains are, in fact, seven kings. In the following image, we see this is the way it is translated in almost every major English Bible.

Revelation 17:9-10

(ASV) and they are seven kings
(ESV) they are also seven kings,
(NIV) They are also seven kings.
(NASB) and they are seven kings
(HSB) They are also seven kings:
(RSV) they are also seven kings
(Geneva) They are also seuen King
(ERV) and they are seven kings
(NAB) and they are seven kings

Grammatically, a major reason for this is that the Greek word εἰ σ ιν *(eisin)*, which in the KJV is translated as "there are," is the third-person plural of ε ιμι *(eimi)*, meaning "I am," which should be rendered "they are." When describing the ten horns a few verses later, a similar phrase occurs: *deka basileis eisin*. There, the KJV and NKJV translate the phrase correctly, without substituting "there" for "they," as is done in verse 10.

Revelation 17:9-10

And here *is* the mind which hath wisdom. The seven heads are **seven mountains**, on which the woman sitteth. And **there are** εισιν [eisin] **seven kings:** five are fallen, and one is, *and* the other is not yet come; and when he cometh, he must continue a short space. - Rev 17:9-10 (KJV)

And **the ten horns** which thou sawest are **ten kings**, - Rev 17:12a

I am not a Greek scholar, and I wouldn't want anyone to believe me based solely on my grammatical explanation, so let's move on to showing that the angel is indicating the seven mountains are seven kings by the context of the passage and by comparing Scripture with other Scripture.

I want to reiterate that all the other times in chapter 17 that the seven-headed beast with ten horns is mentioned, John seems to go out of his way to use phrases used back in Revelation 13. We know the beast in Revelation 13 has many of the same characteristics as the one in Revelation 17. They both have seven heads and ten horns; they both have names of blasphemy on their heads; they both are referred to by their having been killed yet living; they both have the earth dwellers "wonder" at them when they see their apparent resurrection; and they both have people whose names were not written in the Book of Life worship them. I know this seems obvious, but the view that the seven mountains are seven hills of a city prevents people from seeing the most basic point— the seven-headed, ten-horned beast in Revelation 17 is the same beast of Revelation 13, which is obviously the Antichrist.

Our passage goes on to say that one of these heads, which are kings, is the same king who "was and is not" (Revelation 13) and gets the mortal wound. Let's flip back to Revelation 13:3 to check it out: "One of its heads seemed to have a mortal wound, but its mortal wound was healed, and the whole earth marveled as they followed the beast."

We see here that one of the beast's seven heads is said to have a mortal wound. This is an exact match with the Revelation 17 beast. Therefore, Revelation 17:9 has nothing to do with physical hills in Rome, Mecca, Jerusalem, or anywhere else. I mean, do you really think that one of the hills in Rome is going to be mortally wounded and then come back to life, or that everyone marvels at and begins to worship a hill? In other words, the woman/city is riding the Antichrist. This passage is not conveying the type of ground she is sitting on; she *is* the city, and she is riding the Antichrist, not hills.

Objection 2—Found No More

One of the best arguments against the theory that Jerusalem is Mystery Babylon is rooted in the following verse:

> "And a mighty angel took up a stone like a great millstone, and cast it into the sea, saying, 'Thus with violence shall that great city Babylon be thrown down, and **shall be found no more at all.**'" (Revelation 18:21, emphasis added)

The argument here is that Jerusalem can't be Mystery Babylon because this passage says it shall be found "no more at all" and we know Jerusalem is in existence during the millennial reign. We also see the so-called New Jerusalem in the eternal kingdom. This is a very good argument, and it requires a very good answer. How can I say, on the one hand, that Jerusalem will be destroyed and be "found no more" and, on the other hand, say that it will be around forever?

The answer lies in the last eight chapters of the book of Ezekiel, where we find one of the most intricate, detailed building plans for the Israel of the Millennium. Ezekiel contains chapters and chapters of technical details regarding how Israel will be divided, the new temple complex, and Jerusalem and its surrounding areas. To say this is different than what we currently see in Israel is a bit of an understatement.

There are those who have taken all the technical specifications of things like the division of the land in the millennial reign and plotted it all on a map. The twelve tribes of Israel are given parallel rectangular allotments of land, one on top of the other, from the north border of Israel to the south, and each tribe's allotment extends along the entire east/west border of Israel. It really helps to see all this on a map to visualize what I'm saying.

In the middle of these allotments of land is a rectangular portion that Ezekiel calls the "holy portion." The priests and Levites, who service the temple equally, divide this land. There is some debate as to where exactly the temple is in this section. Some say it is in the middle of this land and others say that it is just north of the city, but it doesn't appear to actually be in the city itself, which is very different from Jerusalem now.

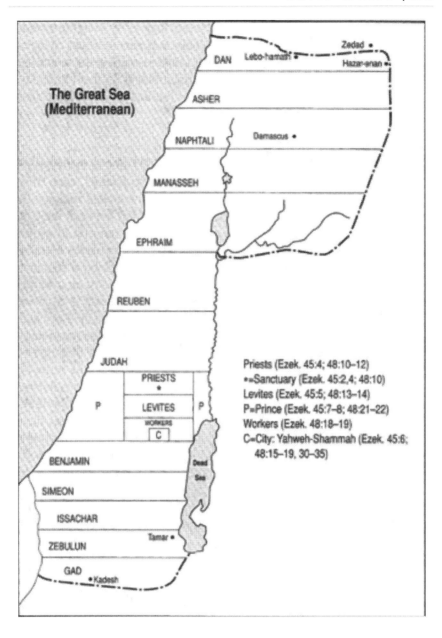

Priests (Ezek. 45:4; 48:10–12)
*=Sanctuary (Ezek. 45:2,4; 48:10)
Levites (Ezek. 45:5; 48:13–14)
P=Prince (Ezek. 45:7–8; 48:21–22)
Workers (Ezek. 48:18–19)
C=City: Yahweh-Shammah (Ezek. 45:6; 48:15–19, 30–35)

Appendix 4
The False Prophet

Not too many places in Scripture discuss this person who will come to be known as the False Prophet, but the information we do have about him strongly supports the idea that the Antichrist will claim to be the Jewish Messiah.

I am convinced that the False Prophet will claim to be Elijah the prophet. Most of us know that the prophet Elijah, who was carried up to heaven in a whirlwind, was prophesied to come back to prepare the way for the Messiah.

> "Behold, I will send you Elijah the prophet before the coming of the great and dreadful day of the LORD." (Malachi 4:5)

> "The voice of one crying in the wilderness: 'Prepare the way of the LORD; Make straight in the desert a highway for our God.'" (Isaiah 40:3)

The idea of Elijah coming back is so important in Jewish religious culture, it is hard to imagine that any Messiah figure could be considered by the Jews unless he had a sidekick who claimed to be Elijah.

We could spend quite some time talking about Jewish traditions regarding Elijah—things like setting out a chair for him during circumcision ceremonies or putting out a cup for him at the Passover meal. Even the *Havdalah*, a hymn that concludes every Sabbath, makes reference to Elijah's return: "Elijah the Prophet, Elijah the Tishbite, let him come quickly, in our day with the Messiah, the son of David."[92]

We are given strong evidence that the False Prophet will claim to be Elijah because the only prophetic "sign" he is specifically mentioned to do is call down fire from heaven (Revelation 13:13).

This apparent miracle is crucially important. To anyone else in the world, calling down fire from heaven would be a neat trick but nothing more. But to a Jew, a prophet calling down fire from heaven is almost the same as declaring himself to be Elijah, the only prophet to perform such an interesting action, which he did three times. Combine this with the fervent Jewish expectation of Elijah's return, and it's easy to see that by this one act, the False Prophet is setting himself up as Elijah. Once the False Prophet has convinced the people that he is Elijah, he will be expected to point to the true Messiah. These miracles appear, then, to be a means by which to fulfill his primary duty of promoting the Antichrist (Revelation 13:12).

It is interesting that, around the same time in Jerusalem, the two witnesses, one of whom may very well be the real Elijah, will be able to stop the rain (Revelation 11:5). Stopping the rain is another major miracle Elijah performed. If one of these witnesses is Elijah, I wish I could say that he will be getting more attention than the fake one (the False Prophet). But, based on the joyful reaction of the people of Jerusalem when the two witnesses are killed, it seems that it is not to be. The people in Jerusalem celebrate and give gifts to one another when the two witnesses are killed (see Revelation 11:10).

---

[92] Joesph Telushkin. *Jewish Literacy*. (New York: William Morrow, 2001).

It may seem that the two witnesses have the False Prophet "out-Elijahed," because they throw fire around and stop the rain as Elijah did, whereas the false Elijah is only calling down fire from heaven. However, there are some interesting reasons to believe that the False Prophet will do one of the other major miracles of Elijah—probably the most impressive of all: to seemingly raise someone, namely, the Antichrist, from the dead. If the False Prophet does raise the dead, call down fire from heaven, and point to the Messiah, then it will be a very strong deception indeed for any Jew waiting for Elijah.

So, the acts of the False Prophet seem to be his attempt to pass himself off as the long-awaited, returning Elijah. Since we know the False Prophet uses his powers for the sole purpose of directing people to the Antichrist, it seems obvious that he is therefore going to claim the Antichrist is the Messiah.

Appendix 5
The Seven-Year Covenant

"Then he shall confirm a covenant with many for one week; But in the middle of the week He shall bring an end to sacrifice and offering." (Daniel 9:27a)

Here in the last verse of Daniel chapter 9, we have a reference to the Antichrist making some kind of covenant with many people. Even until very recently, I've assumed this verse was referring to a "seven-year peace agreement." It has become so common for people to refer to this verse as a peace treaty of some sort that I confess I took it for granted.

However, there is no reason to think this covenant is speaking of a peace treaty. In all the Bible versions I have available to me through Bible software and the Internet (a considerable number), the word *peace* is not mentioned or even implied. In addition, I suggest whatever this covenant is that the Antichrist makes must be a covenant that was already in place, based on the underlying Hebrew text.

I believe this verse is referring to the Antichrist trying to fulfill the modern Jewish expectations of a "new covenant" that the Messiah will make in the last days. This concept is detailed in many places in the Old

Testament, but a notable one is in Jeremiah 31:31, which states:

> "Behold, the days are coming, says the LORD, when I will make a new covenant with the house of Israel and with the house of Judah."

Both Christians and Jews believe this verse is messianic, but their two views of this "new covenant" are vastly different. The Jews believe this means that when the Messiah comes, He will reconfirm the covenant they already had; that is, the Messiah will make it possible for them to once again abide by the laws given by Moses, especially regarding the daily sacrifices in the temple. The Jewish view of the phrase "new covenant" is no more than a renewed national commitment to abide by God's laws.

Jewish scholar Uri Yosef, PhD, , concludes his paper called "Will the Real New Covenant Please Stand Up?" this way:

> "It is evident that Jeremiah's use of the term בְּרִית דָּהָשׁ , a new covenant, does not involve the replacement of the (eternal) Torah by the New Testament. Rather, it signals a renewal of the original Sinai Covenant."[93]

JewsForJudaism.org states:

> "Jeremiah's 'new covenant' is not a replacement of the existing covenant, but merely a figure of speech expressing the reinvigoration and revitalization of the existing covenant."[94]

---

[93] Uri Yosef, PhD. Jeremiah 31:30–36[31-37]1 "Will the Real 'New Covenant' Please Stand Up?" 2001–2011 for the Messiah Truth Project.

[94] Gerald Segal. "Is Jeremiah's 'New Covenant' (Jeremiah 31:31–34) a Prophecy Fulfilled by the New Testament?", n.d., http://jewsforjudaism.org/knowledge/articles/jeremiah/is-jeremiahs-qnew-covenantq-jeremiah-3131-34-a-prophecy-fulfilled-by-the-new-testament/.

Keep in mind that Uri Yosef and the writers of the article in JewsForJudaism.org, like many Jewish people, would agree that this renewing of the Mosaic covenant will happen when the Messiah comes. They believe that one of the ways He will do this—probably the most important way—is by reestablishing the sacrificial system.

Interestingly, this is exactly what Daniel 9:27 states with the words "he shall 'confirm a covenant'" (NKJV). This phrase, "confirm a covenant," is very interesting, and the Hebrew words are apparently difficult to translate into English. Note a sample of how differently it is translated in popular versions of the English Bible:

> **NET Bible (NET):** "He will confirm a covenant."
> **English Standard Version (ESV):** "And he shall make a strong covenant."
> **King James Bible (KJV):** "And he shall confirm the covenant."
> **Young's Literal Translation (YLT):** "And he hath strengthened a covenant."

Notice that it isn't just the words, but their core meaning, that vary. In the NET translation, "he" is confirming an *already existing* covenant; in the ESV, "he" makes a *new* strong covenant; in the KJV, "he" confirms *the* covenant, suggesting it is the Mosaic covenant; and in the YLT, "he" is strengthening an *already-existing covenant*. Of the nineteen versions of the Bible I checked, eleven have the Antichrist confirming or strengthening an already-existing covenant as opposed to making a new covenant altogether.

The obvious question is: Which one is right? I will add a discussion about the details of this linguistic problem in the footnotes,[95] but I believe the original Hebrew expresses a confirming or strengthening of

---

[95] And he shall confirm the covenant—literally, "he shall make strong"—והגביר vehîgebîyr. The idea is that of giving strength, or stability; of making firm and sure.—*Barnes Notes on the Bible* (Daniel 9:27). (See also the following footnote.)

an already-existing covenant. The idea of the covenant being strengthened comes from the fact that the Hebrew word sometimes translated "confirm" carries the meaning of making something strong. I would even suggest that this covenant was meant to be understood as *the* covenant (i.e., the Mosaic covenant). Some translations, like the KJV, even render the word *a* as *the*, which suggests a reference to a particular, preexisting covenant. Contextually, that must be the Mosaic covenant.

There seems to be confirmation that we're on the right track with this idea, because the second part of Daniel 9:27 says: "But in the middle of the week He shall bring an end to sacrifice and offering," as if to suggest that it is obvious that the covenant being strengthened began by starting the daily sacrifices. This verse is contrasting these two ideas; it's like the verse is saying: He confirms the covenant (which started the daily sacrifices), but then (three-and-a-half years later) he stops the sacrifices. The words presuppose that the reader understands the covenant began with restarting the daily sacrifices.

If this is speaking of the Antichrist trying to fulfill the Jewish expectations of the "New Covenant" of Jeremiah 31, then the singling out of the daily sacrifice here and in other places where this event is mentioned is pretty interesting, because without the daily sacrifice it is very difficult, if not impossible, to truly keep the Mosaic covenant. It is the first and most important of all sacrifices to the Jews, it made daily atonement for their collective sin, and it's believed that this sacrifice must start again for God's blessing to rest in its fullness on the Jewish people. In the Jewish mind, the reinstatement of the daily sacrifices is tangible proof that the Messiah has come and Jeremiah 31:31 has come true.

If this scenario is true, the idea that the Antichrist will announce a seven-year covenant, as opposed to announcing an eternal covenant, is absurd. He would not say, "Hey, everyone, I'm the Messiah, and now you have a new covenant, but it's really not eternal; it's only going to last seven years." Here again, I think we are victims of modern Bible prophecy teaching. Scripture never says he will say he is setting up a seven-year covenant. It only says that the covenant will last seven years. In fact, according to a lengthy study on grammar by the *Pulpit Commentary*, linked in the footnotes, the underlying Hebrew suggests this, too. That study concludes by translating that part of the verse in this way: "The covenant shall prevail for many during one week."[96]

So, it seems clear that the seven-year time frame will not be announced to the people who are agreeing to it. The Antichrist will in, all probability, say that this will be an eternal covenant. The mention of the seven years is, therefore, just God telling us how long this false covenant will really last. Note also that Scripture says it will continue to last the entire seven years. It won't go away at the midpoint. Only the daily sacrifices will be taken away.

I believe the covenant made by the Antichrist is an argument in favor of the case that he will claim to be the Jewish Messiah. The Jews are wholeheartedly expecting the Messiah to do the exact thing Daniel 9:27 is saying the Antichrist will do—that is, confirm a covenant and start the daily sacrifices. We can be sure that whoever does this will be looked at as the Messiah by the Jews as well as by many Christians, who may see this as the beginning of the millennial reign of Christ.

---

[96] The clause, "the covenant shall be strong (δ υ ν α σ τ ε ύ σ ε ι) upon many," is a doublet of the clause, "when he shall confirm the covenant to many weeks." The clause, "and after seven and seventy times and sixty-two years," is a doublet of the beginning of the twenty-sixth verse; "Till the end of the war, and the desolation shall be taken away," is an alternative version of the last clause of the twenty-sixth verse. When those extraneous elements are got rid of, we have left a rendering of the twenty-seventh verse, which may afford us light as to the text. "The covenant shall be strong upon many" is a possible rendering of the Hebrew (see Psalm 12:5).—*Pulpit Commentary* (Daniel 9:27).

Appendix 6
Will the Antichrist Claim to Be Jesus?

The question of whether the Antichrist will claim to be Jesus is more difficult than we might think. However, a number of passages might help us come to an answer. In the Olivet Discourse, Jesus warns His followers about "false christs" on a few occasions; for example, Matthew 24:24 says "false christs and false prophets will rise and show great signs and wonders to deceive, if possible, even the elect."

Here we are warned of false christs. I would remind the reader that the word "christ" simply means "messiah"; it doesn't necessarily refer to Jesus. So, it is difficult to determine if any of these christs will claim to be Jesus, based on the use of this word alone. It could be referring to someone claiming to be the Messiah to the Jews, or it could indicate someone claiming to be Jesus.

The plural "christs" is interesting here, because in another verse in the same chapter, Jesus makes it clear that "many" of these false christs will come. I take these references to many false messiahs to mean that the end times will be marked by great messianic expectations. Messianic fervor, and with it messianic pretenders, always have arisen during significant Jewish events in history. For example, of the twenty-five or so false Jewish messiahs who have arisen over the centuries, most were piggybacking on noteworthy events in Jewish history, when expectations of deliverance or victory were very high. The end times, as I understand them, will be nothing if not a series of significant events for Israel. So the fact that many false messiahs will put their hats into the ring during that time is to be expected.

It is clear that, although Jesus warns of multiple false christs, He intends the reader to understand that one of these false messiahs stands alone as the main one—that is, the Antichrist—and these warnings also apply to the Antichrist. Of all the warnings Jesus gives in this chapter, He spends the most time describing the danger of the "abomination of desolation" spoken of by Daniel the prophet "standing in the Holy Place" (Matthew 24:15), where only the Antichrist is in view. Paul explains and expands on this particular teaching of Jesus in 2 Thessalonians 2:2–11 which is one of the most detailed descriptions of the doctrine of the Antichrist in Scripture. Paul describes in great detail this man's actions: sitting in the temple declaring himself to be God, etc. In addition, Jesus mentions the false christs and false prophets showing "great signs and wonders to deceive," a phrase Paul attributes to the "lawless one" in 2 Thessalonians 2:9. This seems to suggest that Paul saw Jesus' warnings about the false messiahs to directly apply to the Antichrist. So there is a solid basis to believe that these phrases about the many false christs also pertain to the main and final False Messiah, the Antichrist.

One verse that seems to suggest the Antichrist will claim to be Jesus is found in Matthew 24:5:

> "For many will come in My name, saying, 'I am the Christ,' and will deceive many."

In parallel passages of this verse, like Mark 13:6, some translations use the words, "For many will come in My name, saying **I am he**," instead of "I am the Messiah," but it should be noted that the original Greek does not contain the word "he," and it often appears in italics because it is an addition of the translators. The NET Bible includes a footnote after the "I am he" phrase which says: "That is, 'I am the Messiah.'"

The first part of this verse, "For many will come in My name," seems to suggest that many of the false christs will claim to be Jesus because of the phrase "in My name," though the second part of the verse, which gives us an example of what they will say, "I am the Christ," leaves the matter open to debate. Is Jesus saying that the "many" will use His name specifically, or is He using the phrase "in My name" in the way that it is used in other places, to say that the they will be claiming His rightful title or authority?

One of the reasons I'm not too quick to say that this verse means the Antichrist will claim to be Jesus is because of the use of a similar phrase in a similar context found in John 5:

> "I have come in My Father's name, and you do not receive Me; if another comes in his own name, him you will receive." (John 5:43)

This says the Antichrist will come in his *own name,* which seems to contradict the idea that he comes in Jesus' name in Matthew 24:5. A resolution could be that in this verse, coming in someone's "name" refers to coming to do that person's will, as opposed to that person calling himself by that name. Jesus, in the chapter where we find this verse, makes it clear that He has come to do His Father's will (John 5:19, 30, 36), which is why He says He has come in His *Father's* name; whereas the Antichrist, who is sometimes called the "willful king," is said many times to do his *own* will (Daniel 11:16, 36). This is why Jesus says He comes in His *own name*. In Matthew 24:5, however, coming in Jesus' name must mean something different, because we know the false messiahs are not coming to do Jesus' will, although they are said to come in His name. If this is true, it would be good evidence that the Antichrist will claim to be Jesus.

One of the reasons I lean toward the view that the Antichrist will in some way or another claim to be Jesus is because of Matthew 24:23–27, which says:

> "Then if anyone says to you, 'Look, here is the Christ!' or

'There!' do not believe it. For false christs and false prophets will rise and show great signs and wonders to deceive, if possible, even the elect. See, I have told you beforehand. Therefore if they say to you, 'Look, He is in the desert!' do not go out; or 'Look, He is in the inner rooms!' do not believe it. For as the lightning comes from the east and flashes to the west, so also will the coming of the Son of Man be."

This was spoken to people who were followers of Christ and understood there would be a *second* coming of Christ. After all, the disciples' question cited at the beginning of this chapter was, "What will be the *sign of Your coming*, and of the end of the age?" It seems to me that Jesus is warning His followers about false messiahs who are claiming to fulfill the second coming of Christ, which means the people He is warning them about, who are in the desert or inner rooms, must also be claiming to be Jesus, if they want believers to think the second coming has occurred. Jesus says these weak attempts at a second coming will not be true, because *His* coming will be as "the lightning comes from the east and flashes to the west." In other words, it will not be something that will be easily mistaken or missed. So, because Jesus seems intent on warning Christians about false messiahs claiming to be carrying out the second coming of Jesus, a first coming is presupposed, and these people necessarily must be claiming to be the return of Jesus.

If it is true that the Antichrist intends to deceive Christians into thinking that he is the second coming of Jesus, then that whole scenario will depend on either an ignorance of Scripture or a willingness on the part of professing Christians to minimize Scripture. I say this because the Antichrist is said to come on the scene as either a political or military leader from a place with ten kings or kingdoms. He presumably rises in the ranks and has a very earthly, though tremendously successful, kingdom. It is absurd for a Bible-believing Christian to think the second coming of Christ will be so mundane. The idea that His return will occur by rising in the ranks of some earthly kingdom as a political or military leader as opposed to a sudden and glorious appearance in the clouds with angels is just not possible unless one is willing to seriously allegorize and minimize the Scriptures, which state so clearly that His coming will be glorious and unmistakable. However, Jesus' warnings in this passage seem to be against just such an error. He essentially says not to be fooled: "My coming will not be so obscure."

Let's explore some of the implications and questions that arise from the view that this false Jewish messiah will also claim to be Jesus. The first thing that comes to mind is how much more powerful this deception would be for professing Christians who would see the Antichrist, claiming to be the return of Christ, miraculously conquering and subduing the Muslim world, and setting up a look-alike millennial kingdom. It would give new meaning to the warnings Jesus gave to His followers about the power of the end-times deception of the elect.[97] The only thing that would prevent Christians from believing this lie, other than the Holy Spirit, would be a solid knowledge of the Scriptures. As we have seen, although the Antichrist will do a pretty good job of looking as if he is fulfilling the Scriptures concerning the return of Christ and the setting up of a millennial kingdom, there are numerous things that he won't be able to do. For example, he almost certainly will not build the millennial temple Ezekiel describes, which is larger than the entire city of Jerusalem, nor will he be able to make a new heaven and new earth. I doubt lions will lay down with lambs under his reign, either.

This brings us to an important point: If the Antichrist does claim to be Jesus, he will be a much different Jesus with a very different doctrine. As I have said, he must minimize the Scriptures to a large degree, perhaps even forbidding the reading of the New Testament, claiming, like so many cult leaders before him, that it has been perverted.. Though we can only get glimpses of the Antichrist's doctrine, no matter how we look at it, he will be teaching a perverted version of the Scriptures. We can only guess about the specifics of those teachings; unfortunately, we must wait to see.

---

[97] Matthew 24:4, 24.

Moving on to the Jewish view of the Messiah, it is very difficult to see how a man claiming to be Jesus could be embraced by the Jewish people who currently reject Jesus with such a passion. I am reminded of a quote from Rabbi Elaine Rose Glickman, who, in the book, *The Messiah and the Jews: Three Thousand Years of Tradition, Belief and Hope,* answers the question of how Jewish people will keep from falling for another false messiah:

> "We will know [who the Messiah is], Judaism counsels, as long as we seek redemption rather than a redeemer. After all, anyone can claim to be our redeemer, and many have. But not even the most successful Messianic pretenders were able to achieve redemption. It is so simple, and yet so clear and true: we will recognize the Messiah not because of the way he looks, not because of a forceful personality or esoteric origin, but because he will accomplish the Messianic tasks.[98]

Glickman defines those Messianic tasks as the "revival of the temple in Jerusalem" and the "triumph of Israel over enemies who sought her destruction." So, it may be that if the Antichrist can offer these things, which Scripture says he will do, they will be willing to accept him, even if he claims to be Jesus.

Although I favor the idea that the Antichrist will claim to be Jesus in some way— even a perverted version—I don't consider any of the verses we have studied in this chapter conclusive enough to become dogmatic about the point. We need to be prepared to see a false messiah who blasphemes Jesus and claims that He wasn't the fulfillment of the Scriptures, as well as a false messiah who claims to be the returning Jesus.

---

[98] Rabbi Elaine Rose Glickman, (2013-02-21). *The Messiah and the Jews: Three Thousand Years of Tradition, Belief and Hope* (Kindle Locations 615-624). Jewish Lights Publishing. Kindle Edition.

More From Chris White

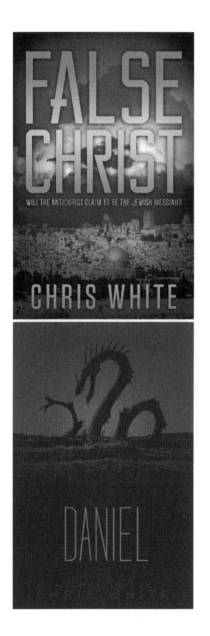

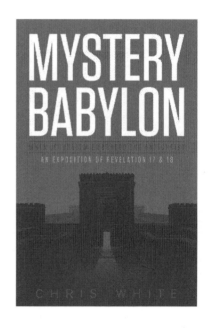

◇◇◇◇

You can subscribe to Chris White's Bible Prophecy Talk podcast at the following links:

Bible Prophecy Talk RSS:
http://feeds.feedburner.com/bibleprophecytalk/NcwG

Bible Prophecy Talk Itunes:
http://itunes.apple.com/us/podcast/bible-prophecy-talk/id482171080

◇◇◇◇

Sign up for Chris' mailing list on the front page of his website:
http://BibleProphecytalk.com

You can contact him directly at chris@BibleProphecytalk.com

◇◇◇◇

If you enjoyed this book please consider reviewing it on Amazon. Every review helps the message of this book reach more people.

◇◇◇◇

Manufactured by Amazon.ca
Bolton, ON

12323087R00164